NON-VIOLENCE VS TIGER FORCE

HARI PADA ROYCHOUDHURY

Notion Press

No.8, 3rd Cross Street,
CIT Colony, Mylapore,
Chennai, Tamil Nadu – 600004

First Published by Notion Press 2020
Copyright © Hari Pada Roychoudhury 2020
All Rights Reserved.

ISBN 978-1-64899-887-4

The book is dedicated to the Victims of
"Non-Violence" Movement of Gandhi

CONTENTS

A SHORT SYNOPSIS OF THE BOOK

The book is about Assam's origin, Assam's natural and Cultural beauty, and Assam's political history of destruction. The remarkable feature is that Assam is full of Coal and wealth of oil besides its fertile river valley of Brahmaputra. Although Coal and oil is explored through mining and refinery but that was not up to the satisfaction of the people where the most oil rich only state of India why not reached to a stage that it could provide sufficient job opportunity to its citizens. So to say the residents of oil reach state is passing their days in uncertainty of future destiny. The fertile river valley of Brahmaputra was utilized by the British before independence in the creation of several hundreds of Tea-gardens to siphon the revenue to the British land keeping the state in a state of starvation and after independence the central Indian government siphons the oil of the state to other states keeping the very oil rich state in a strain of poverty of unrest. To nullify the crying protest of the youngsters of Assam the powerful Center had disintegrated the United Assam into different smaller states to stop the outcry and further converted the beautiful Assam into a site of destructive state without fighting against poverty and unemployment. In order to keep the burning problem under carpet, the powerful central government now has brought the new issue of CAA and NRC. By the advent of new phenomenon, the administration had not only destroyed the Capital of Delhi but even its value of democracy in the international arena.The permanent peace and stability of Assam rests with the removal of all immigrants once for all by the reunion of all the units of Assam to build a new united Assam. It also underlines how Assam came under Bengal administration and gets destroyed along with Bengal by the division of Bengal in the formation of East Pakistan.

NECESSITY TO REMEMBER

[If anyone does not know the role of Gandhi, the under current mystery and how he played with politics to finish the Bengalis of Bengal (+Assam) by creating famine and in bringing the ultimate holocaust for which the Indians suffered in 1947, – how religious fanaticism was nourished by Gandhi to bring "Calcutta Killing" and how the Congress under Gandhi supported the Khilafat movement, the real facts would remain in dark forever. As such without the discussion of the past history of India, the destiny of despair of Assam and the destruction of the image of Delhi by recent communal rioting would not be fair and justified].

[A Picture of Bengal famine of 1943 is in front, a creation of Gandhi to enlighten him as a man of falsehood of humanity and a man of peace. Gandhi was against the British in World War-II, for which British had created the famine by closing the passage of rice from Burma to Calcutta Port and from any other place, just to finish Bengal and Bengalis as the Bengalis were made fool by Gandhi to oppose British in the war making Calcutta, a hard center of Protest.]

1. A SHORT REVIEW OF INDIA AND PAKISTAN

[1.1]

Religious tension has divided the country India into India and Pakistan but now the fear of Corona Virus has integrated the humanity irrespective of the country, why not the unity of India and Pakistan? Let us discuss the matter under the column of a review. Religious tensions existed between Hindus and Muslims for centuries. With the introduction of British-style representative politics based on the policy of **"Divide and Rule"** it was inevitable that religion based grouping would be seen as well. Indian politicians with a modern and secular view like Gokhale and Jinnah wanted to bring Hindus and Muslims together by keeping religion out of politics and concentrating on a political dialogue. In this respect the 1916 Lucknow Pact based on political demands was the zenith of cooperation between the two communities. At the same time the Home Rule League was making progress using constitutional methods to bring about self-rule for India. Incidentally, MA Jinnah, aptly named the greatest ambassador of Hindu-Muslim unity, was the star of Indian politics at that time.

Gandhi had only recently returned to India, and though he had already thought he had achieved international name and fame in South Africa but practically he was nothing but a cunning politician, thought for self image and not for pubic with patriotic heart. He had fuelled the Hindus by the Hindu religious politics of "Non-Violence" in the effort to create Ram-Rajya and also tried to make fool the Muslims even Jinnah by the religious movement of Khilafat but failed in the end. But again posing as a harmless simple person as good as a SAINT under the cover of FAKIR Dress as if he was without any political ambitions, he was able to make fool a many. One of the men, who were deceived by him once, was no other than Jinnah who made Gandhi the president of Home Rule League.

Some of the Muslim leaders started the Khilafat Movement. This was a religious movement; however, over the last few years orthodox religious leaders among the Muslims had been mostly sidelined through the efforts of Jinnah. But here Gandhi gave them a new lease of life. Gandhi who had openly declared that he was a Hindu first and anything else later just to counter Jinnah as Jinnah said he was an Indian first and Muslims afterwards putting his full support behind this orthodox Islamic movement calling Indian Muslims to rise up in jihad to save the Turkish Caliph.

Gandhi had established himself, a saint-like figure among the Hindus and among the Muslims through his show of piety in social work. His support encouraged the Khilafat Movement, which was of no benefit for the Indian Muslims, a life of its own. Gandhi by dint of his clever hidden policy of politics, he could win the heart of ordinary religious minded Hindus by the nature of a SAINT and again in a clever way wined the heart of Muslims by supporting the Muslim Religious Movement of Khilafat. Because of his immense popularity due to Hindus as well as of Muslims no one could dare to oppose Gandhi, for to do so, one had to oppose a SAINT and thus that would at that atmosphere as good as equal to political suicide – hence, everyone joined the Khilafat bandwagon. Gandhi toured every nook and corner of India along with radical Muslim leaders like the Ali brothers stirring up religious frenzy by using the evergreen slogan *'Islam khatraymeinhai'* (Islam is in danger) for the first time. (Ref. 1)

The result was that Muslim League lost its popularity and Muslim political leadership was taken over by the orthodox religious leader Gandhi from the control of secular leader like Jinnah. (Ref.2), (Ref.3)

K.A. Karandikar was writing "Gandhi was responsible for jettisoning sane, secular, modernist leadership among the Muslims of India and foisting upon the Muslims, a theocratic orthodoxy of

Maulvis". The rise of religious sentiment based on Muslim pan-Islamism was falsely blamed Iqbal, but it was actually Gandhi who greatly encouraged this and it was not an upsurge in just Muslim communal fanaticism. (ref.4)

It was only an imagination of a fool that would have expected that the sight of the Ali brothers bringing vast crowds to the edge of religious frenzy when calling for 40 million Muslims to lay down their lives for Islam will not have had any effect on Hindus, who had not forgotten the real and imagined atrocities they had suffered during the times of the Muslim rule. Indeed Professor Beni Prasad rightly warned that Gandhi's actions will lead to Hindu revival and contribute to political separation.

As regards Jinnah's stance on Khilafat movement, it is true that concerned about his political career in a country where the Khilafat Movement had been made into a Holy Cow. Jinnah may not have viciously denounced it at his first thought for his future leadership as such he even compelled to say some tactful words that looked like his sympathy for it. But to claim, as some historians do, that Jinnah was a supporter of Khilafat Movement is as absurd as claiming that Mustaffa Kemal was a protector of the Khilafat!

In the 1918 session of Muslim League, held in Delhi, Jinnah warned the delegates not to dabble in the Khilafat issue as it does not concern India and declared it as a false religious frenzy of which no good will come out for India. Finding the members opposed to this view, he along with some others walked out of the session (Ref 5). However, under the circumstances all the Muslim religious leaders lambasted Kemal Pasha, and considered Jinnah a great leader and visionary. After wards Jinnah resigned at the Congress Nagpur session of 1920 where he said:

"I will have nothing to do with this pseudo-religious approach to politics. I do not believe in working up mob hysteria, after all politics is a gentleman's game".

And this mob hysteria and violence had been amply demonstrated by the non-violent supporters of Gandhi during that session where no one who had opposed Gandhi and his Non-Coop/Khilafat marriage was allowed to explore by a jeering crowd, where leaders and delegates were coaxed, bribed and intimidated into voting in favor. Gandhi politics made him familiar among the Hindus as well as among the Muslims and thereby he might have made his personal future straight and clear but he had done the greatest harm to the nation by bringing religious ethics in the Indian Politics. This was the beginning of the two nation theory. By recalling the earlier incidents the RSS leader Sudarshan had said that Gandhi had done something for his personal benefit at the time of Non-Coop/Khilafat marriage but Jinnah tried to do something for the Indian people and he even recently praised Jinnah's secular outlook: "When Mahatma Gandhi supported the 1919 Khilafat movement, Jinnah opposed it. He had argued that Indian Muslims had no connection with the Khalifa of Turkey. But nobody heeded Jinnah."

Thus it is quite clear to see how religious communalism had resulted fanaticism. It was introduced into Indian politics when it was in its formative years. This affected both Hindus and Muslims but Muslims were more affected as:

Khilafat Movement was an Islamic religious movement but Gandhi was a religious Hindu leader who entered into it to make it more aggressive and fanatic to accomplish his secret desire under the noise of everyone as he was one of the cleverest politicians. He was a SAINT in appearance but he was a super –intelligent person who could make fool not only the Hindus but the Muslims too. This indeed was the watershed dmoment to remember when the dream of Hindus and Muslims living together in an independent India was irreversibly shattered by Gandhi but again how Indians have accepted him as the **FATHER** of the nation, was a game of hidden politics under the cover of emotions.

The memory of past history reminds everyone that the Muslim politics of India never recovered from the damage caused by Gandhi and the Khilafat Movement. It became quite clear for anyone wanting support among the Muslims that the religious card was the trump card. And afterwards under the existing political atmosphere Jinnah himself, at a later stage, played this card in what in his opinion was a game of bluff, but even he did not know the extent of damage that had been done for the seeds of religious frenzy planted during the Khilafat Movement days had by then become toxic trees. Jinnah had predicted the planting of toxic tree in the form of mixing religion and politics would bring bloodshed, chaos and Hindu-Muslim divisions and that had been proved prophetic.

To increase his popularity Gandhi in January 1925 formed a Cow-Protection Sabha and became its chairman but later the same year he announced his retirement from active politics, a job well done for a clever SAINT VS Politician. And along the way he had killed the Home Rule League in 1921, something which delayed India's independence by several years.

It was surprising to know that the same religious fanaticism was imported into Pakistan by those who had actually once opposed the idea of Pakistan (The Ahrars and Jamat-i-Islamietc), along with the constant slogan of *Islam bachao* (save Islam) and the ideology of a pan-Islamic Khilafat, jihadi militancy and violence has the nation in its loud voice. No doubt these jihadist have similar ideology to the leaders of the Khilafat Movement who were ready to use violence in defense of their Islamic Khilafat where Gandhi was a supporter of Khilafat, a very few could understand the Gandhi politics.

Reference:

1. Ref: P.C. Bamford, *Histories of Non-Cooperation and Khilafat Movements*, Delhi, 1974, p. 49)

2. Ref. Tara Chand, *History of the Freedom Movement in India,* Vol III, 1972, p. 418)

3. Ref. K.A. Karandikar, writing in *Islam-In India's Transition to Modernity* (New Delhi, 1968, preface page vii) states:

4. Ref: Sir C. S. Nair, *Gandhi and Anarchy,* Madras, 1922, p. 51.

5. Re: ChaudaryKhalliquzzaman, *Pathway to Pakistan,* Lahore 1961, p. 43-44.]

2. DELHI VIOLENCE & FACE OF INDIAN DEMOCRACY

[2.1]

The Supreme Court, the highest custodian of Judiciary has brought allegation against Delhi Police for failing to act "professionally" to check the violence in north-east Delhi which has left 27 people dead and now increased to 38 and also many injured more than 200. The Indian Prime Minister Narendra Modi appealed for peace and brotherhood but it would have been better if law was imposed strictly hanging the rioters.The Congress could rightly say that the Centre and the Delhi government were responsible for the deadly communal violence in the city. The demand of Home Minister Amit Shah to resign for the failure of maintaining law and order at Delhi is not absolutely unjustified. Moreover he was not a clean person as because he was summoned by a Gujarat Court in connection with 2002 Gujarat rioting.

By the time he had increased his image by abolishing 370 in Kashmir and by solving lawfully "Tin Talac" and "Mandir-Babri Majid issue". Kashmir was one of the bigger Muslim princely states having with a King of Hindu Sikh. So long there was no Hindu-Muslim conflict in India, Hindu and Muslims were living as brother and sister. The division of country based on religion has destroyed the brotherly feeling of Hindu-Muslims. The British granted the independence to India with provisions that (i) division of British India into the two new dominions of <u>India</u> and <u>Pakistan</u>, with effect from 15 August 1947 and the partition of the provinces of <u>Bengal</u> and <u>Punjab</u> between the two new countries. The two new countries, would establish their own office of <u>Governor-General</u>.

To settled the Hindu-Muslim conflict the British government proposed a plan, what was known as **3 June Plan of 1947**, that included few principles which were (i) Principle of the partition of British India accepted by the British Government (ii) Successor governments given <u>dominion</u> status (iii) autonomy and sovereignty given to both countries (iv) both the countries given the authority to make their own constitution (vi) Princely States were given the right to either join Pakistan or India or become a separate nation other than Pakistan or India. Pakistan made Muhammad Ali Jinnah the <u>Governor-General</u> of Pakistan while India made Lord Mountbatten the <u>Governor-General</u> of India. The reason remained behind the secret understanding in between Edwina Lady Mountbatten and Mr. Nehru in the Simla Hotel. The fact of the matter was that the couple shared an extraordinary love. Their deep attachment lasted from the moment they met in 1947 in New Delhi until the day Edwina died 13 years later. The relationship was known even to Lord Mountbatten but his self confidence found it best to turn a blind eye for the cause of any kind of benefit at this crucial time of historic change of British administration, the responsibility being rested upon him. It is also assumed that it was Edwina Lady Mountbatten who gave incentive to Nehru to become the Prime Minister of India instead of Congress elected candidate Petal with the weapon of threat that all the Princely states would revolt instead of joining India if Nehru was not given the post of PM. It was not unlikely that in order to satisfy Lord Mountbatten, he had been posted as the <u>Governor-General</u> of India under the patronage of Nehru instead of taking any Indian for the post of the <u>Governor-General</u> of India. It signifies the important facts that although the Indians have vacated the British from the administration yet the Indians are not very confident to rule the country on its own. Thus a British was kept at the top of administration as Governor – General for advice and guidance at the time of need.

Pakistan a Muslim majority country expected Kashmir being a Muslim majority Princely State would join Pakistan. The King of Kashmir did not join either Pakistan or India. Under the instigation of Pakistan few tribal Muslim insurgents occupied a part of Kashmir. Finding difficulty in maintaining law and order Maharaja Hari Singh had approached to India for protection. Accordingly the Instrument of Accession was executed by Maharaja Hari Singh.

The Instrument of Accession is a legal document executed by Maharaja Hari Singh, ruler of the princely state of Jammu and Kashmir, on 26 October 1947. By executing this document under the provisions of the Indian Independence Act 1947, Maharaja Hari Singh agreed to accede to the Dominion of India.

In a letter sent to Maharaja Hari Singh on 27 October 1947, the then Governor-General of India, Lord Mountbatten accepted the accession with a remark, "it is my Government's wish that as soon as law and order have been restored in Jammu and Kashmir and her soil cleared of the invader the question of the State's accession should be settled by a **reference to the people**. In order to complete accession process thus a plebiscite was necessary. The accession of Lord Mountbatten's remark and the offer made by the Government of India to conduct a plebiscite or referendum to determine the future status of Kashmir led to a dispute between India and Pakistan regarding the legality of the accession of Jammu and Kashmir to India. India claims that the accession is unconditional and final while Pakistan maintains that the accession is fraudulent as it is not done by plebiscite. However, the fact of the matter was that the Governor General accepted the accession on 27 October, the day the Indian troops were airlifted to Kashmir, although plebiscite was not completed.

Some scholars have questioned the official date of the signing of the accession document by the Maharaja. They maintain that it was signed on 27 October rather than 26 October. However, the fact that the Governor General accepted the accession on 27 October, as such the matter ended there but Pakistan continued in its effort to acquire Kashmir with the question of plebiscite.

[2.2]

Who was Amit Shah? He was an Indian politician serving as the current Minister of Home Affairs who has been once President of the Bharatiya Janata Party (BJP) for the period from 2014 to 2020. He joined the BJP in 1987. He was elected to the lower House of Parliament of the Lok Sabha in the year 2019 from Gandhinagar. He became the youngest serving full-time Home Minister at an age of 54. He was a close assistant of PM Narendra Modi.

Shah was given the BJP's charge of Uttar Pradesh, India's largest and politically most crucial state during the 2014 Lok Sabha elections. The BJP and its allies swept the state, registering their best performance, by winning 73 out of 80 seats. As a result, the image of Shah rose to national prominence and was appointed as the party's national president in July 2014. In his initial period of two years, the BJP achieved success in Legislative Assembly elections in Maharashtra, Haryana, Jammu & Kashmir, Jharkhand in 2014 and also in Assam but lost ground in Delhi and the larger eastern state of Bihar in 2015.

Moving to the earlier history, Shah was involved with the Rashtriya Swayamsevak Sangh since childhood, worked as RSS volunteers but he came into limelight for his excellent management when he was the election campaign manager for Lal Krishna Advani in Gandhinagar during the 1991 Lok Sabha elections. During the time period of 1995-2001, Shah served as Modi's informer assistance in Gujarat. Shah became an MLA in February 1997 after winning the by-election but he was succeeded to retain his seat even in the 1998 Assembly elections. During Narendra Modi's twelve-year period as the Gujarat CM, Shah having being worked as the most trusted assistant of Modi emerged as one of the most powerful leaders in Gujarat. After winning the 2002 elections, he became the youngest minister in the Modi government. In 2013, Shah was accused of having Snoopgate, who ordered illegal surveillance on a woman in 2009, during his tenure as a home minister.

After Narendra Modi became the Prime Ministerial candidate of BJP, Shah's influence also increased rapidly in the party. The two have been accused of sidelining other BJP leaders such as Lal Krishna Advani, Sushma Swaraj, Murli Manohar Joshi and Jaswant Singh. By this time, Shah had gained recognition as an excellent election campaign manager, and had been assigning as "modern-day Chanakya", Shah was appointed as a BJP general secretary, and was given the charge of Uttar Pradesh (UP). He was chosen not by Modi, but by Rajnath Singh, who had been impressed by the skills that Shah displayed in wresting Congress in Gujarat. The decision did not go down well with many among the party workers as they saw him as a liability owing to the criminal charges against him.

Uttar Pradesh general elections: Shah's political career, which had declined after his arrest on 25 July 2010 in connection with the Sohrabuddin case but again revived after BJP's victory in the 2014 general election. Shah had been made in charge of BJP's UP campaigning on 12 June 2013, less than a year before the elections. Since February 2012, Shah had spent considerable time in UP, trying to understand the reasons for the Samajwadi Party's winning performance in the 2012 UP Assembly elections devising the methods how to defame Samajwadi Party. Shah realized that the voters were dissatisfied with the Samajwadi Party, which he believed had failed to keep its election promises after the win. He also took advantage of the OBC voters' displeasure with the UP government's decision to create 4.5% reservation for the minorities within the 27% OBC quota in government jobs and education. He found out the plan how to satisfy the voters. In UP, where Shah was made the chief in-charge, of the election, BJP and its allies won 73 out of 80 seats. Shah also played an important role in BJP's election campaigning strategy outside Uttar Pradesh. In 2018 the party although lost power in the states of Chhattisgarh, Rajasthan and Madhya Pradesh but in the next year in 2019, the BJP Party won 303 seats to get majority in Indian general election, making Shah the most successful BJP President.

Now the aggressive Saha turned his attention towards Muslims as "illegal infiltrators" to generate votes. In 2018, Shah said millions of "illegal infiltrators" have entered the country like "termites" and should be "uprooted". Shah led BJP to victory in the 2019 Indian general election, becoming the most successful BJP President ever, in the process. During the election campaign, he visited 312 out of 543 Lok Sabha constituencies, carrying 18 road shows, 161 public meetings, and over 1,500 BJP Party meetings. Winning the election, he became a Minister. Shah took oath as Cabinet Minister on 30 May 2019. He took office as Minister of Home Affairs on 1 June 2019. After a thumping victory he wanted to show something spectacular as such on 5 August 2019, Shah moved a resolution to scrap Article 370 in the Rajya Sabha and reorganize the state of Jammu and Kashmir as one of the union territory and Ladakh region is separated out as a separate union territory. After looking to people's joy he became anxious to show another spectacular event with respect to NRC. On 19 November 2019, Shah declared in the Rajya Sabha of the Indian parliament that the National Register of Citizens (NRC) will be implemented throughout the country very soon.

Forgetting the growth of the country through trade and cooperation of all and the nearby friendly countries, he had engaging himself in vote gathering process for the Party. In December 2019, he introduced the Citizenship (Amendment) Act, a bill, which grants Indian citizenship to religiously persecuted minority communities who migrated to the country before 2015 from the Muslim-majority countries of Pakistan, Bangladesh and Afghanistan. In North-East India, including Assam people were very much concerned about the impact of immigration on the culture and politics of the local people as such people are protested against the Act. Elsewhere, the opposition parties criticized the Act's exclusion of Muslims as detrimental to India's theory of democracy to live with all maintaining the rule of equality. Shah, however, insisted that the bill was not anti-Muslim on his own because it did not change the existing path to citizenship available for all living in India. Saha is no longer a man of BJP but also now Home Minister of India. His line of thinking must be above Party Politics. He must work for the people of the country irrespective of religion, language or community. His activity must reflect as the nature of humanity. It is now not the time to remember the religious politics what was shown by Gandhi, Nehru or Petal and divided the country. Now the politics must be towards integration and not towards disintegration. Petal implemented June 3 Plan of British, Gandhi agreed to division and Nehru get delighted to become the PM of India through his secret weapon of threat given by Edwina Lady Mountbatten in the case of accession of Princely states. Now that days have gone, the Muslims who are now living in India have passed more than seventy years in terrible condition of mental strain without going to Pakistan, where in India they were being looked down for no fault of them as the supporters of Pakistan. Truly speaking it was the Hindu leaders particularly Gandhi himself compelled Jinnah to think otherwise. It is now the past history, now we have to live together regaining the lost brotherhood of Hindu-Muslim only when we could see a bright future like in any other country.

He was a close associate of Prime Minister Narendra Modi and held executive portfolios in the state government during Modi's tenure as its Chief Minister. During the 2014 Lok Sabha elections Shah was the BJP's in-charge for Uttar Pradesh, and had shown spectacular success. It has increased Shah's importance and then he has been appointed as the party's national president in July 2014. In his initial two years, the BJP achieved success in Legislative Assembly elections in Maharashtra, Haryana, Jammu & Kashmir, Jharkhand in 2014 and also in Assam but lost in Delhi and Bihar in 2015. In the 2019 Indian general election BJP won 303 seats to get a clear majority. Apart from all success he was look down by many because of his involment in the case of the extrajudicial killings of criminal Sohrabuddin Sheikh; however Shah dismissed all the accusations against him as politically motivated. But again Shah was arrested on 25 July 2010 in connection with the Sohrabuddin case. He was charged with the murder, extortion, and kidnapping among other charges. Besides these he has other controversies. Shah was again accused of sidelining the police officers who testified against the Gujarat government in cases related to the fake encounters and the 2002 riots.

All these prove beyond doubt that he was not a clean man with a clean mind. A Home Minister of a country should be above all suspicions. He should be above religion, community or caste. His work must be for the country men irrespective of Language, Caste or Religion. The loss of so many persons in the capital city by rioting in no way justify the efficiency of the Home Minister where the allegation from the public front as well as from HC that "Police remain inactive" at the time of rioting.

Independence has come to India for more than 70 years before but still the anguish between Hindus and Muslims has not vanished. Yes, it was true the country India and Pakistan was formed on the basis of religion because of short sided leaders where the favorite leader Gandhi said the country would be divided over my dead body but he was the pioneer for the division of the country at the back door just to get rid of Jinnah. Now the Indian people forgetting the religious division must live together, with brotherhood, equality and fraternity. But for that primary effort must come from political leaders. All soldiers work under the command of Army Generals; similarly all party workers or public in general would work under the command of Patriotic Leaders who are holding the post of Ministers.

On 5 August 2019, Shah moved resolution to scrap Article 370 in the Rajya Sabha, and also reorganize the state such as Jammu and Kashmir region serving as one of the union territory and Ladakh region separated out as a separate union territory, the decision was a right decision, the people in general liked it, but how the Article 370 was imposed right at the beginning only in Kashmir unlike the integration of other states remain a misty. Now the right of Article 370 has acclimatized the people of Kashmir, and suddenly the abolition of that right due to 370 would bring a kind of unhappiness among the people. But in the long run people would forget the unhappiness if they could realize that we are all the equal citizens of India connected with each other by the bond of friendship, equality and fraternity.

The history of Kashmir gives us good or bad lesions of humanity. When the Indian favorite leader Gandhi was at the peak of his

"Non-Violence" movement only with Hindus mainly along with few Muslims, Jinnah was with Muslim League militant volunteers. Jinnah succeeded to convince Suhwardy, the then Prime Minister of Bengal and succeeded to carry out "Calcutta Killing" and finally Gandhi agreed to divide the country on the basis of religion and make the Muslims enemy to Hindus forever. At that volatile atmosphere, Kashmir, a Muslim majority state did join neither India nor Pakistan. Under such situation the newly formed Pakistan attacked Kashmir. The King of Kashmir compelled to take **accession** to India as per the declaration of British government to hand over the administration to Indians. Fighting started between India-Pakistan and at last stopped but Kashmir was divided in between India and Pakistan due to their occupation in the specific area bringing pain and agony to the people of Kashmir of both the regions. What kind of humanity had shown by the leaders of both the nations which could not be seen in any other region of any country in the world?

Even in the atmosphere of communal tension few Muslim leaders of Kashmir prefer to remain with India thinking a better future. Does it not signify a sense of humanity above religion among few individuals? In course of time in India political leaders failed to keep religious harmony in India although it is declared India, a secular country. The communal atmosphere in India vitiated the mindset of the young Muslims of Kashmir. The Muslims of Pakistan had taken the advantage of the existing communal atmosphere and infiltrated the militant volunteers to carry out massacre of killing Kashmiri Pundits and compelled the Pundits to leave Kashmir. Thus the virtue of humanity that once tempted the Kashmiri Muslims to live with Kashmiri Pundits and with Indian people now changes in the opposite direction. Here we find a change of humanity. Thus humanity depends upon the patriotic nature of the individuals involved in politics who prefers to dedicate his service for the cause of humanity but many among them prefers to take advantage to enjoy the personal life with glory of luxury along with name and fame.

After so many changes of heart, Kashmir was living with India along with a new provision of right under 370, the abolition of that right would bring resentment but the future course of the treatment of humanity would bring back the brotherhood of humanity above religion or anything else. The formation of Pakistan on the basis of religion was a mistake of Indian political leaders and the religious leader Gandhi. It is now expected in near future the name of Gandhi would vanish from India when the depth of brotherhood between Hindus and Muslims would increase a step further.

[2.3]

Expansion of humanity: What was seen by the people of Europe that the Scientific Revolution had changed human understanding of the world and that led to the Industrial Revolution, a major transformation of the world's economy? At the beginning of the Scientific Revolution in the 17th century that had little immediate effect on the industrial technology. It is only in the second half of the 18th century that scientific advances began to be applied substantially to practical invention and expansion. The Industrial Revolution began in Great Britain using new modes of production—the factory, to manufacture a wide kinds of goods in faster and in a larger quantity using lesser number of labor than previously required. The refreshment as well as enlightenment also led to the beginnings of modern democracy in the late-18th century. American and French Revolutions brought a change in the system of life. Democracy and republicanism had brought a profound effect on the world events and on quality of life. All people get inter related with the exchange of culture, trade and what not. Because of industrial progress Europeans had achieved influence and control over the Americas, but imperial activities turned to the lands of Asia and Oceania.

In the 19th century the European states had social and technological advantage over the Eastern lands. Britain gained control of the Indian subcontinent starting with Madras and Bengal, Egypt and the Malay Peninsula; similarly the French took Indochina. The British also colonized Australia, New Zealand and South Africa with large numbers of British colonists and also taking large number emigrates from the

British colonies. Similarly Russia colonized larger pre-agricultural areas of Siberia. In the late 19th century, the European powers divided the areas of Africa. Within Europe, economic and military challenges created nation of states, and ethno-linguistic groupings began to identify themselves as distinctive nations with aspirations for cultural and political autonomy. This nationalism would become important to peoples across the world in the 20th century. The people learn to live together unlike India guided with short sided political leaders, who only thought for few community based on language and religion and above all, who thought for the pleasure of personal life having with public name and the power of chair.

During the Second Industrial Revolution, the world economy became reliant on coal as a fuel, as new methods of transport, such as railways and steamships, effectively shrinking the world and beginning the new civilization of living together as human beings forgetting religious politics of India, the worst of humanity.

The advantage was that Europe had developed by the wealth generated by the Atlantic trade but the economy of the country developed by the the Industrial Revolution. Indian politicians remained busy with the religious politics in the process of capturing power but remain completely indifferent in the art of learning administration and the art of trade. The art of trade brings wealth and wealth is the source of prosperity and happiness of every individuals. The happiness keeps away rivalry and brings love of brotherhood and real love of pleasure of humanity.

Silent War of Super-powers: The 20th century opened with Europe at an apex of wealth and power, and with much of the world under its direct colonial control or its indirect domination. Again the other remaining part of the world was influenced by heavily Europeanized nations, the United States and Japan.

As the century unfolded, however, the global system dominated by rival powers was subjected to severe strains, and ultimately yielded to a more fluid structure of independent nations organized on Western models. This transformation was catalyzed by wars of unparalleled scope and devastation. World War I led to the collapse of four empires – Austria-Hungary, the German Empire, the Ottoman Empire, and the Russian Empire – and weakened Great Britain and France.

In the aftermath of War, the powerful ideologies rose to prominence. The Russian Revolution of 1917 created the first communist state, while the 1920s and 1930s saw militaristic fascist dictatorships gain control in Italy, Germany, Spain, and elsewhere. Ongoing national rivalries, exacerbated by the economic turmoil of the Great Depression, helped to precipitate World War II. The militaristic dictatorships of Europe and Japan pursued an ultimately doomed course of imperialist expansionism, in the course of which Nazi Germany orchestrated the murder of six million Jews in the Holocaust and of millions of Poles, Russians, and other Slavs, while Imperial Japan murdered millions of Chinese. An earlier model of genocide had been provided by Turkey's World War I mass murder of Armenians.

The World War II defeat of the Axis Powers opened up the ways for the advance of communism into Central Europe, Yugoslavia, Bulgaria, Romania, Albania, China, North-Vietnam, and North-Korea. World War II ended in 1945, but immediately the United Nations was founded in the hope of preventing future wars, as the League of Nations had been formed following World War I. The war had left two countries of all, most equal in strength, the United States and the Soviet Union, concerning with principal power to influence the international affairs. Each was suspicious of the other and feared a global spread of the other's, ideology, the ideology of capitalist or the ideology of communist, whereby to build up the political-economic model. This led to the Cold War, a forty-five-year stand-off and an undisclosed arms race between the United States and its allies, on the one hand, and the Soviet Union and its allies on the other hand to make each of them stable and stronger. With the development of nuclear weapons during World War II, and with their subsequent proliferation, all of humanity of different nations were put at risk of nuclear war between the two superpowers, as demonstrated by many incidents, most prominently the October 1962 Cuban Missile Crisis. The powerful nations are now in the process of industrialization on the one hand and again on the other hand, the other countries such as USA are working in the exploration of space works to know the future strategy. In China, Mao Zedong implemented industrialization and collectivization reforms as part of the Great Leap Forward (1958–1962). In between 1969 and 1972, as part of the Cold War space race, USA send twelve men to be landed on the Moon and safely returned to Earth.

The Cold War ended in 1991, when the Soviet Union disintegrated, in part due to inability to compete economically with the United States and Western Europe. However, the United States likewise began to show signs of slippage in its geopolitical influence. In the early postwar decades, many colonies in Asia and Africa of the Belgian, British, Dutch, French, and other west European countries won their formal independence. But the newly independent countries faced challenges in the control of poverty, illiteracy, and endemic tropical diseases. Most Western European and Central European countries gradually formed a political and economic community, the European Union, which expanded eastward to capture some of the former Soviet countries.

Silent War in space studies: Both the nations USA or the Soviet Union is in the process of space study in the discovery of moon. It is nothing but the preparation of third world war to know technologies in jet aircraft, rocketry and electronic computers. In the World War II, these advances led to jet travel, artificial satellites with innumerable applications including global positioning systems (GPS), and now the Internet—inventions that have revolutionized the movement of people, ideas, and information and what not.

However, all scientific and technological advances in the second half of the 20th century not required only for an initial military impetus but also that period saw ground-breaking developments in the discovery of the structure of DNA, the consequent sequencing of the human genome, the worldwide eradication of smallpox, the discovery of plate tectonics, manned and unmanned exploration of space and of previously inaccessible parts of Earth, and foundational discoveries in physics phenomena ranging from the smallest entities (particle physics) to the greatest entity (physical cosmology).

Someone use the human Civilization in the destruction of humanity for the cause of fulfilling his desire. Having being tortured by the Force of US, the Victim as well as the sympathizers like Osama bin Laden in 2001 had undertaken an effort in the destruction of New York City's World Trade Center killing lots of human being. That was happened on day of the 11 September 2001 by the attack of Al Qaeda designed by Osama bin Laden. That attack influenced to change the U.S. foreign policy for which US has started the longest war in the history of the United States attacking the forces of Al Qaeda in Afghanistan.

This period has also seen by the expansion of communications with mobile phones and the Internet, which have caused fundamental societal changes in business, politics, and individuals' personal lives and in war techniques. The Internet and mobile telephony have also equally utilized by the criminals for the criminal activity. The longest war in the history of the United States, in Afghanistan, has brought vast economic disparities, and dissatisfaction in the United States. But behind the seen a revolutionary wave of uprisings had happened in North Africa and in the Muslim worlds that led to a resurgence of authoritarianism and the advent of reactionary groups like the Islamic State. Thus the mankind is fighting to bring back the ideals of humanity. So long the deals of humanity are not restored; the real peace in the universe of mankind could never be restored.

[2.4]

Forgetting Humanity of Gandhi if we turn our attention towards CAA and NRC, could we not see another mistake we are going to do to increase the difference between Hindus and Muslims just to destroy the existing friendship, equality and fraternity that had been grown up by the time period after independence. On 19 November 2019,

Shah declared in the Rajya Sabha of the Indian parliament that the National Register of Citizens (NRC) will be implemented throughout the country. It is good to hear National Register of Citizens (NRC), but it is equally true that we are dissatisfying a large section of the people particularly the Bengali people Hindus or Muslims. Why? CAA is giving Citizenship right to all Hindu Bengali refugees after six years and that after affidavit or documents, if failed he or she would be non-resident. For Bengali Muslims residents have to give the necessary documents. Thus there might be a section of non-resident who failed to produce documents.

The experiment already has been tested in Assam, at the beginning 40 lakes have been detected non-residents but afterwards that had been reduced to 19 lakhs. Now if it is in the populated state of Bengal, the number is likely to be not few lakhs but few cores. If so will it not bring the question in front how that number would be accommodated in the detention camp apart from the question of expense? The question of uncertainty is likely to arise in the minds of such category of people. The question of uncertainty has led few of them to choose the path of suicide.

It is also equally true no country will permit illegal immigrant to stay in the country. But here in the country of India, there lies a difference. Who are these illegal immigrants? These people are no other persons than the people of India once, who were under compulsion, became a resident of a new country formed due to the pleasure of few political persons. At the time of partition the consent of these people was not taken or their forefathers' consent have never taken, no referendum being ever held. Thus India has a moral obligation to look after these people unlike any other country.

The question of illegal immigrants arises in Assam after a long period of agitation of student movement. Why Assam alone would take the responsibility of illegal immigrants of East Pakistan or Bangladesh? It is true but where is the past history? A mistake of present would bring sufferings in the future. A parent tries his best to educate his children so that he or she could pass a better life. If he could not he has to suffer. Gandhi could not educate his first child; he became a drunker and turned to Muslim for which he has to suffer a lot. After return to India, Gandhi changes his activity according to the situation of the country to make himself a leader of the nation although he failed to become a successful father but later he was successful to become the father of the nation. In doing that he applied the best art of his liberty no one could think of where he could change the title of Indira Nehru-Khan to Indira Gandhi and afterwards, Rajiv Gandhi, Rahul Gandhi and so on. Thus M K Gandhi gets heritage benefit of Nehru Dynasty forgetting the loopholes of his Gandhi family. In the end Nehru house get converted into a Gandhi house. But among all success the image of humanity could not be kept hiding. The Title image could not revive the personal image. The country was divided to kick out Jinnah. The division of country based on religion brought the ever ending enmity of Hindu-Muslim. Now in India Hindu- Muslims fighting is going on since 70 years forgetting the development of the country.India, although achieved Independence but not achieved Independence with joy of happiness because it was at the cost of the partition of the country and also hurting the humanity of the Indians.

With the change of time history changes but the virtue of humanity never changes. The brotherhood in between England and French changes to enmity for more than hundred years to fight with each other but now they are living as inseparable brother sisters due to the virtue of humanity. Gandhi fought for independence through "non-Violence" but ended with a divided India. Netaji fought for independence through "Azad Hind Force" and sacrificed his life. History has forgotten Netaji but remembered Gandhi for which today Gandhi is the FATHER of the nation. Here the virtue of humanity existing in dark and in future one day the darkness would go away and the light of truth would reappear. A falsehood cannot survive for long.

Bangladesh was liberated by India, when Bangladesh declared a secular country whereby Hindu-Muslim or Christian all can live together. Assassination of Majab family happened in Dacca; a new government came to power and declared Bangladesh an Islamic country. History changes with the change of atmosphere but humanity never changes, sometimes it existed in dark. Good sense would come back once again when all human beings would live in harmony bringing the virtue of humanity in front submerging the ethics of religion.

It is shocking to remember that India is lacking in the existence of farsighted leader with great heart of humanity. At the outset the creation of Pakistan on the Eastern part as well as on the Western part of India based on the similarity of religion was nothing but a blunder and a destruction of the virtue of humanity. The Pakistan in the Eastern part was a future danger for the whole of the South Eastern Regions of India, the then Indian leaders either could not think of or mostly the Northern Leaders thought of their benefit and future only neglecting the Eastern Region and giving goodbye the whole region in their inner mind. A farsighted leader could easily assess that East Pakistan would have been completely a Muslim country in future when no government could go against the Muslim religion as the country is formed based on religion, and population increase through multiple marriage would go on until the country would have been absolutely an Islamic country. What practically had happened? 3 cores have now increased to nearly 20 cores. It was not the fault of the government because no government could go to power imposing restriction over birth control, or any law against the dictum of Quran.

No country could live in peace keeping huge possibility of danger at the border or nearby regions where the area was once a continuous region of one nation. Realizing the insecurity of Delhi for the Chinese submarine in the Chittagong Port under the Ministry of Pakistani Government, India under Indira Gandhi indulge in the liberation of the country in the opportune moment of unrest in East Pakistan. Getting the opportunity to rectify the earlier mistake of blunder, India did nothing but Kashmir and that too nothing but a foolish agreement and released the 90 thousand captive soldiers. If the stalwarts of Northern leaders really thought for the Eastern

Region, the regions of Assam, the India government could make agreement for the safety of communication through sea as well as through land and thereby the Indian government could restore the safety of communication as well as the safety of trade of the region. At the time of liberation war at least one core population had taken shelter in Assam, Tripura and in the Eastern regions of West Bengal as such an agreement under joint military command was necessary for the safety of the region so that in future if such a staggering influx any time happened that could be stopped at anytime and handled with joint command of force. A permanent joint military head quarter at the capital Dacca could have been set up for the cause of future safety such as in the case of (i) assassination of Mujib family (ii) Communal rioting or any kind of unrest in the country, or for the reason of any kind of unrest that would going to disturb the peace of the North East of India including the Assam region. If so the North Eastern Region never could face with the problem of illegal immigrant. The Northern leaders of India never thought for the future safety of Assam or the adjacent regions. Rather in the difficult atmosphere they prefer to say goodbye to Assam. The people of Assam never could forget that in 1962, during Chinese aggression, the Indian Prime Minister of Northern Region Mr. Nehru never hesitate to say goodbye to Assam by saying "My heart cries for the people of Assam".

Assam was under East Bengal before partition but Assam became an independent state after independence. The district Sylhet was a part and parcel of Assam since 1874. At the time of independence Sylhet was given to referendum and finally to East Pakistan but the people were permitted to live anywhere. The history changes but the virtue of humanity prevails. To-day most of the Hindu people and few Muslim people are living in Assam including the Barak Valley region. The economic condition did not permit all people to migrate immediately to Assam just after the partition. The change of history has brought in front the CAA and NRC to prevent them to migrate to Assam but the virtue of humanity would one day permit them to come to Assam as because they (the people of Sylhet) were once a part and parcel of Assam, which might not be true for the people of other regions of Bangladesh.

In December 2019, Home Minister Amit Saha introduced the Citizenship (Amendment) Act, 2019 bill, which grants Indian citizenship to religiously persecuted minority communities who migrated to the country before 2015 from the Muslim-majority countries of Pakistan, Bangladesh and Afghanistan. In North-East India, people concerned about the impact of immigration on local culture and politics protested against the Act. Elsewhere, the opposition parties criticized the Act's exclusion of Muslims as detrimental to India's pluralism. Shah, however, insisted that the bill was not anti-Muslim because it did not change the existing path to citizenship available for them.

AAP (AamAadmi Party) leaders Sanjay Singh and Gopal Rai urged the Centre to deploy the Army in the affected areas of Delhi to bring the situation under control that justify the rioting situation was beyond control. Public resentment appeared against few BJP leaders due to which no FIR was lodged. In rioting, Jafrabad a place just 10km away from PMO burns but no action on the part of police was taken. What a wonder an intelligence Bureau officer found dead in Chand Bagh area of Northeast Delhi. Deadly Delhi riots were encouraged by one Mr. Kapil Mishra. Who is Kapil Mishra? He was initially a member of AamAadmi Party. He was an elected member to Delhi Legislative Assembly from Karawal Nagar on an AAP ticket in the 2015 election. He was the water resource minister in the then Arvind Kejriwal-led government but later on he left APP and join BJP. Thus an AAP neta-turned BJP firebrand, a devoted prince member did a lot to encourage the people and what to do in the carnage of destruction. Supreme Court refuses to entertain pleas, related with Delhi violence; Army was not calling in by the govt. An 'unfortunate' state of security existed in Delhi on the day of the visit of American President Trump. Congress thought to march to restrapati Bhavan. It was like that of Delhi violence when a horror film existed during anti-Sikh riots. Death toll rises to 38, injured few hundred. Arvind Kejriwal expressed his desire to call Army to control violence. Congress

Working Committee tried to meet together in order to discuss Delhi violence. At last Ajit Dival of NSA has taken the responsibility to maintain peace in Delhi and accordingly he would enlighten the cabinet on Delhi Violence. BJP targeted APP leader Arvind Kejriwal to take the responsibility of giving aid to the victim families. NSA Ajit Doval thought to visit the riot-affected areas of Delhi once again and meet with the representatives of both the communities, so that the situation in the riot-affected areas comes under complete control and also he would do his best to bring confidence so that no side feels anyone being neglected.

[2.5]

So many incidents happened in Delhi violence: A 22-year-old man's scrotum and penis were ripped apart, and his anal region suffered severe injuries during police firing in Delhi's Mustafabad on Tuesday, a man, Mohammad Imran, a welder, was to wed in May, he get injured, he is recuperating at LNJP Hospital, again According to Shamshuddin, his father, who is a carpenter, he and his son were standing inside one of the lanes of Mustafabad, when the police starting shooting and releasing tear gas to quell the crowd. "It happened within seconds. He was just standing there when he shouted and fell down. His trousers had turned red. We rushed him to the house and realized that it was a big wound."

Few reported cases: AAP councilor Tahir Hussain was charged for killing of IB staffer but he denies his involvement. On Thursday, reports emerged saying that bits of broken bricks and glass were found on the terrace of the AAP councilor's home. Later in the day, he was booked on charges of murder and arson. Hussain, however, has denied involvement in the killing and called the allegations against him "baseless".

Ankit Sharma (26), who worked for the IB, had gone missing on Tuesday and his body was found in a drain near his home in northeast Delhi's riot-hit Chand Bagh area on Wednesday. His family members claimed that the local councilor and his associates were behind the killing. Hussain rejected the allegations.

Nearly 7,000 central paramilitary forces have been deployed in the affected areas of northeast District since 24 February, according to the Ministry of Home Affairs. All these indicate the depth of Delhi violence, how it happened, why? All questions go towards Home Minister Amit Saha. He should be above religion as he was holding the Home Ministry and the Delhi Police Depart is under his custod.

A nation is known by the image of few Patriotic persons with Patriotic character. Abraham Linolmn of the USA, who after becoming President created his own force and fought against the white as well as against the black to stop the cry of separation and thereby he never hesitated to kill to the extent of four million people but the country remained united as such today the USA is the Superpower where all kinds of people are living in peace maintaining friendship, fraternity and brotherhood.

India is the largest democracy; it should preserve its democracy like that of the USA. The tragedy is the division of India based on religion under the guidance of religious leader Gandhi. Pakistan was formed for the Muslims of India, but Gandhi failed to form India for the Hindus of India. Now after 70 years few political leaders thought of creating India for Hindus. Many people doubted the present government under the leadership of Amit Saha, who is thinking to create a Hindu Rashtra without declaring in public. The implementation of CAA and NRC is the first step in that direction. But if it is really so, it would be disastrous for India when India would never see the light of prosperity. A country could reach to the goal of wealth and prosperity if it could live with all with equal opportunity. Thus to-day people could see the grain of prosperity in the USA and also in the Arab Land. Trade with the neighbor state is another criterion of progress; as such maintenance of good relation with neighbors is the primary need for prosperity.

The integrity of Delhi carnage: No major incident of violence was reported from the riot-hit northeast Delhi in the last 36 hours, the Home Ministry said on Thursday night. The ministry issued the statement after Home Minister Amit Shah reviewed the situation in the violence-hit parts of the city in a meeting with senior officials and top police brass. It is a disgrace for Home Minister to fail in maintaining law and order in the Capital City Delhi of India. Had it been in remote area, the administration could bring many excuses such as lack of information, bad road condition etc. But no such excuse justifies the carnage at the Capital Delhi.

The death toll in the violence that broke out in **northeast Delhi** five days ago reached 42 after a 60-year-old man was beaten to death **in Shiv Vihar** early Friday morning, despite heavy police deployment in the area. According to police, 123 FIRs have been filed so far following the violence in the area, 630 people detained and 47 peace committee meetings held in affected localities. "We have controlled the situation in northeast Delhi," Additional CP M S Randhawa told reporters.

The reality appears to be different. A report of Delhi Violence that has exposed the truth of story which is as follows, a young Muslim woman had taken a reporter around a riot-hit Delhi locality. Chandbagh area of Delhi is one of the most devastated areas in violence-scarred North East Delhi.

The girl is pointing to the charred remains of the Chand Baba mazar in Delhi's Chand Bagh neighborhood. For three days, the women of Chandbagh stayed locked up in their homes they were listening to the terrifying sounds of violence raging outside their homes, and fearing for their own lives and also the lives of their families. Only on the Thursday morning, as signs of life returned to the area, they finally stepped out to see a neighborhood ripped apart, littered with the debris of a riot.

They walked around the neighborhood in small groups to see the depth of devastation until the police pushed them back into their lanes. Two elders shouted at them for coming out: "Go back home, don't crowd together or else the police will use it to beat us again." A 19-year-old girl ZebaSaifi came forward and began to tour Baba's mazaar, and across the road, the petrol station how all these were burnt. The shrine of Chand Baba was burnt by a mob. Painstakingly, ZebaSaifi pointed out every shop, showroom and house that has been burnt on the road. All these belonged to Muslims but on the other hand nothing has happened to the Hindu homes and the temple in the area.

At the entrance of B-Block of the neighborhood, from behind an iron grill gate, Zaitun, a woman in her late sixties began to speak, her voice trembling with anger and grief: She said "People are blaming

Tahir for the violence, they are blaming us for the violence, and no one is naming the real culprit, Kapil Mishra." Tahir Hussain is a councilor of the AamAadmi party who has been charged with the murder of an Intelligence Bureau policeman whose body was found in a drain during the riots. Kapil Mishra is a leader of the Bharatiya Janata Party, who delivered a provocative speech on the very day of violence that was Sunday

Another Hindu woman came in front and said "We have been living alongside each other for 40 years without any trouble." Shakuntali Devi stepped up to nod in agreement. The nearby Durga temple was not damaged. But a madrasa a few lanes away had been burnt in the violence. A wall was painted with the Indian flag written the tricolor is the pride of Muslims and Hindus; it is the symbol of India. A message painted on a board on the wall of madrasa that was burnt by a mob. ZebaSaifi said arguments from both sides had been occurring in several lanes across colonies like Chandbagh. "These arguments are started from both sides but if violence breaks out, we know it is the Muslims who will have to bear the consequences, so many are fleeing their homes," assuming more trouble. Many more families were leaving Delhi for safer locations.

The women of the houses had not been able to feed their children or babies properly. "When life and breath are under threat, it is hard to draw attention to life's daily needs for young children," one woman said. "Even in the midst of war, they cry for their food and their milk."

[Women gathered in a lane of Khajuri Khas to mourn a death in the eighborhood.]

Deep inside Khajuri Khas' of Sri Ram Colony, many women assembled in large numbers inside a lane to mourn a death in their neighborhood. Earlier in the day, Shehnaz's husband, Babbu Mohammad, had died at the Guru Teg Bahadur Hospital where he had been taken after he was injured during the riots. Babbu Mohammad was the sole earner, supporting his parents, his wife and three children, the eldest of who was not yet four. Babbu Mohammad's mother took out a passport size photo of her son. She then showed to everybody two more images of her son, one which shows him with serious head injuries, bleeding, his eyes glazed, and the other on a hospital bed, unconscious. She cried why men kill innocent people and finally collapsed on the ground. The women gathered in the room tried to console her. "Today we are crying not just for Babbu and his family. These tears are for all of us. In the past three days, we were too scared even to cry," said one woman.

At last incidentally, National Security Advisor Ajit Doval had visited the area and Home Minister Amit Shah had held a meeting to discuss the situation. Funeral procession of a riot victim is being carried out in northeast Delhi's Mustafabad area. Police have so far identified 36 bodies of victims of the violence. Apart from Ayub, the others identified were Mubarak Husen (28), Dilbur Negi (20), Monis (21), Babbu Salmani (33) and Faizan (24).

Who were the victims of Delhi violence auto driver, scrap collector and waiter, many among them are dead, a victim is saying -"My father had been at home for the last few days because of the violence. Today, he left around 4 am-5 am to collect scrap. I was woken up when some unknown people brought him to our home. He had injuries on his head, body and legs. He was still conscious at the time and told me that some men had stopped him in ShivaVicar and asked him his name. Once he answered, they beat him," he said. Salman claimed that few people called UP Police who didn't provide him with a vehicle. "I carried my father to a nearby private clinic on the cart in which we keep the scrap material," he said.

Salman, who also works as a scrap collector, said the clinic provided first-aid and bandaged the wounds. "But I could not get him admitted there because I was told it would cost us Rs 5,000," he said, it was the Fifth day but no closure of death incident. Outside Delhi mortuary, many of my relatives said waiting is endless. "It was clear that my father needed further medical attention, so I let him rest for some time and then took him in an auto to GTB hospital. But on the way, I could see him weakening and bleeding. He died on the way," said Salman, weeping outside the mortuary in the afternoon time.

Both of them used to earn Rs 300-400 per day, Salman said. "I have nobody left in this world," he said, adding that his mother no longer lived with them.The northeast district, meanwhile, saw peace meetings and police flag marches as residents attempted to pick up the pieces after days of violence. At Farrukhiya mosque in New Mustafabad, residents gathered on the roof for Friday prayers in batches around 1 pm. On Tuesday, a portion of the mosque and the neighboring madras had been destroyed.

It becomes the belief of the people that "Our rulers want an India that thrives on cruelty, fear, division, and violence".

Delhi Police says 21 victims succumbed to gun shot wounds: The majority of the victims (21) died of gunshot wounds, four each of "stabbing injuries" and "assault", three due to "assault with burns" while the cause of death was not known for four more people, said Delhi Police. Of the deceased, 15 were Muslims and 10 were Hindus, while the religious identities of the others are not clear. In the Capital of Delhi the killing of Muslims by Hindus and the killing of Hindus by Muslims enlighten that India is not a civilized country, where India was partitioned based on religion. Gandhi was the pioneer in the creation of the country through the falsehood of "Non-Violence" where he injected in every mind the hidden violence. Unless his image is vanished from Indian soil, the Hindu-Muslim violence of hatred would not vanish from the Indian soil.

[2.6]

Delhi Violence is erupted centering CAA Protest: The USA government asked the Indian government to look after the killing and burning of Muslim houses in Delhi. India in reply said to US government "Don't interfere in the Indian administration". But anywhere when human beings get affected to the extent of killing and burning, any human being of any country can interfere because it concerns humanity of human being. This signifies in India no one is present who could realize human pain and the call of humanity. Gandhi was falsely recognized as a man of peace although people know it very well that Independence came by division through bloodshed due to rioting where "Calcutta Killing Day" was an open declaration day calling for human killing who would oppose Pakistan. When thousand of human killing was going on in the streets of Calcutta in the presence of Non-Violence activity of Gandhi in Calcutta, how Gandhi could be called a man of peace. So many Hindu-Muslims rioting happened in India during the period Gandhi, and also during the period of the Prime Ministership of Nehru and many others. Very recently Mujaffapur rioting took place where was

Indian Patriotic leaders? Indian leaders always think for Party and not for the people.

At least 22 people have been killed and over 200 injured in communal violence that broke out in northeast Delhi three days ago. Jaffrabad, Maujpur, Babarpur, Yamuna Vihar, Bhajanpura, Chand Bagh, Shiv Vihar are among the areas mainly affected by the riots. National Security Advisor Ajit Doval said he has been sent by Prime Minister Narendra Modi to personally visit the affected areas. "I give you my word of honour that we will do our best (to control the situation)," Ajit Doval said while interacting with locals. Pulling up the Delhi Police, the Delhi High Court today asked why it has not registered FIRs against politicians for giving hate speech. The court asked when FIRs are registered for arson and deaths, why are FIRs not being registered for hate speech. Hearing the pleas on the violence in Delhi, the Delhi High Court has said it doesn't want to enter into the question whether Army should be deployed to contain violence in North East Delhi. "We should focus on the issue of registration of FIR right now," the court said.

Delhi violence, a matter in Delhi High Court: On the plea of deployment of Army in the violence-affected areas, court says 'We don't want to enter into the question of deployment of Army. We should focus on the issue of registration of FIR right now.' No reason not to lodge FIR against 3 BJP leaders, HC asked Delhi govt. On violence in Delhi, government's standing counsel Rahul Mehra contended in the high court that there is no reason not to lodge FIR against three BJP leaders. In the matter of Delhi violence, the Delhi Court even said we cannot let another 1984 happen in this country. In the middle of the night the HC Judge has been shifted to Punjab.

Twenty people, including a Delhi Police head constable, have died so far in the riots that broke out on Monday in Maujpur and Jafrabad areas of Delhi's North East district. Nearly 150 were wounded and property-cars, homes, shops and a petrol pump-were set on fire amid heavy stone-pelting and violence that was unleashed on the streets of India's national capital. What makes this more disturbing is that most instances of violence have occurred within a radius of just 12 km from India's most secured area--the Raisina Hill. It is an area that houses the Parliament House Complex, the Rashtrapati Bhavan, the Prime Minister's Office and the defense and home ministries, among other high-profile offices. Is it BJP's planned conspiracy behind Delhi violence questioned Sonia Gandhi.

Sonia Gandhi further said, "There is a planned conspiracy behind the violence. The country also saw this during the Delhi elections. Many BJP leaders made inciting comments creating an atmosphere of fear and hatred. One such inciting comment was made by a BJP leader last Sunday."Sonia Gandhi in her press conference said it is "rather shocking" to see the silence of the top leadership of the central government and the Delhi government in wake of the violence in Delhi. Are you serious you haven't watched speeches of Kapil Mishra, Anurag Thakur: HC said to police?

The Delhi High Court said it is disturbing that the Delhi Police has not yet watched video clips of controversial speeches made by BJP politicians Kapil Mishra, Anurag Thakur and Parvesh Verma. The court had asked the Delhi Police if it has taken any action against these three BJP politicians for their hate speeches. To this, the Delhi Police told the court that it has not seen videos of their speeches. The Supreme Court on Wednesday termed unfortunate the incidents of violence in Delhi but refused to entertain pleas on them. A bench comprising Justices S K Kaul and K M Joseph said it will not expand the scope of petitions filed in connection with the protests at Shaheen Bagh by looking into the pleas on violence. Supreme Court's observation pointed out Delhi Police over lack of professionalism.

The Supreme Court on Wednesday pulled up the Delhi Police saying there was lack of professionalism. The SC said had the police acted in accordance with the law; many problems wouldn't have taken place. These things would not have happened had police not allowed instigators to get away, the Supreme Court said. Justice Joseph gave example of police in the US and UK, and said that force has to act professionally as per law if something goes wrong. As per the autopsy report, Delhi Police Head Constable Ratan Lal was shot during violence over CAA. The autopsy report has revealed that it was not a stone but a bullet injury that proved fatal. The bullet had entered from Ratan Lal's left shoulder and was removed during autopsy. Delhi HC has already directed police to respond by 12:30 pm on plea for action against those involved in inciting violence in northeast Delhi over CAA. The High Court has said police need not wait for the court's direction and should take action on its own in connection with northeast Delhi violence.

At last NSA Doval has given responsibility to end Delhi violence. Doval was an established responsible officer who understands the duty of the greatest democratic country of India. Let us know who is he? Doval was born in 1945 in the village in Pauri Garhwal in United Provinces, now in Uttarakhand. Doval's father, Major G. N. Doval, was an officer in the Indian Army. He received his early education at the Ajmer Military School in Ajmer, of Rajasthan. He graduated with a master's degree in economics from the Agra University in 1967. Ajit Doval was also conferred with an honorary doctorate degree in philosophy by Amity University, in November 2018.

Doval joined the Indian Police Service in 1968 in the Kerala cadre. He was actively involved in anti-insurgency operations in different regions like the regions in Mizoram and also in Punjab. He was involved in much insurgency operation. On 30 May 2014, Doval was appointed as India's fifth National Security Advisor. In June 2014, Doval played a crucial role in ensuring the secure return of 46 Indian nurses who were trapped in a hospital in Tikrit, Iraq. He is widely credited for the doctrinal shift in Indian national security policy in relation to Pakistan. Switching from 'Defensive' to 'Offensive' as well as to the 'Double Squeeze Strategy' was his strategy. It was his speculation the September 2016 Indian surgical strikes in Pakistan.

In October 2018, Doval was appointed as the Chairman of the Strategic Policy Group (SPG), which is the first tier of a three tier structure at the National Security Council. On June 3, 2019 he was reappointed as NSA for 5 years and was given Union Cabinet Minister

Rank. National Security Advisor (NSA) Ajit Doval left from the Ministry of Home Affairs (MHA) after his meeting with Union Home Minister Amit Shah. Home Secretary Ajay Kumar Bhalla and Delhi Police Commissioner Amulya Patnaik were also present during the meeting. During this meeting, NSA Doval gave a detailed description of the violence-prone area to the Shah. He also told the Shah that the situation in Delhi is now becoming normal and there is peace.

National Security Advisor (NSA) Ajit Doval has briefed Home Minister Amit Shah about the prevailing situation in North East Delhi where communal violence has claimed at least 22 lives. Ajit Doval met Amit Shah soon after his visit to the riot-affected areas of North East Delhi. This was the NSA's second visit to the violence-hit localities in less than 24 hours. NSA Ajit Doval briefed Amit Shah about the current law and order situation in North East Delhi and steps taken to bring back normalcy there, a home ministry official said. As per sources in the government, NSA Ajit Doval has been given the charge of bringing Delhi violence under control. The NSA will be briefing the Prime Minister and the Cabinet on the present situation in Delhi. NSA Doval had last night visited Jaffrabad, Seelampur and other affected parts of northeast Delhi to review the situation.

The NSA has made it clear that lawlessness would not be allowed to remain in the national capital & adequate number of police forces and paramilitary forces have been deployed. The police have been given a free hand to bring the situation under control. National Security Advisor (NSA) Ajit Doval had visited the area affected by violence in northeast Delhi last night and reviewed security arrangements. Ajit Doval had on Tuesday night reached North East Delhi for an on the spot inspection and to get a stock of the situation. NSA Ajit Doval reached Seelampur to get a briefing on the situation minutes after Home Minister Amit Shah called for a third meeting with Delhi Police and his ministry officials on Tuesday evening.

US lawmakers expressed concern over Delhi violence, said world is watching. Delhi violence has drawn sharp reactions from US lawmakers who have called the situation horrifying. Reacting to the violence that has claimed at least 13 lives, US Congress woman Pramila Jayapal said the "deadly surge of religious intolerance in India is horrifying". "Democracies should not tolerate division and discrimination or promote laws that undermine religious freedom," she said in a tweet, adding that the "world is watching".

Congressman Alan Lowenthal too termed the violence a "tragic failure of moral leadership". "We must speak out in the face of threats to human rights in India," he said. National Security Advisor (NSA) Ajit Doval visits northeast Delhi early on Wednesday morning. Ajit Doval visited several violence-hit parts of northeast Delhi such as Seelampur, Bhajanpura, Yamuna Vihar and Maujpur. He was accompanied by the Deputy Commissioner of Police. National Security Advisor (NSA) Ajit Doval leaves from the office of Deputy Commissioner of Police North-East in Seelampur to review the security situation in different parts of North-East Delhi, on the intervening night of 25-26 February, All Delhi Metro stations have been reopened, including Jaffrabad, Maujpur-Babarpur, Gokulpuri, Johri Enclave and Shiv Vihar, that were shut for two days over the incessant violence and clashes in northeast Delhi.

Parts of Delhi has been on the boil over the past three days while communal violence over the amended citizenship law further escalated in northeast Delhi on Tuesday. A total of 13 have died while over 200 people have been injured in the clashes across different parts of northeast Delhi, such as Chand Bagh, Bhajanpura, Gokulpuri, Maujpur and Jaffrabad.

Police struggled to check the rioters who ran amok on streets, burning and looting shops, pelting stones and thrashing people. After overnight incidents of arson, tension shouldered in the national capital and as the day progressed. Several localities like Chand Bagh, Bhajanpura, Gokulpuri, Maujpur, Kardampuri and Jaffrabad saw pitched battles between the members of two groups who also hurled petrol bombs and opened fire. A curfew was imposed in parts of northeast Delhi and rumors flew of Delhi Police issuing shoot-at-sight orders, which the police later denied. As Delhi Police faced allegations of inaction, Union Home Minister Amit Shah held a meeting at noon with Delhi Lieutenant Governor Anil Baijal, Chief Minister Arvind Kejriwal, city police commissioner Amulya Patnaik and others on steps to restore peace. The meeting resolved to take measures to stop rumor-mongering and also use drones at the protest sites to identify miscreants.

It needs to be unraveled who is responsible for the current riots in Delhi, the Sena said while referring to the "language of threats and warning used by some BJP leaders". It further said that the violence could potentially spread the message that the Central government has failed to maintain the law and order situation in Delhi.

[2.7]

Indian Democracy under BJP: BJP-led govt had not only destroyed democracy but turned democracy into an activity of tyranny, chaos, and anarchy. Violent clashes erupted in the Indian capital as sectarian violence engulfed parts of India's capital last month.

(i) Women in Delhi mourn relatives who were killed in the communal violence.

(ii) People carry the body of a riot victim during a funeral procession in Delhi last month.

The hospital overflowed with patients as the violence outside raged for five days. Rickshaw puller Prem Singh's family found him there the day after Ansari's death. Singh had stepped out to buy milk for his three children and never returned. He was one of the unidentified bodies recovered from the roadside and placed at the mortuary. He was shot dead by a Muslim mob targeting Hindus in the area.

Heart-rending reports of human misery, and cruelty, have poured in from the neighborhoods of New Delhi that were ravaged by groups of rioters even as US President Donald Trump was visiting the Indian capital last month. Armed with guns, petrol bombs, sticks and rods, they fought pitched street battles, attacked people and homes, set fire to shops, markets, schools and vehicles, and desecrated mosques and cemeteries. Large swathes of northeastern Delhi were laid waste in an orgy of violence that could well have been mistaken for war-torn Syria.

Thousands have been displaced and lives and livelihoods destroyed beyond repair. The toll, which currently stands at 53 – including 33 Muslims and 15 Hindus – is being updated as more bodies are discovered, the grievously injured continue to die in hospitals, and corpses are identified, sometimes only from their half-burnt limbs. Narendra Modi's monopoly over power and his vision of India through the eye of most talented art of assistant Amit Saha gets shattered not only in India but all over. Last week, angry opposition leaders threw a pertinent in parliament, demanding a discussion under a thrust of outrage the incidents of violence. Enraged by the House Speaker's decision to defer the discussion with the pretext of Holi, they balled up pieces of paper and threw them at him. That is what Indian parliamentarians can carryout of the outburst of anger. They also rush to the "Well of the House" – a space for secretarial staff near the Speaker which MPs occupy as a traditional form of registering protest.

Public in general had lost the confidence with the political leaders both in for or against the government. If the opposition leaders were sincere for the well fare of the public, they could raise their voice earlier. Had the opposition leaders been get agitated a couple of weeks earlier and ventured into the restive areas of the city with the same urgency, dozens of people might still be alive and thousands of families saved from impoverishment. Throughout the time Delhi burned, or in the days building up to the violence, none of them showed any interest in mobilizing their cadres to organize peace marches or initiate other community interventions. Protesters can shout slogans afterwards making a rally demanding the resignation of Home Minister Amit Shah for his alleged inaction in stopping the deadly communal violence in Delhi but without any effect, the dead soul would not get back the life.

It is not that the clashes that erupted or the targeted violence that followed were a complete surprise. Modi's Bharatiya Janata Party (BJP) has for some time been openly inciting its flock for a bloody showdown. Once the hotheads on both sides had been sufficiently warmed up, the final act would begin. And, it needed to begin soon, as the BJP's crushing defeat in last month's Delhi state election indicated that it was losing its Hindu majoritarian narrative to the recent spurt of secular protests against a new law, the law of formulating NRC with a new pattern throughout the country had seen as anti-Muslim. The bloodbath in Delhi is the culmination of months of protests against a controversial law that gives preference to non-Muslim refugees from neighboring Islamic nations over others in granting Indian citizenship. Together with a proposed national citizenship verification drive, the law is seen as a tool to single out Muslims for disenfranchisement while protecting Hindus and other minorities who lack sufficient documentary proof of citizenship. No country in the world gets its development by the discrimination of its citizens. The real destroyer was Gandhi who initiated the discrimination by starting "Non-Violence" only with the Hindus. Now the activity of BJP is only for capturing power and not with neither the majority of Hindu votes, nor the development through the economic prosperity of the nation similar to the activity of Gandhi, who only did everything to keep the image of "Non-Violence" and not the unity of the country nor the economic prosperity of the nation unlike other political leaders of other nations. Thus BJP leaders are selfish for making BJP government while Gandhi was selfish for keeping "Non-Violence" for his name as a man of peace and no one was thinking for the prospect of the nation and the economy of the nation.

Considered by many as an affront to India's secular constitution that does not discriminate on the basis of religion, the law has triggered rallies, marches and boycotts across the nation. Largely led by students, activists, intellectuals, artists, film personalities and the liberal middle class, the protests have been the first mass outpouring of popular rage against Modi's government. One area in Delhi in particular, called Shaheen Bagh, where elderly Muslim women have led a peaceful sit-in since December, has become an iconic protest site. It has inspired copycat, non-violent demonstrations across the country, which triggered the violence in Delhi.

Senior BJP leaders have been openly urging followers to attack the protesters. "Shoot the traitors" has become a popular slogan for party workers, who like to see the protests as a purely Muslim phenomenon and hence deserving of a bloody reprisal. The BJP tried to whip up majoritarian anger against Muslim protesters in the recently concluded Delhi state elections but failed miserably, as the local AamAadmi Party (AAP) swept back to power with an overwhelming majority. Rather than accept the people's verdict, a local BJP leader threatened protesters with violence if they did not end their sit-ins. That inflammable speech set the stage for the clashes between Hindu and Muslim mobs days later. What began as rioting by both sides soon descended into a massacre of Muslims, as hordes of armed Hindu men brought in from outside Delhi went about targeting Muslim homes and businesses.

In the time-honored tradition of Indian mass murders, such as Gujarat in 2002 and Delhi in 1984, the overwhelmingly Hindu police force remained inactive, either choosing to look away or ordered to stand down and allow the bloodletting by their political administrators. To regain the image of Indian democracy particularly in abroad, Modi's federal government, has swung into action – although it is late. Now an uneasy peace is returning as the Delhi police force, was engaged into action to control the situation from further deterioration.

Security personnel were engaged to patrol roads in Delhi following the communal violence. Delhi as the nation's capital allows for its police force to be controlled by the federal government unlike all other state governments where the police forces remain under the control of State Government. Delhi's ruling AAP, which grew out of an anti-corruption movement in 2012, uses this as an excuse to pretend helplessness in the matters related to law and order. AAP the newly formed party was thinking to emerge as a national party. It gave emphasis on basic services, such as health and education;in contrast to the **denominational** politics of BJP Party keeping focus on religion and caste that party often resorts to. AAP was rewarded handsomely for its development agenda in the Delhi elections, but on the raging issue of the BJP's Hindu-first thrust and the larger national debate over assaults on the secular character of the Indian state, the AAP has chosen the convenient path of silence.

The AAP neither pressed its substantial cadres into action nor did it exhibit any urgency in ramp-up the city's medical services to help riot victims. It was a Delhi High Court judge, S. Muralidhar, who had due to the urge of humanity convene a midnight hearing at his home to order police to ensure safe passage for the injured to hospitals, after reports that ambulances were being blocked by rioters.The AAP government was also slow in setting up health and relief camps for the victims after the violence subsided in order to keep his image as a balanced politician. Afterwards Delhi chief minister, Arvind Kejriwal, came to taking action on the riots praying peace for everyone.

When the partitioning of the subcontinent into Hindu-majority India and Muslim-majority Pakistan triggered widespread riots at the time of India's independence in 1947, Mahatma Gandhi, Congress' guiding light, stayed in Calcutta restoring peace otherwise militant Muslim League volunteers might have finish many of Hindu political leaders when there might be no body to rule Hindu India what had happened once in the capture of Delhi by Babur. In early 1948, when communal violence again gripped Delhi, Jawaharlal Nehru rushed to the scene and urged the rioters to stop. The startled rioters, recognizing India's first prime minister retreated.

India's current prime minister was hosting Trump at a carnival dinner less than 10km away from where violence erupted. Even if Modi was not otherwise engaged, nobody would expect him to intervene personally to stop the riots. His detractors hold him responsible for allowing 2002's violence in Gujarat – where he was then the chief minister – in which more than 1,000 people, mostly Muslims, were butchered. His Hindu supremacist followers admire him for much the same reason. He has a reputation, and a constituency, what he protected for few years as Hindu Chief Minister efficiently. What is the excuse of those who claim to oppose Modi's ideology and swear by Gandhi and Nehru?

The Delhi riots are but one of the many instances of the failure of Modi's so-called secular democratic identity "Sab Ka Sath, Sab Ka Bikash"has exposed his government a Hindu-centric politics at the national level. Even though they have had some success in state as well as in central elections, where the national parties like Congress have been in disarray ever since Modi rose to power. The BJP sees Modi's thumping re-election in last year's national elections as the stamp of popular consent on the party's majoritarian project of remaking India as a Hindu state, it seems now after the declaration of NRC going to impose all over India have created mistrust, and that had been reflected in the verdict of Delhi Election where many opposition leaders may have come around to a similar view as well.

In reality, the BJP Party has actually been more honest in its hatred of Muslims than the "secular"parties that cynically use to garner votes. The protests against the citizenship law are the first time in six years of Modi's rule that indicates a sincere alternative idea of India by the other political Party. Modi's rule is increasingly being compared to the 18-month "Emergency" that former Prime Minister Indira Gandhi imposed between 1975 and 1977, when she suspended all civil liberties. There is a similarly because of the climate of existing a fear cycology. Any kind of Criticism is ruthlessly punished by branding the critic as unpatriotic. Political rivals are kept in surveillance. In Kashmir, the government locked up elected leaders and thousands of others since August with the plea of national security and without any other explanation.

In Kashmir, the citizenship law and a citizenship verification drive in Assam have caused India's score to fall the most among the world's 25 largest democracies of the year, according to a new report from US democratic center of observation. "The Indian government's alarming departures from democratic norms under Prime Minister Narendra Modi's BJP have downgraded its value as the world's biggest democracy even compare to Hong Kong, where protests demanding democracy have been raging for months.

Hopefully independent institutions key to a democracy, such as the central bank, the military, the media, and even the judiciary, have been witnessing gradually authoritarian control. Justice Murlidhar, a judge as well as a humanitarian who convened the midnight hearing to ensure the safety of riot victims and criticized the Delhi police for not prosecuting BJP leaders' hate speech, was quickly transferred to another court. Preserving democracy is after all not solely the ruler's responsibility, but also of the leader of opposition. If Modi is wrecking India's democracy, the opposition's failure to even put up a fight renders it equally guilty. Failure of democracy is nothing but the loss of economy of the country. Modi's Hindutva populism, backed by naked threats against India's Muslim minority and the suppression of dissent, is crashing India's economy and its democracy.

Using all its tools of propaganda and tactics of intimidation, Narendra Modi government is broadcasting the message that all is well in India. But it isn't. The truth is different, India, as a nation, is going through a great turmoil - economically, politically and socially according to many author, activist and writers. The Indian economy, once the world's fastest-growing economy, is now sick. According to Arvind Subramanian, Modi's former Chief Economic Advisor has written that the Indian economy is "headed for the intensive care unit." He even noted that growth has slowed "to just 4.5 per cent, the worst for a long time," and also the other economic indicators, such as "goods and services, exports, imports and government revenue are all in negative trend. Unemployment record is high, and the agricultural sector, is facing crisis.

Consumer food price inflation is 8% high. The price of a core foodstuff, such as onion has shot up by 173 percent in November. The Modi government has wrongly adopted economic policies such as "demonetization," that had decimated the world's fastest-growing economy, and brought it down to its knees. However, Modi is loudly boasting of saving the economy from disaster.It's not just the Indian economy that is facing a crisis but also India's democracy is in danger.

Thriving on communal politics, Modi and his Home Affairs minister, Amit Shah, have turned the world's largest democracy into an authoritarian state. It is true Gandhi has created the communal feelings of Hindu-Muslim under the cover of "Non-Violence" and misleads the people with religious ethics having a dress of half naked FAKIR and finally divided the country as the country of Hindus and the country of Muslims just to kick out Jinnah and made his name as a man of peace. Now seventy years have passed Indian people should not suffer any longer due to the mistake of few selfish leaders. The BJP government should not count votes keeping alive the earlier sentiment of Hindu-Muslim. A country cannot develop without the 100% devotion of the people of the country.

In Kashmir, for instance, after scrapping Article 370 which ensured a special constitutional status for the region, the Modi government arrested three former ministers, democratically elected members of Parliament who opposed the change in Kashmir's status, invoking "national security" as a reason to keep them in detention for months together. Also in the name of "national security," the Modi government imposed a colonial-era law, Section 144, suspended the internet, blocked all telephone lines and imposed a total communications blackout in Kashmir. By the ending of few months, the people of Kashmir have had to endure a great deal of suffering – but there is almost no free flow of information to the outside world, and therefore in no way of holding the Modi government accountable.

[2.8]

What is the future of democracy in India? Yesterday's hard core enemies are getting united for power (Lalu and Nitish), there is no agenda for a few political parties still ruling the states (TMC), power of state level parties is increasing which can influence the national government, calling social engineering parties are ready for any compromise (SP, BSP), partners in coalition government are acting like opposition parties (Shivsena), parties who criticized each other in the pre-election campaign come together to form Government (BJP and Jammu and Kashmir Peoples Democratic Party). Literally no political party for exception has any agenda for economic, social and cultural development; rather the political parties are driven by mass pressures to maintain their vote banks. People are getting misguided and provoked by religious and cultural threats. Emotions are riding rational thinking. It is the time for the people to think for the best as India is heading towards anarchy. Antisocial, uneducated, uncultured and corrupt people are entering politics and people are electing them again. Politics has become a money making business. Established politicians are busy in establishing their dynasty.

Delhi incidents: 25 Feb, 2020, the Home Minister appreciated the participation of all parties and urged them to exercise restraint, rise above party lines to tackle the situation, according to an official release. He also urged leaders to avoid giving provocative speeches and statements which could flare up the situation. Addressing the Delhi Assembly on violence in the parts of Delhi, Delhi Chief Minister also announced that AAP government will give Rs 1 core compensation to Head Constable Ratan Lal who was killed during the violence.

As per eyewitnesses who were inside Farooqia masjid offering evening namaz, a group of armed men broke the doors of the mosque and assaulted those inside. Mohammad Masjid, an eyewitness, said, "They were wearing helmets and we could not see their faces. They hurled petrol bombs." The mosque is next to the Mustafabad anti-CAA protest site, which was also torched. Within hours, the worst Hindu-Muslim violence in India in years was exploding. Gangs of Hindus and Muslims fought each other with swords and bats, shops burst into flames, chunks of bricks sailed through the air, and mobs rained blows on cornered men.

Though property belonging to Hindus was burned, the destruction was much heavier on the Muslim side. In Muslim areas, shop after shop was destroyed and entire markets were burned down. Dozens of Muslim residents have accused police officers of standing passively while the destruction was underway. On Wednesday, the few people out on the streets walked quietly past the blackened car hulks and smashed homes. The whiff of charred materials still hung in the air, in what some scholars said was an eerie echo of previous religious bloodletting in India.

The common public is the victims of emotions. The religious emotions created by our previous leaders are now to be removed for the betterment of the country, for the prosperity of the country and above all for the dignity of humanity. The purpose of life is to be happy. From the moment of birth, every human being wants happiness and does not want suffering. It is clear that we humans, who live on this earth, face the task of making a happy life for ourselves. Therefore, it is important to discover what will bring about the greatest degree of happiness. Happiness never confines to self, it extends to surroundings and it extends to others. Unless the surrounding is good, happiness cannot persist, unless you learn to love others, the joy of happiness, you can not realize in mind and spirit.

A healthy economy makes a family happy; a disciplined family makes the surrounding happy, a feeling of love for others makes the humanity happy. The creation of love begins with association with others, having the exchange of mind and exchange of heart. We the Indians unless we live together, we cannot think of a 'Nation of a great India'. Religion is a teaching of love, faith and devotion. Political leaders have used our faith and devotion towards religion for their benefit inacquiring power. Instead of using love to decrease the distance between people to people, our political leaders had used love to increase the distance by the weapon of hatred.

The British utilized the 'Divideand Rule Policy" to rule India. Gandhi utilized Hindu religious policy through "Non-Violence' to keep the Muslims away so that Jinnah would be away of India, Petal utilized the Hindu-Muslim hatred policy in the acceptance of two nation theory of British proposal, Nehru utilized the hatred policy of Hindu-Muslim in the acceptance of the division of the country to become the PM of India. But nobody thought of the future of the country after the division of the country. Nobody learnt any lesion from other world leaders, how they preserved the unity of the country. The people of India became the victim of partition of India caused due to the power greedy nature of our Indian leaders. Even now our political philosophers are thinking in the same pattern. They never could think of why England and French fought for hundred years but today they are the closest friend in the world.

What were the objective of the political leaders of India?: To describe the sufferings of Assam it is necessary to give an outline of the political leaders of India how the leaders of India thought for Assam and to what extent for themselves in the affairs of their comfort and luxury of life. Even after winning World War-II, the British was willing to take leave off from India as the Labor Government thought the ruling of India any longer will be injurious from economic point of view as well as from administrative point of view. The mindset of police force in India was completely changed after the war with the Azad Hind Force of Netaji. But on the other hand, the Indian political leaders were busy with how to capture the power of Chair. If there be anybody at the top, who was no other than the Great Gandhi, who had no other skill except the orthodox religion, although he had a law degree from Inner Temple, but he failed in practice completely at Bombay High Court. He was after his image how to make himself a man of peace through his new discovery of "Non-Violence"

In the course of progress it appeared that Gandhi, a man of Gujarat and Nehru a man of Allahabad became close enough to each other and finally both became the renowned persons in the World with secret understanding. Nehru became the PM of India after independence due to Gandhi and Gandhi became the father of the Nation due to Nehru. Motilal Nehru was the Congress president till the end of 1920. Gandhi came in contact with Motilal Nehru and became an active member of Congress. However he became

Congress President in 1924 due to good wishes of Motilal Nehru and that was the turning point of Gandhi's life as a political leader. He spread the Congress activity in every cities and every villages, by the message of non-violence but again he supported violence, he supported the Khilaphat Movement, a violent Muslim movement for the cause of preserving Khilafat in Turkey, earlier he supported the British by joining World war I, all activity was for his popularity to establish himself as the Supreme leader, no matter with the ethics of "Non-Violence" or ethics of violence. For the sake of popularity he never hesitated to join the British in the war, and supported the violent activity of the war or to join the Khilaphat Movement where the Muslims of India doing violent activity against the British in India in support of the Muslims of Turkey.

After failure in Khilafat Movement, he again started Salt Satyagraha and then the "Non-Violence" activity in Calcutta in 1930, only with the Hindus, no Muslims joined the movement. He joined the round table conference at London but failed to nullify the demand of Pakistan of Jinnah with logic. Finally he agreed indirectly the British proposal of 3June 1946, two nations, for two religions. At the outset the Congress rejected the proposal but after "Calcutta Killing" Congress surrendered and agreed to the British proposal of two nations. Jinnah, the Leader of Muslim League succeeded to achieve Pakistan, but Indian leader Gandhi and others failed to achieve an United India, Nehru twisted the failure of Gandhi to success by saying India achieved Independence by Gandhi's Non-Violence whereas the Independence was due to the Muslim threat of "Calcutta Violence". Gandhi was indirectly agreed to the British proposal of partition against his earlier promise of united India in order to fulfill his inner desire to kick out Jinnah from India and become absolute man of importance of India.

The country was divided whereby Pakistan was formed. 2% ML volunteers carried out "Calcutta Killing" and 90% Indians remained as silent spectators under the leadership of Gandhi. Gandhi once publicly said "country would be divided over my dead body".

But that commitment remained as commitment. The young Nehru became PM of India and in 1962 Nehru gave good-bye to Assam in the event of Chinese onslaught over Assam crossing Arunachal.This was the love of Indian leader with the people of the remote corner of India of Assam.

But after partition it appeared almost all the Hindus of East Pakistan had been thrown out of East Bengal but no Muslims from Bengal or from Assam had been thrown out of India. Instead of that a Nehru-Liquate Ali Pact was made in between Indian Prime Minister Nehru and the Pakistan Prime Minister Liquat Ali Khan whereby more Muslims came back to Assam as well as to West Bengal. Liquate Ali Khan, a man of Pakistan a leader of Indian Muslims once; never have forgotten the safety of the Muslim people although Pakistan was formed for few Muslims of India. He thought himself lucky for the creation of Pakistan where Muslims could live like that of the Sultan period or Mughal period of India but he was in distress of mind for the future safety of the Muslims remained in India after the partition. The problem was more in East Pakistan as he had initiated the exodus of Hindus with the secret method of violence and burning of Hindu houses in the night and lifting of households in the daytime. Millions of Hindus evacuated the seventeen districts of East Bengal and had taken shelter in the nearby regions of Bengal and Assam in the month of January and February of 1950 reducing the Hindu percentage from 37% to 7% (at present). He was worried with the repercussion in Bengal and Assam. But surprisingly he gets a call from Indian PM Nehru. Immediately he responded, fixed a date and had formed the Nehru-Liquat Ali Pact so that displaced Muslims can be settled in their own house in India even after the formation of East Pakistan. Thus Liaquat Ali, a leader of Muslim remained in peace after stabilizing the future safety of the Muslims in India even after the creation of a separate Muslim country for the Muslims of India. There lies his successes of leadership and peace of mind unlike Indian leaders who were in mental peace for their personal success. But Nehru, the PM of India, a man of Uttar Bharat how could he think for the people of Assam or Bengal? If so how did he allow the Muslims of East Bengal in addition to the Bengali Hindus to live in Assam and Bengal to make the life of the people of this region miserable? Population explosion is the reason of unrest in these regions. Thus Muslim leaders did everything for the Muslims for their better future, while the Hindu leaders of Delhi did nothing for the people of these regions after the division of Bengal and Assam based on religion except exploiting the people with the false hope of industry and job opportunity.

Thereby the agony of Assam was increased step by step. Thus instead of reducing the sufferings of the people of Assam, the government of India was increasing the sufferings and hence the agony of Assam. Thus the people of Assam are agitating against CAA.

[Indian Prime Minister Narendra Modi and Bangladeshi Prime Minister Sheikh Hasina after a meeting in New Delhi on October 5, 2019 agreed to sign number of agreement.]

Recent political developments in India have opened up a Pandora's Box, to say the least. The developments in regards to CAA and NRC in India are overtly targeting the country's largest minority, Muslims. With an increase in hate crimes particularly against Muslims in recent years, there is fear that India, long known as the world's largest democracy, has going dangerously intolerant to Muslims under the ruling of Bharatya Janata Party (BJP).

For the Awami League government in Bangladesh, which shares a border with India on three sides, India's National Register of Citizens (NRC) and Citizenship Amendment Act (CAA) were regarded as "internal matters," or so it was declared to the people of Bangladesh Government that NRC or CAA is the internal matters of India. However, this nonsense stance of India is not accepted by the people of Bangladesh. A government remains in power with the desire (votes) of the people. Realizing the fact, the Government of Bangladesh is now not cooperating with India in many respects. It might be the reason why did Bangladesh deny sending his foreign Minister to India to an important meeting, although in the last October, Bangladeshi Prime Minister Sheikh Hasina signed seven bilateral treaties with her counterpart Narendra Modi in India. It is unfortunate on the part of Modi government to destroy the good relation with Bangladesh for a better future prosperity.

At a time when anti-India sentiments are profound among Bangladeshis, New Delhi assured Dhaka that the NRC and CAA would not affect Bangladesh. However, the people as well as the government are not satisfied only with the assurance. There are genuine concerns and apprehensions in Bangladesh that the NRC and CAA might unleash an exodus of Muslim Bengali-speaking people from Assam to escape persecution in India. After having taken in nearly a million Rohingya refugees fleeing persecution in Myanmar, Bangladesh cannot take in any more.

It is a pity that India's spirit of being known as "the world's largest democracy" has been infected by the Modi regime, giving rise to the fundamental question: What is the future of Muslims in India? Furthermore, how will the ethnocentric anti-Islamic reign of terror in India affect Bangladesh? Everybody, every citizen of Assam irrespective of Hindu, Muslim, Bengalis, Assamese, non Assamese, Tribals, Adi-Bashi and all other groups of Assam want development along with India. Let a peaceful atmosphere be prevailing in India as well as in Assam for the development of Assam which was neglected so long.

Reasons of enmity of Responsible persons: The formation of Pakistan, a separate homeland for the Muslims of India what was created on 1947 on the basis of religion had created new problem for the genuine Muslims of India, who did not choose to go to Pakistan or even consented to form Pakistan. They were as bonafide citizens of India as anybody else. The leaders of India and the leaders of Muslim League under the guidance of Jinnah and under the guidance Gandhi had never thought it necessary to ask for their consent before agreeing to the decision of dividing India. The leaders were over whelmed with the joy of power of chair and joy of international name and fame that they had no time to think anything else. The partition made the identity of the Muslims of Assam &West Bengal as well as the Muslims of whole of India, very problematic and questionable. What should be their status in view of the formation of a newly created national state based on the religious identity taking into account only of a few Muslims of Muslim League? Of course, the identity crisis of the Muslims was not altogether a product of the partition although the partition added a new dimension to it. There had been an age-old dichotomy existed between the identity of the Muslims and the Hindus. The identity of the Muslims of Bengal (including Assam) had been partitioned long before as the Hindus of Bengal, in general, believed that the Muslims of Bengal were not Bengalis by the birth of heredity. The Hindu Bengali intellectuals of Calcutta had seen that the majority of the Muslims of Calcutta were non-Bengali in origin, who used to speak in Hindustani Urdu. Moreover, to increase the social status the upper class Muslims always gave stress to their foreign origin publicly. The Muslim speaks Bengali language with a style of inscribing with some Urdu and Arabic words, although at the lower level, both the Hindus and the Muslims shared almost the same language. With the formation of Pakistan due to the demand of a section of the Muslims, the loyalty of the Muslims as a whole was put to question in India. It was quite natural that since partition time, Muslims would be labeled as anti-national and constantly looked upon with a degree of suspicion. Who were responsible for that, definitely, not the genuine Muslims who loved the country not less than anybody else. It was the few leaders of Muslim community as well as the few leaders of Hindu community had remained responsible for their immediate gain. They had made a compromise among themselves in sharing the chair of power and name and fame. It was pity to see that even today; Muslims were required to prove that they were not anti- nationals in many of their activity.

[2.9]

Gandhi's leadership inquisitiveness: Gandhiji's method of political mobilization of the masses was nothing less than magical. Gandhi after his arrival took extensive tour all over India to get to know firsthand information regarding the plight of Indians under the British Raj. Meanwhile he maintained silence and continued to study the existing Indian leaders keeping an eye on the political situation of India. He participated in the session of Indian National Congress and the Muslim League but chose to remain neutral. Gandhi had on his own that the constitutional and political methods which were in momentum in the colonial country could not do anything unless these movements were started based on the principles of Satyagraha. The Indian National Congress up to 1916 remained as an organization of moderates but since 1916 the Indian National Congress appeared to be turning to an extremist organization. After the advent of Gandhi, the Congress ceased to be either a 'Moderate' or an 'Extremist' body, but Gandhian, because he gave the Congress an ideology of "Non-Violence" for mass gathering movement and less hostile to government for prolonging the movement and making him the prime leader. His magical power as crowd puller lies in his words which were regarded as **sacrosanct** as religious rituals which were perhaps the sole mover of Gandhi to a political height. He had long realized that to the majority of Indians what mattered was religious sentiment and Gandhi left no opportunity to grab that. When Gandhi's call for non-cooperation against the Rowlatt Act paid no dividend, he turned towards the Khilafat movement card. The Indian national Congress passed a resolution at the Calcutta session in September 1920 and demanded for the establishment of an atmosphere of Swaraj. Poet Rabindranath Tagore, M.A. Jinnah and many others opposed the resolution. M.A. Jinnah thought that it would throw the unprepared ignorant mass into a serious kind of disaster but no one could dare to stop Gandhi.

Gandhi rejected Jinnah's advice. Gandhi said that he did not rely merely upon the lawyer class or highly educated men to carry out all the activity of non-cooperation. His hope was more with the masses, so far as non-cooperation are concerned. M.A. Jinnah lost faith with Gandhi and he stood for his Muslim people who were in utter loneliness particularly after the 1920 Congress session, who did not endorsed Gandhiji's methods but at the same time he refused to acknowledge any voice of dissent. Jinnah although had the same bitterness as Gandhi against the British but his methods and styles seemed to exercise cautions and restraint and avoided to throw his people into the abyss of civil war. Both the leaders began to differ on various issues together with their achievements in political field. Both were looking for public benefit but again also for personal image how to be a bigger leader. Finally they got separated at the height of political development when Jinnah finally sought for an independent and separate country of his own.

The question of Equality: In the secular, democratic India, all citizens are equal in the eyes of law. But in actual practice, it failed to satisfy the minorities, particularly the Muslims, who were treated separately on the ground of national security as their loyalty was suspected. It was also true, the partition and subsequently the formation of Pakistan had created religious bitterness and also enmity. The Muslims of Pakistan would leave no stone unturned to instigate a few of the Muslims of India to work for sabotage activity on behalf of Pakistan to hackle India. In the process of investigation genuine Muslims were also sometimes punished, which would lead to resentment and generate feeling of downgraded citizen, an unbearable and painful state of situation. The country had to face this situation why? It was due to the luxury of few Indian leaders for occupying the power of Delhi's chair at the cost of the division of the country. In West Bengal, the Muslims were historically far behind the Hindus in respect of wealth, power and education, because the Muslims once in the earlier time had discarded the learning of English. It was only during the last two decades of the undivided Bengal that the Muslim upper class and middle class came out to challenge the superiority of their Hindu counterparts. With the partition, the situation had changed drastically, because of the arrival of the educated middle class refugees from East Pakistan, the pro-Hindu attitude of the employers came in their way as an obstacle to get a job of honor because of existing communal atmosphere. All kinds of crisis were the cause of economic backwardness of Bengal.

It was neither the British nor the Delhi government gave necessary attention to improve the economy of the nation particularly the economy of Eastern India including United Assam and Bengal. It was nothing but to fight for food and survives. Thus, the partition had a disastrous effect not only on the Hindus of East Bengal but also on the Muslims of Bengal and Assam as well. For the sake of argument it could be said that Muslims had got what they had wanted, the Pakistan, the East Pakistan, what else had remained here for them? But the fact of the matter was that all Muslims did not want Pakistan, it was Jinnah, who wanted Pakistan for his desire to be the Chief of the nation centering Punjab which is nearby to his birth place but very cleverly he could utilize the Muslims of Bengal for his benefit taking the issue of religion to instigate the simple minded common people of Bengal who thought all the (Allah) is the only hope for survival in the case of any disorder and despair.

The creation of Pakistan in the Eastern wing of India was a necessary step for Jinnah to full fill the demand of Pakistan by the "Calcutta Killing" through Bengal PM Suhawardy. He knows it was impossible to achieve his goal of attaining Pakistan without the Bengali mighty force, who never went back to raise their voice for

Pakistan and later even by the use of mighty sword. He did not start the direct action from Delhi or Lucknow or any part of UttarBharat, the centre of Mughal Emperor or from South, the place of TipuSultan, but he started the direct action from Bengal itself, although many Muslims did not like the voice of Pakistan. But for no reasons many genuine Muslims were penalized. It was the creation of power greedy politicians. The formation of Pakistan was originally thought of by Jinnah for the Western regions including Punjab, but initially he did not get sufficient response from the region of Punjab, the center of military force, because Punjab was at that time neither with Muslim League nor with the Congress but with a Punjabi Hindu (Sikhh)-Muslim united Party what was the Unionists Party. But Jinnah after the successful operation of "Calcutta Killing" carried out by the militant Muslim League Volunteers under the command of Bengal Prime Minister Suhwardy, had succeeded to destroy the unity of Unionists Party and brought the Hindu-Muslim hatred, rioting and violence even in Punjab. People were afraid to talk against those politically powerful leaders. Of course even today in independent India it exists, it carries dangers to speak against any powerful political leader. This is what the Indian Democracy is!

The age-old friendship and brotherhood between Hindus and Muslims were totally destroyed by the clever policy of partition of Delhi leaders involving Hindus and Muslims under the guidance of Jinnah and under the guidance of the Congress President Nehru and Petal keeping Gandhi as the prime architect behind the scene. It was because the more the destruction of Bengal, the less was the obstacle for the Delhi leaders to occupy the chair of power. It was the Bengal and Bengali people in the British administration that stood as the pillar of British Rule. After the driven out of the creamy layer of the Muslim society from West Bengal, the remaining Muslims who stayed behind were progressively marginalized in every aspect of life. During the first two decades after partition, the Muslims faced a tremendous communal hostility, by the arrival of refugee from East Bengal in everyday with the vivid memory of human atrocity. Who is to blame-- Muslim League or Congress or the power greedy political philosophers? Who was destined to claim an International political philosopher, how he could forget to visualize the eventful situation of post-partition era and remained idle without taking effective steps to remove the sufferings of the people. The look-out was the Chair and not the sufferings of the people. Had it has been in mind, the division of the country would have been rejected. Muslims were isolated, alienated and their identity was fragmented. Therefore, it is now the time for reconstruction of brotherhood and friendship and thinks for the Unity of Hindus and Muslims.

Peace in Unification: Although partition has long been used as a tool of resolving ethnic and communal problems, but it never gave a permanent solution. Partition means breaking, what is used as for the solution of the problem in order to bring peace and happiness. But the philosophy of happiness dictates that 'happiness and real peace' rests in unity while 'enmity and bitterness' rests in disunity. As the culture and scientific evolution is expanding day by day, the unity among mankind is growing faster and faster. UNO is the example of unity of nations and sustaining peace since World War Second. Following the pattern of territorial partition, the Partition of Germany, Cyprus, Korea and Vietnam, the British Indian Empire followed the same tradition to divide India and the State of Punjab and Bengal aswell. The partition theorists might have argued that physical separation of warring ethnic groups may be the only possible solution to prevent civil war but such kind of solution is nothing but a temporary solution. Korea was divided into North Korea and South Korea under the influence of two superpowers. But were the two countries in peace? War threat is continuing between the two countries concerning with little matter. So partition could not bring peace except temporary peace. The East German and the West German again under the two super powers remain separated since 1945. To prevent the flow of people from East to West, Berlin Wall was erected. But again on 28 November 1990, the reunion occurred with the fall of Berlin Wall. Thus it is seen 'Peace lies in Unity'. Vietnam was in constant fight, North Vietnam against South Vietnam under the influence of big powers. But the untiring efforts of Ho ChiMinh brought the unification of two Vietnam and that exerted real peace in Vietnam. So peace lies in unification. Looking to Cyprus, the conflict started since1974, after the Turkish invasion of Cyprus.

In the threat of mass massacre, transfer of large number of people took place forming the Turkish Cypriots in the North and Greek Cypriots in the South. The conflict never had ended. UN Secretary, Koff Annon proposed for referendum in 2004. Division or Partition never solves the problem. Partition of India was a mistake and the issue was to capture the seat of power. And the Partition of Bengal was to crush the Hindu elite, who ruled during British Period and the Bengal so that Bengalis never could turn back towards Delhi. The leading partition theorists like ChaimKaufmann, John Mearsheimer and Stephen Van Evera and Donald Horowitzer provided the basic arguments in favor of partition for the fact that it is a humane way of dealing with an ethnic conflict through negotiation avoiding war & loss of lives. But the reality is different. Did the division of India bring peace with Pakistan? It has brought enmity between the two nations. It would not go until the unity is restored. Did the division of Bengal bring the end of rioting and torture? No, it had brought religious hatred and destroyed the feelings of brotherhood.

Hindu–Muslim unity is a religiopolitical concept in the Indian subcontinent which stresses members of the two largest faith groups Hindus and Muslims working together for the common good. The concept was championed by various rulers of India, such as Mughal Emperor Akbar, leaders in the Indian independence movement, such as Mahatma Gandhi (correctly more for Hindus through Hindu ethics of 'Non-Violence") and Khan Abdul Ghaffar Khan as well as by political parties and other movements, such as the Indian National Congress, KhudaiKhidmatgar and All India Azad Muslim Conference.

In the earlier time in Mughal India, the emperor Akbar advocated for Hindu–Muslim unity, appointing both Hindus and Muslims as officials in his court. Akbar participated and promoted festivals of both Hinduism and Islam, he also created feasts such as PhoolWalon Ki Sair to be celebrated by citizens of all faiths. Chhatrapati Shivaji also tried to promote Hindu-Muslim unity. Maratha HindaviSwarajya also kept many Muslims in high posts. Shivaji's personal security, his most trusted courtiers were Muslims. A Muslim general had led the Maratha troops once in the battle of Panipat. In the First War of Indian Independence in 1857, the Hindus and Muslims of India mobilized to fight together against the British. Reflecting on this in 2007, Manmohan Singh once the PM of India stated that these events "stood as a great testimony to the traditions of Hindu–Muslim unity that held out as an example for subsequent generations".

The Lucknow Pact of 1916 was an example that could be seen as an "important step forward in achieving Hindu–Muslim unity" during the era of the Indian independence movement. Muhammad Ali Jinnah advocated Hindu–Muslim unity in early years of his political career. Gopal Krishna Gokhale stated that Jinnah "has true stuff in him, and that freedom from all sectarian prejudice which will make him the best ambassador of Hindu–Muslim Unity". In summary it could be concluded that Jinnah was liberal but Gandhi was communal and Gandhi was responsible for the division of the country.

Threats to Hindu–Muslim unity: In the First War of Indian Independence, known as the Indian Rebellion in 1857, Hindus and Muslims in India joined together as Indians to fight the British. The British became concerned about this rise in Indian nationalism and therefore henceforth the British set up communalistic feelings in their administration among Hindus and Muslims so that they might not again unite to try and overthrow any rule of British crown. The author of Composite Nationalism and Islam, Maulana Husain Ahmad Madani, a Deobandi Muslim scholar and proponent of a united India, argued that the British were attempting to "scare Muslims into imagining that in a free India Muslims would lose their separate identity, and be absorbed into the Hindu fold", a threat that "aimed at depoliticizing the Muslims, weaning them away from struggle for independence." In the eyes of Madani, support for a two-nation theory resulted in the entrenchment of British imperialism.

In the same vein, Kashmiri Indian politician and Supreme Court judge MarkandeyKatju **wrote in** The Nation, up to 1857, there were no communal problems in India; all communal riots and animosity began after 1857. No doubt even before 1857, there were differences between Hindus and Muslims, the Hindus going to temples and the Muslims going to mosques, but there was no enmity or animosity. In fact, the Hindus and Muslims used to help each other in their festivals even in the religious festival; Hindus used to participate in Eid celebrations, and Muslims in Holi and Diwali. The Muslim rulers like the Mughals, Nawab of Awadh and Murshidabad, Tipu Sultan, etc were totally secular; they organized Ramlilas, participated in Holi, Diwali, etc. In 1857, the 'Great Mutiny' broke out in which the Hindus and Muslims jointly fought against the British. The British government thought to start the policy of divide and rule policy after 1857.

[2.10]

Who was Communal Gandhi or Jinnah? Gandhi and Jinnah both was friend and both of them played the important role in India's freedom struggle against the British colonial rule, but they were enemy to the people of partition victims. They were good to the people of the country as they brought independence to them but they were the worst creature of humanity as they brought inhuman misery to the people who lost many of their near and dear ones in rioting and passing their lives in distress. They have shown their common concerns on leading the country to the goal of freedom, but in the end instead of unity of the people and unity of the country they divided the people as well as divided the country. However, Gandhi differed from Tilak (Bal Gangadhar Tilak) who got himself closely associated with the orthodox sections of the Hindu society as well as with the militant revolutionary. Tilak laid down the foundation of militant Hindu party working for the nation as anti-British as well as anti-Muslim. Although Gandhi was an orthodox Hindu, but never dare to be anti-Muslim on political ground because he was a man of weak mind prefers "Non-Violence" for his image in the absence of any desire or capacity for the creation of militant Hindu group. Gandhi was attached with the basic dogma of truth, kindness and service to humanity but bias towards the Hindus. The Dalit intellectuals criticize Gandhi for endorsing the Caste system in Hindu religion.

His decisions to show affiliation with Khilafat Movement indicates he was principle less and suffering with a dilemma of what is good or what is bad. It is also alleged that he lent his support to the Hindu Mahasabha's appeal for one million rupees for carrying out the specific work. He was also not other than a communalist when he is shown to be a deep rooted orthodox Hindu not ready to reconcile with any one and boast of his religion on the top of others. Jinnah never allowed religion to dominate his political outlook or activity. He hated caste violence and also communalism. Jinnah disliked Mullahs for which once he was to appoint a backward Hindu Jogindarnath Mandal as the first Kazi of sovereign republic of Pakistan which he was to create as the Quaid-i-Aam. If he was communal how he could keep a large number of intimate friends who were no other than Hindus and Parses. Jinnah was essentially a politician and had no live consciousness of his religion. The birth of Jinnah as a Congressman incidentally occurred at a time when All India Muslim League was born in 1906. Jinnah did not join the Muslim League at first. Rather Jinnah in those days was persuading the Indians and particularly the Muslims to join Congress. He bitterly opposed for reservation and highly critical of Communal Electorates in 1908.Thus it was seen the role of M.A. Jinnah for over two decades was dedicated to the cause of Nation. He only in 1912 became a member of Muslim League as well with a condition that Muslim League has to revise its constitution and to work for Hindu-Muslim Unity.

He warned the Leaguers in the Muslim League Session held in 1918 in Delhi, not to dabble in Khilafat issue as it did not being concerned with India. Again he opposed Gandhian politics solely because of Gandhi's approach and methods which had potential to jeopardize the whole concept of national unity. M. A. Jinnah was a strong believer in secularism and a leader with specific objective.

Gandhi was never a strong believer in secularism but biased with orthodox Hindus and Hinduism. He was after his image through "Non-Violence". Jinnah was a true ambassador of Hindu-Muslim unity but not Gandhi. Gandhi was responsible for the division of the country to become the FATHER of the nation by removing Jinnah and bringing Nehru in the Chair. M. A. Jinnah was never a communal person or a communal Muslim, although he had been towards Muslims to create Pakistan because of orthodox Hindu Gandhi. M.K. Gandhi was a communal person by birth; he was always with the Hindus to create a Hindu Rastra and always in the endeavor of how to be the FATHER of the nation by removing Jinnah from the country and bringing Nehru in the Chair. Now Indians should think why a communal person should be honored as the Father of the nation who destroyed the country by division and destroyed the Hindu-Muslim brotherhood by division of the people by the movement of "Non-Violence". The pain of destruction of brotherhood was not forgotten even after more than 70 years of Indian Independence, the recent "Delhi Violence "is the real testimony.

Therefore, it is now the time for reconstruction of brotherhood and friendship and thinks for the Unity of Hindus and Muslims and not Delhi rioting through the non issue of CAA and NRC. The CAA is a issue that is concerned with department of Foreign Affairs and NRC is also an issue concerned with particular Department concern but both were brought in public front by the government by passing laws in Parliament just to bring a sense of sentiment that the present government is working for the right of Hindus, so that the Hindus (Majority) would support the government and the BJP party would remain in power even in future. Therefore the issue is nothing but the issue of partition based on two nation theory out of religion. The creation of two nation was originated by Gandhi starting with his own discovery of "Non-Violence" movement taking only the Hindus most vigorously in Calcutta since 1930 creating a community of Bengali Hindu a supporter of "Non-Violence" and another a community of Muslim, the non supporter of "Non-Violence" who created later the militant Muslim League (ML). Thus who was the destroyer of the nation with the creation of Hindus and Muslims, no other than Gandhi? A destroyer should not live in peace but he was recognized as the FATHER of the nation by twisting the history. Now it is Corona Virus that had made all the Indians together as one forgetting who is Hindu, who is Muslim, who is of higher caste or who is of lower caste. Let us think of British India; we are all of one region we must fight against the enemy Corona Virus all together. Gandhi had divided us once based on Hindi-Muslim, but the pain of division had not yet gone that was why Delhi violence and the destruction of the Capital Delhi, the destruction of democracy of India. Our religious leader Gandhi had failed to unite us and agreed to divide the nation for his name and fame discarding many like Khan Abdul Gaffer Khan, Rajjaji and many others, Jinnah a non-communal leader became communal under the communal atmosphere of India and compelled to divide the country based on two religion, two country but we could see the division of segregation could not bring real peace of happiness of life and in addition we are now suffering with an invisible force what is called Corona Virus. It is now necessary to fight against the invisible enemy "Corona Virus" by a force of unity of British India what is urgently required to survive in the universe. Now it is the call of the all-mighty to get united and fight for the unknown enemy Corona. If we could defeat Corona Virus, we could defeat the divisive policy of Gandhi's "Non-Violence" and the two nation theory of Jinnah, where we could live again together like French and British as one British India.

3. WHO WAS GANDHI? IS HE FATHER OF THE NATION OR KILLER OF THE NATION?

[3.1]

To know Gandhi one has to go to the place where he built up his early life. He was born in a village of Gujarat called Purbandar where the people were passing their days remaining under the custom of orthodox Hindu religious prejudices. The effect of prejudices of the orthodox Hindu religion bestowed over him at his early life that never went away from him even in his later life.It is heartening to remember that when he was about to go to London for the study of Law, he was warned by the villagers that if he was determined to go to London he could not come back later in the village as he would take alcohol in London. Under these circumstances he had to promise by touching the feet of his mother and the feet of his Brahmin Priest that he would never drink alcohol. He was a Hindu and he would follow the ethics of tolerance in the later life. The ethics of tolerance led him to engage in the movement of "Non-Violence". Mohandas Karamchand Gandhi (Mahatma Gandhi) was born on October 2, 1869, into a Hindu Modh family in Porbanadar, Gujarat, of India. His father, Karamchand Gandhi, was the Chief Minister (diwan) of the city of Porbanadar and his mother, named Putlibai, was the fourth wife; the previous three wives died in childbirth. Gandhi was born into the vaishya caste, a business class society. He married Kasturbai (Ba) Makhanji at the age of 13, through his parent's arrangement. They had four sons. Gandhi learned tolerance from Hindu religion. He never eats meat, or tasted alcohol. Gandhi studied law by going to London, and became a law graduate from the **Inner Temple** law court in 1891, and then he was admitted to the bar of England.

Very soon he returned to Bombay and began to practice law. But he failed in practice of law in Bombay Court. Finally he returned to his place of primary family home at Rajkot. He was a Burette law graduate from London but not very successful in the practice of law at Bombay. The humiliation of failure in Bombay Court began to hurting him very much mentally. Dada Abdulla, a merchant in South Africa once approach to him and requested him for going to South Africa to deal with his cases. Getting the chance he gladly accepted his proposal just to get rid of the humiliation having being a Burette Law graduate from London, but failed to practice in any reputed Court of India and as such he agreed to go to Durban, Natal in South Africa.

Very soon he experienced racism there when he was thrown off a train while holding a valid first class ticket and pushed to third class. Later he was beaten by a coach driver for refusing to travel on the foot-board to make room for a European passenger. He was barred from many restaurants because of his race. When he raised the voice of protest he found many people gather around him and support him for his right. This had given him a hidden power of strength to fight for the cause of right. In 1894, Gandhi founded the Natal Indian Congress. They focused on the Indian cause and British discrimination in South Africa. In 1897, Gandhi brought his wife and children to South Africa. But he was not good and happy enough with his eldest son as because he preferred to remain most of the time under alcohol. He was once attacked by a mob of racists. Gandhi became the first non-white lawyer to be admitted to the bar in South Africa.

In 1906 Gandhi, for the first time, organized a non-violent resistance against the Transvaal government's registration act. He called upon his fellow Indians to defy the new law in a non-violent manner and suffer the punishment for doing so. He was jailed on many occasions along with thousands of his supporters. Peaceful

Indian protests caused a public outcry and forced the South African Smuts authority to negotiate a compromise with Gandhi. Finding difficulty to control his son and harassment due to racists act in South Africa he thought to return to India. Coming to India he desire to do politics through the concept of non-violent resistance to become a leader.

Back in India, Gandhi became active and engaged himself in the struggle for Indian Independence. He spoke at the conventions of the Indian National Congress, for starting non-violent movement. In 1918, Gandhi opposed the increasing tax levied by the British during the devastating famine in non-violence manner. He was arrested in Champaran, in Bihar, for organizing civil resistance of tens of thousands of landless farmers. He was arrested and kept in jail, but Gandhi went on a hunger strike in solidarity with the famine stricken farmers. Hundreds of thousands of his supporters gathered around the jail. Finally he was released. He was delighted for his effort on seeing the success. At last the tax collection was suspended and all prisoners were released.

During "non-Violence" in Punjab the Jallianwala Bagh massacre occurred in Amritsar, on 13 April 1919 under O'Dwyer's tenure as Punjab's Lieutenant Governor. Gandhi immediately declared that all violence was evil after the Amritsar massacre of 379 civilians by British troops, which traumatized the Indian nation. As the leader of the Indian National Congress party Gandhi launched "Swaraj", a campaign for independence and non-cooperation with the British authorities. He urged Indians to replace British goods with their own fabrics and goods. He was imprisoned from 1922-1924, but released after the discovery of his disease. To keep the emotion of independence active Gandhi and Jawaharlal Nehru issued the Declaration of Independence on January 26, 1930.

The religious hatred was originated between Hindus and Muslims due to divide and rule policy of the British administration. Gandhi protested against the salt tax of the British to be paid by the poor people of the country. Gandhi wrote to the Viceroy, Lord

Irwin: "If my letter makes no appeal to your heart, on the eleventh day of March I shall proceed with co-workers of the Ashram as I can take, to disregard the provisions of the Salt Laws. I regard this tax to be the most iniquitous of all from the poor man's standpoint. As the Independence movement is essentially for the poorest in the land, the beginning will be made with this evil."From March 12 to April 6, 1930, Gandhi made the famous Satyagraha of the Salt March to Dandi. The long distance he walked on foot to the ocean in protest against the British salt monopoly and salt tax. He led thousands of Indians on a 240 mile (400 km) march by foot from Ashram Ahmadabad to the village of Dandi on the ocean to make their own salt, what is known as 'The Dandi March' or 'Salt Satyagraha'.

People became sympathetic towards Gandhi on seeing the two-mile long procession for 23 days. On April 6, Gandhi reached to the destination and collected a grain of salt and declared, "With this, I am shaking the foundations of the British Empire." Gandhi's plan worked because it appealed to people in every region, and every class. The British government imprisonment people over 60,000. The British even opened fire on the unarmed crowd and shot hundreds of demonstrators. Gandhi was arrested on 4th May 1930. At last the British government, represented by Lord Irwin, signed the Gandhi-Irwin Pact in March 1931, agreeing to free all political prisoners. Gandhi was invited to London as the leader of the Indian National Congress, but he could not win over Jinnah to demand India's right jointly. Gandhi campaigned to improve the lives of all including the untouchables; Jinnah campaigned to improve the lives of Muslims. He returned and fought for independence only with the Hindus as he failed to convince Jinnah. At the beginning of the Second World War, Gandhi had done the greatest mistake by declaring that India could not be a party in the war, while Jinnah very cleverly had supported the British in the War to become a favorite person. The result was Jinnah became a favorite man of the British but Gandhi became an unwanted person although he never raised sword against the British. He could get independence through sword in a shorter period of time as happened in the case of USA or other countries. But he preferred "Non-Violence" to give British a longer period of time to remain in power but at the same time he wanted his new experiment of "Non-Violence" get popularize so that he could make name out of "Non-Violence" as a man of peace.

India won independence in 1947, followed by the Indo-Pakistani War of 1947, and partition of India. Gandhi said, "Before partitioning India, my body will have to be cut into two pieces." About one million people died in the bloody riots until partition was asserted by Gandhi as the only way to stop the Civil War. He urged the Congress Party to accept partition, and launched his last "fast-into-death" campaign in Delhi, calling for a stop to all violence. Gandhi also called to give Pakistan the 550,000,000 rupees in honor of the partition agreement. He tried to prevent instability and anger against India through "non-Violence".Gandhi was shot three times in the chest and died while on his way to a prayer meeting, on January 30, 1948. His assassins were convicted and executed a year later. The ashes of Gandhi were split in portions and sent to all states of India to be scattered in rivers. Part of Gandhi's ashes rest in Raj Ghat, near Delhi, India. Part of Mahatma Gandhi's ashes is at the Lake Shrine in Los Angeles. Why? Gandhi could not give a United India, failed to prevent massacre of people in different places then why did people honor him for his "Non-Violence". It was due to the imposition of the then Prime Minister, Nehru. The matter was simple. Gandhi made Nehru the PM and Nehru made him the FATHER of the nation and made him immortal by his ashes in different places. But the British PM Attlee coming to Calcutta after winning the War-II said British could not rule India any longer as the British lost its forces in the War fighting against Netaji's Azaid Hind Force. If so why Gandhi was honored so much in India? Why did his birthday (October 2nd) get celebrated in India as a national holiday calling it 'Gandhi Jayanthi'?

Why did several major roads in most of the larger metropolitan cities in India name in his honor, as M.G. Road? Why he should be called Mahatma? The title "Mahatma" (meaning "great-soul") was given to him in 1915 wrongly by Rabindranath Tagore. He was nominated for the Nobel Peace Prize five times between 1937 and 1948 but very rightly Nobel Committee never awarded the Prize because in the name of "Non-Violence" he created the situation of violence, the situation of rioting and massacre whereby millions of people get displaced, get killed and created Hindu-Muslim rivalry for the past, present and for the future.

Gandhi was a politician under the cover of a Hindu Saint just to mislead the Hindu people in the name of independence of India through a movement calling it a "Non-Violence" movement. He convinced the people through religious ethics to create "Ram-Rajya". The movement of "Non-Violence" was for the independence of United India but he created a situation whereby rioting happened in between Hindus and Muslims and the country gets divided. But he became the FATHER of the nation due to his clever politics.

The Partition Plan of British, popularly known as June 3 Plan, was neither opposed by the Muslim League nor by the Congress in true sense. The leaders did not think even to carry out referendum or think it necessary to take the opinion of the majority of Muslims of India. Rather June 3 Plan was imposed over the public through rioting and "Calcutta Killing". That only justified the fact that the acting leaders were more addicted to the power of Delhi Chair and less to people's suffering. Petal was in a hurry to get independence even by division, how quickly he could be the Prime Minister of India? Gandhi was in the process how to bring Nehru in the Chair only then his image would be protected. Nehru was in the process under the guidance of Lady Mountbatten how to acquire the post of PM. Nobody thought of the consequences of the partition and not at all the people's condition out of division of Bengal and Punjab.

Gandhi became the most popular leader of the country misleading the common simple minded religious Hindu people in the name of "Non-Violence" with the illusion of the creation of a "Ram-Rajya". In public front he said the country would be divided over my dead body. But the Congress and Gandhi finally accepted partition on grounds- that it reflected the will of the people that it was the only way out. On 4th June, Gandhi, after meeting the Viceroy and Congress leaders, said that the CWC had agreed to the vivisection of Pakistan and Hindustan not under any threat of violence.

It was understood that Partition was temporary, that it could be turned back, once the imperialists were out of the picture. Partition was seen by the leaders as better than civil war or balkanization. Out of thrust of power every demand of the Muslim League was acceptable to Congress leaders, no matter with the division. Gandhi or the Congress leaders have no time to think why the leaders failed to convince Muslim to form a United One India. Gandhi's own reading of the communal situation was that both Hindus and Muslims had moved far away from non-violence, as such the first objective was independence at any cost to make name and fame under the shadow of Nehru family as he has no leadership capacity except religious affinity and befooled the people in the name of "Non-Violence".

Congress leaders wanted early transfer of power to take the pleasure of Chair and just get rid of the politics of non-cooperation of the Muslim League. Petal was a selected candidate by the Congress for the post of PM of India, but Nehru was also a candidate backed by the under current guidance of Lady Mountbatten, under such condition Gandhi dismissed rumors of his disenchantment with Nehru by saying that Nehru was the best candidate for PM of India. Thus in the end as a shroud politician he was succeeded to fulfill his last desire to become the man of peace and later the Father of the nation.

Today after 70 years people could not forget the impact of partition, where the leaders thought at the time of agreeing to partition that "Partition was temporary, that it could be turned back, once the imperialists were out of the picture". All these were nothing but falsehood, the impact of partition is present in every corner of India and even among political leaders. India even now could not produce any real patriotic politician to think equally for all people of the country forgetting religion, caste or community. The failure of the maintenance of the law and order in the capital of Delhi is a clear signal of the impact of past mistake what was once created by Gandhi by his "Non-Violence" only with the Hindus, and then agreed to the formula of partition considering partition is a "temporary" affair. What once the leader of the nation Gandhi said "The country would be divided over my dead body" and later at the time of joint meeting, Gandhi considered "Partition is a Temporary affairs" which could be removed afterwards. The creation of any kind of falsehood by any political leader is nothing but an offence and anybody created such an offence is punishable. As the offence is related with the nation, the offence is serious and as such punishment of that kind of offence must be of highest order. The hanging of such an offender being related with the nation only could console the people of the nation. But Gandhi is no more as such removal of his name from the country for ever could bring only some kind of tranquility in the minds of the people of the country. There is no point of keeping his name in the Indian notes and recognizing him as the Father of the nation. If so the real feeling of brotherhood between Hindus and Muslims is likely to regain within existing India and later the feeling must be lead to faraway place Pakistan and other regions of British India when the actual India, a united India would have been turned back what was the earlier Congress stalwart leaders once thought of and divided the country thinking that "Partition was nothing but a Temporary affair".

4. A STUDY OF GANDHI & JINNAH IN FREEDOM STRUGGLE

[4.1]

The emergence of an independent federal nation is an outcry of happiness but the partition of the British India by the creation of Pakistan along with a curse of massive violence ruining the life of millions on both sides is an outcry of pain of suffering. Both these newly independent countries were led by the two famous personalities—Mahatma Gandhi and Qaid-e-Azam Jinnah who were in the mainstream politics of colonial India. They began their journey as the main persons in the freedom struggle movement with the sole purpose of creating an independent united India with a democratic, federal and inclusive polity but later they parted their ways in two different directions. Mahatma Gandhi's method of mass mobilization was based on religion and religious ethics of "Non-Violence". Jinnah opposed the process of Gandhi. Jinnah was disturbed by Gandhi's method of movement. According to him Gandhi's method of movement would adversely affect the principles of democratic governance. He began to differ with Gandhi on many counts, and finally he began to build up the Muslim community under his leadership. Gandhi was claiming publicly that he was representing all communities which were not acceptable to Jinnah as because Gandhi sometimes saying publicly that India would be a Ram Rajya. Despite the commonality of the basic goal of attaining independence, the two leaders differ widely. Jinnah's suspicion of the dominance of the Caste-Hindus led by the Indian National Congress particularly under Gandhi compel Jinnah to claim a new Pakistan for ensuring rights and dignity of the Muslim community. Owing to this type of distrust and disagreements, various measures initiated by the British government but failed to develop consensus between the two leaders. They differed in their appeals to their masses and communities where Gandhi was doing "non-Violence" only with the Hindus again Jinnah was holding meetings with the Muslims. Their disagreements in fact appeared in great differences in their personalities, views, and their methods of building the nation and making constitution. The objective of the leaders was to explore their demands to the British colonial masters and convince them how they could bring equality, justice, development and peace among the people. But the discussion exposes the leaders' major lacunae in the context of freedom struggle, partition politics, and two-nation theory. Gandhi referred as Father of the Nation, an advocate of non-violence and his ethical aspects of "Non-Violence" politics. On the other hand, Jinnah is glorified as Qaed-i-Azam for creating a new nation for the Muslim community to get free from the command of Ram-Rajya. Both the leaders were working for the two different communities.

Their work is a modest attempt to make a comparative study of the two stalwarts in order to draw a closer sketch on the ground. Both the leaders were concern with post-colonial governance of the country. Both the leaders failed to reconcile to create a united India, as both the leaders wanted to keep their hero-like image after independence. The study of an academic discourse would expose their comparative deficiencies in the struggle for a united India in relation to India's freedom struggle. In the context of collusion it could be said that while Mohammed Ali Jinnah kept intimate relations with Western life style and carried a deep influence of the western education and analysis, on the other hand Mohandas Karamchand Gandhi found solace with the Hindu life style, ideology with strong belief in Hinduism and differed with western ideologies in political thoughts. Gandhi was an ardent advocate of the principle of non-violence in both theory and practice. The whole life of Gandhi was directed, regulated and molded by the spirit of Non-Violence. He wanted to keep his image under "Non-Violence". Gandhi-Jinnah conflict first began with simple political overtone but finally ended with communal violence.

Both Gandhi and Jinnah had similar educational background of juridical matters but their views, concerns and commitments were completely different. M.K. Gandhi was committed to the virtues of common truths in all religions with his firm commitment to Caste-oriented Hinduism. He was pointing objections over the wrongs of the British rulers without looking into the fears of the Muslim minority community. M.A. Jinnah was moving towards future welfare of the Muslims. He was facing challenges at two levels—first to get rid of the colonial masters and second, to get rid of Hinduism base on Gandhi ethics. M.A. Jinnah became confident in the celebration of his achievement and in the consolidation of his idea of Pakistan. Gandhi could indeed want to show to the world that he deserved the word Mahatma ascribed to his name when he got the bullets in his chest by Nathuram Godse. But the truth is he was more for the image of "Non-Violence" and less for the unity of Nation. Another additional factor pinching his mind what was the influence of Netaji if he returns any time he would be chosen as the Prime Minister of India instead of Nehru when his image as FATHER of the nation would go away. Hence under all circumstances he remained committed to Hinduism when Jinnah would be ousted to Pakistan with the division of Bengal. The divided Bengal could not come forward with Netaji along with a stronger force to occupy Delhi Chair any time. Thus a compromise with Jinnah was detrimental for his future prospect. A no compromise formula would go for partition of India and Bengal as well which would be better for him when he could be the FATHER of the nation.

Indians are kept in dark about the events that took place in early 1920s either due to ignorance or bias towards religion.What took place in that period of 1919-21 was crucial not only in bringing about the 1947 Partition, but the religious fanaticism that is tearing Pakistan apart.

Religious tensions existed between Hindus and Muslims for centuries. With the introduction of British-style politics it was inevitable that religion based grouping would be seen as well. But the people knows that Indian politicians like Gokhale and Jinnah wanted to bring Hindus and Muslims together by keeping religion out of politics and concentrating on a political dialogue. In this respect the 1916 Lucknow Pact based on political demands was at the height of cooperation between the two communities. At the same time the Home Rule League was making progress using constitutional methods to bring about self-rule for India, when MA Jinnah, rightly named the greatest ambassador of Hindu-Muslim unity, who became the star of Indian politics at that time.

Gandhi returned to India from South Africa. Posing as a harmless simple person with no political ambitions, but he was able to make fool of many. One of the men who were deceived by him was Jinnah who made Gandhi the president of Home Rule League. Unable to compete with Jinnah in secular and constitutional politics Gandhi decided to use religion as his weapon of choice to corner Jinnah. The opportunity came in front of him due to the agitation started by the Muslims on the issue of the Ottoman Khilafat. It was Turkey who recently lost the war and the allied powers despite having promised during the war that they will not do any harm but afterwards the British began to dismember the Ottoman Empire. The Muslims of India felt loyalty to the Ottoman Khilafat who began to fight against the British in India in support of the Muslims of Turkey, Mecca and Medina.

This was a religious movement; however, Jinnah since the last few years tried to sideline these orthodox religious few Muslim leaders. But Gandhi gave them a new lease of life. Gandhi who had openly declared that he was a Hindu first and anything else later to counter Jinnah who said he was an Indian first and Muslims afterwards. In order to increase his popularity among the Muslims he gave his full support behind this orthodox Islamic movement calling Indian Muslims to rise up in jihad to save the Turkish Caliph.

Gandhi had established himself as a saint-like figure among Hindus and Muslims through his show of devotion and social work. His support gave the Khilafat Movement, which was of no consequence for Indian Muslims, a life of its own. He in a clever way increased his popularity among the Hindus as a Hindu Saint, and among the Muslims as a supporter of the Khilafat bandwagon and trying to supersede the popularity of Jinnah and other leaders fighting for Independence. Gandhi toured every nook and corner of India along with radical Muslim leaders like the Ali brothers inciting religious frenzy by using the evergreen slogan *'Islam khatraymeinhai'* (Islam is in danger) for the first time.

The result was that Muslim League lost its popularity and Muslim political leadership was taken from secular leaders like Jinnah by orthodox religious leader Gandhi. No doubt it was an upsurge in just Muslim communal fanaticism under the shadow of Gandhi. For only a fool would have expected that the activity of the Ali brothers bringing vast crowds to the edge of religious frenzy calling for 40 million Muslims to lay down their lives for Islam will not have had any effect on Hindus. Who could forget the real and imagined atrocities, Muslims had done over the Hindus during the times of the Muslim rule. It was indeed an indirect action of Gandhi in the revival of Hinduism to contribute to political separation. As regards Jinnah's stance on Khilafat movement, it is true that concerned his political career in a country where the Khilafat Movement had been made into an issue of Muslim religion, Jinnah was not a supporter of Khilafat Movement like Gandhi but he had sympathy for it to keep his popularity among the Muslim community.

In the 1918 session of Muslim League, held in Delhi, Jinnah warned the delegates not to dabble in the Khilafat issue as it does not concern India and declared it as a false religious frenzy of which no good will come out for India. Finding the members opposed to this view, he along with some others walked out of the session. "I will have nothing to do with this pseudo-religious approach to politics. I do not believe in working up mob hysteria, politics is a gentleman's game". The mob hysteria and violence had been mainly demonstrated by the non-violent supporters of Gandhi during that session where no one who opposed Gandhi and Gandhi thought it was okay for the sake of his popularity against the outrage of Jinnah.

"When Mahatma Gandhi supported the 1919 Khilafat movement, Jinnah opposed it. He had argued that Indian Muslims had no connection with the Khalifa of Turkey. But nobody heeded Jinnah. 'Thus it is quite clear to see how religious communalism and resulting fanaticism was introduced into Indian politics by Gandhi at the outset of his political carrier. But it affected the Muslims mostly, after all Khilafat Movement was an Islamic religious movement. This indeed was the watershed moment when the dream of Hindus and Muslims living together in an independent India was irreversibly shattered under the clever water-tight policy of Gandhi side tracking Jinnah.

The Muslim politics of India never recovered from the damage caused by Gandhi and the Khilafat Movement. Henceforth it became quite clear for anyone expecting support of the Muslims that must be the religious card. And Jinnah himself, at a later stage, had compelled to use this card for the benefit of his personal gain as well as for the Muslim community. Jinnah had predicted bloodshed, chaos and Hindu-Muslim divisions as a result of mixing religion and politics by Gandhi and later this proved prophetic. Hence Gandhi was the architect of creating Pakistan but after Gandhi Nehru made the Indians fool again by making Gandhi the Father of the nation. The present **Delhi rioting** is the after effect of Gandhi politics.

After getting popularity among the **Muslims Khilafat Movement**, Gandhi turned towards Hindus and thereafter on 15 January 1925 he formed a Cow-Protection Sabha and became its chairman and later in the same year he announced his retirement from active politics, a job done in a calculated strategy to sustain his popularity among the Hindus apart from the Muslims. His clever policy of sympathy succeeded him to maintain his popularity among Hindus as well as among the Muslims to a great extent. Anyway by his Hindu-Muslim politics he delayed India's independence by several years.

So anyone who does not know the role of Gandhi how he played his role as a clever politician having with ahalf naked Fakir Dress, in order to mislead the people under the cover of a SAINT divided the country on the basis of religion and in the end became the **Father** of the nation, he could not know real history of India, the real cause of Hindu-Muslim conflict and the Delhi violence due to hidden pain of partition. He supported Khilafat Movement initiated by the Indian Muslims knowing well that many Muslim jihadists have similar ideology to the leaders of the Khilafat Movement who were ready to use violence in defense of their Islamic Khilafat, where they could bring the ultimate holocaust of Calcutta Killing on 16th August 1946. Keeping himself at a distance during massacre of thousands of people in the streets of Calcutta and finally he brought to bring the two religious group together and completed the division according to the June 3 Plan of British. He was afraid of Bengal and the young Bengal leader Subhas. As such his activity of "Non-Violence" mainly remained in Calcutta of Bengal just to finish the economy of Bengal and the strength of Bengal Leaders.

He joined the British Force in the First World War to enhance his popularity but he opposed the British Force in the Second World War in the name of Independence of India but just to finish Bengal and Bengalis as the British would fight to the last against Azaid Hind Force under Bengal leader Netaji, and to finish the Bengalis by famine, by preventing the supply of rice from Burma to Bengal during the War time. Under compulsion Jinnah get satisfied with Pakistan and Gandhi get satisfied with India keeping away Khan Abdul Gaffer Khan, a staunch supporter of United India and also discarding the Rajaji's C.R. formula for the consent of Muslim of Pakistan territory. In the end the question of division of India was finalized between the two Gandhi and Jinnah and nothing spectacular was done because there are many Muslims like Khan Abdul Gaffer Khan who would not agree in the division of the country, when Gandhi's dream of removing Jinnah would not be successful. Thus the success of the division of the country was the success of Gandhi's dream that had made it easy to bring Nehru in the chair to fulfill his goal of achievement "The FATHER of the Nation".

5. THE HISTORY OF ASSAM AND ITS DESTINY OF DESTRUCTION

[5.1]

Gandhi was the most popular leader because of the religious movement of "Non-Violence" based on Hindu ethics of "Tolerance". But he was in danger of two persons, one was Mr. Jinnah, the leader of Muslim League as well as the leader of militant Muslim volunteers who speaks for Pakistan and the other one was Netaji, the leader of Azaid Hind Fouz who speaks for violence "Give me blood I will give you freedom". He said in public front that the country would be divided over my dead body. But in the secret of his mindset he agreed to the proposal of partition to divide India on the basis of religion because without division of the country he could not kick out Jinnah from India. Thus partition brought happiness to his mind although he was against partition in public front. Even after partition of India and giving goodbye to Jinnah, he was not happy because of the uncertainty of the existence of Netaji alive or dead. The dropping of Atom bomb at Japan allowed the British to win the war but the news of Netaji was not known with certainty either alive or dead. In the question of the inclusion of Assam in India, the most of the Congress leaders remained silent as they were afraid of the aggressive Jinnah for the cause of few important places of Uttar Bharat particularly of Delhi, Lucknow or Allahabad, the important territory of Mughal Empire, those places might be out of India if demanded by Jinnah for Pakistan and as such they never wanted to antagonize Jinnah for asking Assam for India. A clever politician Gandhi always thinks ahead. Assuming Netaji alive, Gandhi thought ahead what would go against Netaji if he comes back to India in future. Gandhi was the only Congress person who encouraged Assam to be included in India where he would get the support of Assam if Netaji anytime get back to India.

But again he did not wanted the Bengali speaking district Sylhet of Assam to be included in India as because the increase of Bengali population would go in favor of Netaji, a person who could challenge the post of PM to replace Nehru when Gandhi's image of name and fame would vanish with the removal of Nehru. The district Sylhet was living with Assam since 1874 and by its long standing existence it became an inseparable part of Assam although they differ to some extent in their way of speaking but culturally they became almost one in manner and also one in culture or even in the letter of language of their mother tongue. But it was separated at the time of partition of India to make Assam a homogeneous state.

[Goliath Bordoloi]

Gandhi encouraged the Assam Prime Minister Gopinath Bordoloi to keep Sylhet out of Assam by referring the district for referendum. Finally Sylhet went away from Assam of India, while the people of Surma valley of Sylhet once supported Bordoloi under the direction of Netaji to become the Prime Minister of Assam replacing Saddulla. But forgetting everything Sylhet was removed from Assam at the time of partition of India to make Assam homogeneous. The land of

Sylhet was removed from Assam but not the people as most of the Hindu people shifted to Assam. Now Gopinath Bordoloi could see from heaven that the state of Assam is disintegrated further what was once predicted by the opposition leader Ruhini Chowdhury who said the separation of Sylhet would initiate the disintegration of united Assam. Tiger like other forces, demanded the right of Union Territory, likewise the similar other forces demanded the right of Language, demanded the right of religion and lastly demanded right of community, what had finally destroyed Assam and destroyed the prosperity as well as the beauty of the Unity of Assam. Let us proceed further to look into the facts of sequences and the future what is existed in all living human beings under love, fraternity, and equality. But the thinking of Gandhi was only the ethics of "Non-Violence" due to the emotion of secret desire to make name and fame through the movement of independence how to make himself the architect of the Indian Independence where Assam was a part of India. The people of Assam involved in the "Non-Violence" movement with full energy and sacrificed many of their youths and youngsters. The result was a United Assam State after independence but very soon that State has been fragmented into a mini-state without any further progress of development. The state remains in a state of unrest for no progress and prosperity in spite of its natural wealth of coal and Oil besides Tea and natural beauty.

A farsighted opinion of a Senior Person: A senior person Mr. Joshuda Ranjan Chakraborty of Langoi Road Karimganj has rightly elaborated how the Assam has done the greatest blunder by separating Sylhet just before the time of partition. But instead it could be done afterwards by separating it as a separate state like Mizoram and other states of Assam. Mr. Chakraborty elaborated as such at the time of partition the district Sylhet was the largest and the greatest district of Assam. It was a Hindu majority region everywhere except few town areas of Sylhet and Badarpur regions of Karimganj. During the time of partition of India Bengal and Punjab was partitioned. There was no question of the partition of Assam including Sylhet. Then why did the Hindu majority district Sylhet went to Pakistan? The reason was nothing but "Language". Assam was a land of different tribes of Hills and planes for which at the outset it was named as ASOM (ups and downs), a living place of all kinds of people never in question. It was thought at the time of partition if the populated Bengali speaking district Sylhet is separated then Assam could be freed from the fear of its language. Accordingly a committee was formed and along with Gandhi and other congress leaders a plan was designed how to get Sylhet separated from Assam. Finally, Sylhet was separated except the district of Karimganj for the river line demarcation.

The tragedy of Hindu people get started in Islamic East Pakistan. The leaders of Assam get a sigh of relief after the separation of Sylhet but they could never think of that Pakistan would be an Islamic country, the existence of which was based on religion where Hindus and Muslims could not live together. The original demand of Muslim League was a separate homeland for the Muslims of India. So the question of living Hindus in Islamic Pakistan did not arise. It was certain that the Hindus have to leave Pakistan. Where these people would go? There was no other place for them other than the India. As such India had given the right for the Hindus to live in India. In the course of time Pakistan became violent to make it an Islamic country, the Hindu people of Sylhet compelled to shift to the nearest region Assam to save their lives, family and religion. Now there is a cry in the hearts of many leaders of Assam, "Assam has got rid of Sylhet, but not of Sylhetis". The problem of language remained even after the separation of Sylhet. Practically 90% people of Sylhet had taken shelter in Assam. Centre also agreed in the fact that as Sylhet was a part of Assam, they have every right to settle in Assam.

If the Sylhet had remain in India, the people of Sylhet would remain in India and there would not require for these people to take shelter in any place of Assam, in addition many people of other districts of East Pakistan also could take shelter to certain extent in this region instead of the regions of Assam. There would not be any refugee problem at all in Assam. The language problem also would have been solved easily by the formation of a separate

State including Cachar and the adjacent Bengali regions because the region would have been much bigger regions than Nagaland or Mizoram and economically much more solvent. There would not be any more language problem where the peace loving Assamese people could live in peace. If the proposal of a separate state was given including Cachar and Sylhet under the leadership of Gopinath Bordoloi of Assam instead of giving the economically rich Sylhet to Pakistan, the approval of center easily could have been achieved. If so it could solve problem from both sides. It could save Assam from the problem of refugee as well as the language. To design the refugee of Sylhet as foreign national would not had arisen as they are born and brought up in undivided Assam. The present problem of Assam was due to shortsighted policy of the earlier leaders of Assam based on the question of separation of Sylhet.

[5.2]

Activity of Mahatma Gandhi: Gandhi was assassinated on 30 January 1948 in the compound of Birla House, by a Hindu advocate named Nathuram Godse, had he not being assassinated and lived for another 20 years, then there would have been a change in the country which would lead the country far behind. If Gandhi had been alive in India the condition of Hindus would have been bad to worse. He desired to go Pakistan to make a name for him even after the massacre being occurred in Pakistan. It was because his look out was the personal image and not the people or the country. He accepted the concept of partition on the basis of religion although he uttered in public front that the country would be divided over my dead body. If he would have reached to Pakistan, he would have been killed brutally. The record of history says he was about to be killed in Naokhali, had the local Hindu volunteers not saved him in right time, however his goat, which he carried with him had been killed.

Gandhi was a good man but not a good politician. More over his vision was not wide but circumstances compelled him to change his ideas and thoughts time to time. What he was, he was a LLB graduate from Inner Temple London, and somehow, he returned to Bombay to practice but failed to get a single client, while the case of Jinnah was opposite. He went to South Africa, not very comfortable there, not happy at home due to disobedient son, also not happy in outside because, he was humiliated in the travelling bus, as well as in white restaurant, moreover he was not popular very much in his profession there.

Finally he came back to India, here also he get frustrated as because no client. Finally he came across with Motilal Nehru; there he found some sort of mental stability and happiness. There he thought of discussing the idea of "Non-Violence" with Motilal, who vehemently opposed the movement of "Non-Violence". However, Gandhi was free to discuss anything under the shadow of Nehru family, and then onwards his love for Nehru had grown up. His thought was how he would make himself expose as a saint, or as a politician or as a Fakir to win the heart of common people. Since then two factors were playing in his mind, one the glory of Nehru family and the other the public sympathy which he had seen in South Africa at the time of his experiment in going to Restaurant fixed for whites, occupying the front seat in Bus or Rail reserved for whites and so on.

He started his experiment of sympathy movement in Champaran district of Bihar in 1917, Kheda district in Gujarat in 1918 and against the Rowlett Act on 6 April 1919 whereby massacre happened on 13 April 1919, supported Khilafat Movement (1919-1920) and then the killing of 22 Police personal by the Public in Gorakhpur district in UP on 5th February, and thereby everywhere he failed even he was imprisoned. His idea changes to a different angle now. At that time, it was the place Calcutta where violent struggle was going on. Killing of British in secret mission and the hanging of the culprit or sending the culprit to Andaman jail was the hot news of the day at that time.

Gandhi's attention turns towards Calcutta. It was his thinking how to bring Nehru and Nehru family in the fore front because he thought it was the Nehru family which will make him the great. He knows Bengalis were cultured and most religious minded. He thought of an idea, a religious movement under the guise of a Saint Dressed as a half naked FAKIR to mislead the common people and to win the heart of common Hindu Bengalis, and start the spreading of poison of hatred in between Hindus and Muslims. Why? It was because unless the destruction happened in Bengal, the top most economy of Bengal get destroyed, the power CENTER of Calcutta and Bengali's leadership could not go away, the chance of occupying the power of Delhi would have never been opened up for Nehru.

He thought of a religious movement which was nothing but "Non-Violence". Tolerance is in the ethics of Hinduism, and hence he twisted it to non-violence. When it was proposed in Nagpur session in 1930 it was vehemently objected by Jinnah, but still Gandhi remained adamant to his decision bypassing Jinnah's objection because he could not expose his inner thought to a Muslim leader.

He changed his dress; he became a Fakir, because it was necessary to befool the Hindu Bengalis. He became a saint in posture, living simple, dressed simple, as if a Fakir, although he was not doing the activity of a Fakir, but doing politics behind the shadow of a Fakir. In 1930, he started non- violence in the form of Civil Disobedience Movement in all places of towns and cities throughout of Bengal befooling the most of the Congress leaders except few such as Rabindra nathTakur, CRDas and few others living in Calcutta. Hindus were mad to join the movement as if it was started by the messenger of God, Gandhi, by their religious belief and faith over Gandhi. He mesmerized the masses like a magician. No Muslim joined what he had wanted. That was the first success of Gandhi to bring Nehru in the Chair befooling the Bengali's.

The subsequent part is better not to write, how the atmosphere of hatred created in Calcutta, apparently by Gandhi (could not be shown in the picture because of photo restriction,) but religious violence was everywhere. It was 16th August 1946, Jinnah convinced Suhrawardy, the then CM of Bengal to start direct action. It was declared by Muslim League16 August was the Direct Action Day; it was the Calcutta killing day, if Pakistan was not given. Gandhi remained in silence in his Ashram at Gujrat. Neither had he make peaceful negotiation nor any preparation to stop the senseless killing. Now after massacre and after Pakistan somebody saying he was preparing to go to Pakistan before his assassination to bring peace there, why? Why he did not do it before "Calcutta Killing" and before the creation of Pakistan?

However it was his afterthought. Before the creation of Pakistan he was anti- Muslim in the secret of his mind and in action. He talked of Ram Rajya keeping Nehru in the Chair. But after completion of this part he openly became a spoke person of Muslim, because of two reasons, (1) the Muslims were well prepared by their Militant ML volunteers to carry out massacre anywhere everywhere. (2) His goal of glory lies in Non-Violence.

Now he was in Calcutta just after Pakistan to save the Muslims in Bengal. His weapon was again a religious weapon the **FASTING** which is generally under taken by the Hindus at the time of offering something to God at the time of doing Pujas. Again by his saintly activity he befooled the religious Hindus to stop anti- Muslim activity, thus Muslims remained in peace in West Bengal even after the formation of Muslim East Pakistan. Thus today we find Muslims in East Bengal (now Bangladesh) as well as in West Bengal. After his success he went to Delhi, to clear the MAJIDS of Delhi, which were occupied by the refugees who had arrived here from West Punjab losing everything and in most of the cases half of the family members. Gandhi did not stop here, he asked Nehru, Petal to give cores of money from Indian treasure to Pakistan for running Pakistan administration.

Now to satisfy the Hindus he was spreading the message that he would go to Pakistan to stop the killing of Hindus by Muslims there. How funny it was. Is there any time that he was successful to befool Muslims? Never, he was successful to befool the Hindus because of religious instinct. Muslims never believed him because he was after Ram Rajya. God was favorable to him that was why today he was an international icon and placed along with other international icon of 20th century like Winston Churchill, Roosevelt, Hitler or Moa-Sa-Tang.

Abraham Lincoln sacrificed his life for the unity of America, unity of white and black, while Gandhi became an icon by dividing India and creating a permanent hatred in between Hindus and Muslims and also killing millions of Punjabis and millions of Bengalis and also displacing millions from their ancestral home.

Gandhi favored Nehru many times that had been exposed in public. He was happy by making Nehru the President of the Congress party but he was not happy with Netaji being inducted as President in 1938. In 1939 he openly opposes Netaji by posturing SitaRamPattavia but unfortunately he was defeated against Netaji. Does it indicate his simple life with simple mind or a simple life with crooked mind? Not only that he had discarded the selected candidate Sadder Petal by the Congress party, as first PM of India, he had replaced Petal by Nehru, why? Does it indicate his saintly behavior?

Nobody knows whether India won independence by the act of Gandhi's Non-Violence, but what was known or what had been seen, was that he had done the greatest harm to India to live as a great nation. Had his vision was not limited to Nehru and really think equally for all to create a great country or a Ram Rajya, he could do that. But his idea remained confined in limited area of community, personality and above all in religion. A national leader is always above religion in every country and everywhere. The formation of India- Pakistan on the basis of religion was the first example set up by Gandhi in the world and how the first Indian Prime Minister declared him as the FATHER of the nation unilaterally after his assassination without asking the people remained a question of mystery.

It was too late when Gandhi realized his mistake in carrying out Non-Violence movement only with the Hindus, while Jinnah carried a violent movement under trained ML volunteer, where 2% militant voice prevailed over 98 % neutral cum non-violence voice. To rectify its affect Gandhi followed the policy of appeasement towards Muslims. After Gandhi, Congress followed the same policy of appeasement; thereby Muslims have consolidated their position not only in Pakistan east or west but also in India. Pakistan became one country one law while India became one country but different law.

Muslims got Pakistan but they prevailed Muslim right in every state of India because of their unity, and farsighted thought bypassing Hindu right in many cases on the basis of Muslim's right of personal law.

Gandhi never thought of the development of the economy which could built a united solid foundation what had found to be seen in Japan, USA or UK while Gandhi always thought of capturing the power of chair through the religious thought of unity apart from the thought of humanity. Today the cry is for "Muslims Free India" as said by one of BJP worker, Shakhi Maharaja -Why? Who created the situation, definitely it was created by Gandhi that indicated his lacking power in foresightedness. Pakistan became an enemy country, why? It was because of Gandhi and because of non- violence activity, the activity of appeasement and surrendering to militant force. A country is ruled by its strength and not by surrender, or sacrifice out of religion.

Today Modi is speaking in front of American dignitaries that "Terrorism" is the enemy to humanity and the country who are nurturing the art of terrorism, who are not less than the enemy of humanity pointing finger towards Pakistan, why? It was because of Hindu-Muslim rivalry created by Gandhi through his activity of "Non-Violence". Modhi is asking for action, asking for cooperation of all country, but not asking for Non-Violence. The man, Gandhi who had done the greatest harm for the present, for the past and also for the future, how could Indians are honoring him now, every year in India by performing Gandhi Jyanti, and also in foreign soil and in Indian currency note giving his picture. In summary his contribution was zero, who had created a dark India having a dark future, a future calling the Babur to come to India as it was once predicted by Jinnah that one day Indians will call the Muslims to rule India because the Indian Hindus do not know how to administer a country as because it existed in Muslim blood, who ruled India for many years more than Hindu kings.

In Congress regime Gandhi's' idealism was spread in every country, but could the India preserve it in its own soil. It failed to preserve it with China, had it followed the principle of "non-violence", India had to give off the whole of Arunachal and even the whole of North-East, and had it followed with Pakistan in the last four wars, it had to give off Kashmir, Bangladesh and half the territory of India. Should the Indians would follow Non - Violence or discard Non-Violence forever? Only the unknown power of God will save India if the Indians follow and save Gandhi and preserve Gandhi's idealism of Non-Violence.

To describe the nature of Gandhi, the author has written an answer in 1916 in connection with the reply of a question asked in the **Quora** which is quoted below.

Why did Gandhi support the Khilafat movement in spite of the fact that the Turks had killed 2 million Armenian Christians in the Armenian genocide? [Answered by Author in June 23, 2016.]

Turkish military officials, soldiers and ordinary men sacked Armenian villages and cities and massacred their citizens. Hundreds of thousands of Armenians were murdered. With the change of Government Armenians hoped for the best. But Young Turks wanted most of the people was to be converted to "Turki" by heart in TurK Empire. Accordingly their way of thinking, brought a danger signal for others, non-Turks–and especially Christian non-Turks, who were faced a grave threat to the new state. Armenians organized volunteer battalions to help the Russian army to fight against the Turks in the Caucasus region. These events, and general Turkish suspicion of the Armenian people, led the Turkish government to push for the "removal" of the Armenians from the war zones along the Eastern Front. Thus the Young Turks created a "Special Organization," which in turn organized "killing squads" or "butcher battalions" to carry out the worst genocide of the history. The Young Turks did it because they were dedicated to their religion.

Indian Muslims supported the Turks as because they are also dedicated to Islam.

During the World War 1, Turkey was a party to Central Powers (Germany, Austria-Hungary, and Bulgaria) and very soon it was going to lose against the mighty stronger British Force of British Empire. The Britishers wined the cooperation of Indian Muslims under the condition of the exchange to help or treat the Turks generously after the war. But the war promise was not honored as such the Indian Muslims started the Khilafat Movement in India in support of the Turkish Government. Gandhi supported the movement with a secret mischievous intention to win the Muslims heart. Is it not treacherous and mischievous and against the ethics of humanity? Gandhi is writing letter to Hitler to stop war on the ground of peace for humanity. But here in the movement he is supporting the genocide indirectly. What a contradiction of the ethics of Gandhi!

In Khilafat Movement Gandhi is supporting the Muslims of India who were in favor of genocide to Armenians. Where is your ethics of Non-Violence? When Gandhi is talking of humanity, he should be above of any religion of mankind or community of mankind. He is supporting here the religious force of violence against the ethical force. But in Indian Independence he applied the ethical force against the religious force of "Non-Violence". It was started in 1930 at Calcutta in Civil Disobedient Movement, as a Non-Violence Movement. Non-Violence is the opposite side of Tolerance, which is the ethics of Hindu religion. Muslims did not join the "Non-Violence" movement whereby he was successful to bring communal violence and disunity opposite to Khilafat Movement. Gandhi was acting as saint but he applied the rule of politics in opportune time to fulfill his inner ambition. But again he never forgets to talk of humanity and Mankind. Who can forget that he created Pakistan at the cost of millions of death of Punjabis and Bengalis? Is it not genocide like Armenians? Why? Only ambition was to make Nehru, the PM of India, apparently he was not for any position but he knows Nehru will not keep him down.

[5.3]

It was a known fact that Gandhi applied the ethics of Hindu religion "FASTING" to compel the government to pay Pakistan the part of the money left by the last British government, what India kept it in holding because of unfriendly behavior of New Pakistan in Kashmir matter. Rs 55 Core was paid by the Government to Pakistan by 8th January, 1948. But Gandhi had forgotten that just before independence an interim government was formed where Liquate Ali Khan was the finance Minister, who stopped all sanctions against all congress ministers, when they had no alternative but to appeal to the Hindu Kings to help the administration monetarily. Why Gandhi was silent at that time? Pakistan was happy after getting money as such they invited Gandhi to Pakistan under military cover up as they knew his life was insecure in Pakistan. It was agreed on January 27 that Gandhi would travel to Lahore. But big question had arisen what he should say to the Public in the land of Pakistan- "Gandhi is to appeal to the Muslims to protect the minorities in Pakistan".

If he wishes to appeal why did after finishing of unity and unity of friendship by the strain of blood? Could he not appeal before the formation of Pakistan and before the onslaught of bloodshed? He was supported by more than 80% people, yes his credit was there to bring these people along with him by the bond of religion or whatever it, although he utterly failed to bring any lawfully rich intellectuals with him. A ruler is born to rule but not to appeal throughout the life. By the policy of appeal and tolerance before partition or after partition he had destroyed the county. He went to Noakhali, could he succeeded in stopping rioting. If so, the 90% Hindu would not come to 12%. Rather Gandhi had created a situation whereby the whole region would be a Muslim region in near future. It is now appeared to be true. The 17 core people of present Bangladesh is now sufficient enough to convert the whole of eastern region consisting of Bangladesh, Assam and West Bengal, a Muslim region, a creation of Gandhi.

Somebody is writing such as "Gandhi was a realist. He probably knew that partition could not be undone." Why he had created the situation of "undone". Gandhi became a leader of more than 80% people of India, why did he failed to satisfy Jinnah or failed to give the minimum right to Muslims for the unity of the country? Gandhi became a UK Barrister but failed in the profession, again Gandhi became a champion of religious saint to befool the country men but again failed in politics, failed to convince the people of other religion. Thus to save India now, people of India had to forget Gandhi, forget Non-Violence, forget appeal or sacrifice, and must be strong enough and rule like a RULER. Once Gandhi saved Assam to become a part of East Pakistan but now it appeared that it was not for the love of Assam but for the fear of Netaji, who might reappear again in India as his death was not confirmed in the war although end of war was declared after the dropping of Atom Bomb in Japan. The 1962 Chinese aggression to Assam and the subsequent " goodbye to Assam " by the Indian PM Nehru was a reminder to the people of Assam that the Gandhian policy of "Non-Violence" was not the appropriate policy to keep Assam in India. "Non-Violence" policy of Gandhi, what was implemented by the Center over Assam was the cause of disintegration of the United Assam, which could not be denied by the political stalwart of India.

[5.4]

Everywhere Gandhi was recognized in India as well as in abroad as a "Man of Peace", then why not in India where all people can live in peace and harmony?

So long Indians were ignorant of human being and humanity, and as such people could not live in peace and harmony. Instead of talking of peace and harmony in the world let us concentrate on the talk of peace centering of India and Pakistan only. It depends upon the person or the so called leaders of the region. Here Indians could name Gandhi as the man of importance of the region as he was known in the world as a man of peace.

But in true sense he was the murder of humanity because he created Hindu sentiment by the creation of "Non-Violence" dressing himself as a Hindu SAINT with a half naked FAKIR Dress and again created Muslim sentiment by supporting "Khilafat Movement" a religious Muslim movement of Turkey. It was because he created two religious groups and created Hindu-Muslim rioting between them through the movement of "Non-Violence" as because he started the movement in Calcutta only with the Hindus without taking the Muslims. Why? The inner intention was to bring Hindu-Muslim rioting so that the country gets divided when Jinnah would be out of India, and he could be the only absolute people friendly leader of India. He could make Nehru the PM without any dispute when his name would be known throughout the world. He became a saint with a half naked dress just to fool the Religious Hindu people but under disguise he never forget to give his title to Feroz Khan, the husband of Indira Nehru to make her Indira Gandhi in order to make himself familiar and a custodian of Nehru family just to cover up the naughty activity of his eldest son, who was a drunker. His success of joy lies in the transformation of the Nehru family to Gandhi family. The division of India on the basis of Hindu-Muslim matters a little to him but his extreme pleasure lies in ousting Jinnah for ever from India by the division of India in a clever way keeping himself in dark and finally agreed to the concept of division without protest. Thus peace was not the goal of Gandhi; the goal was the international name and fame. Service to humanity was not his vision of life otherwise he could not give his consent in the division of country to bring tragedy to millions of the country men in the sphere of rioting and displacement of human being beyond imagination.

[5.5]

Now Assam is the eastern most part of India filled with enchanting and picturesque of natural beauty along with a chain of hills and rivers mainly with the Brahmaputra and the Barak. It has been the living place of various people of the places of plain, tribes and immigrant people of the adjacent regions. The dynamics of synthesis and the assimilation of the races of adjacent regions had made Assam glorified but the thinking of local issues had kept the vital economic issues far away and in the end till today, the beautiful region remains in dark and the people became the victim of destiny of despair. The USA, a country of ice became a superpower because of the strong economic power while Saudi-Arabia, a country of desert became a power house of wealth and prosperity because of its huge reserve of oil. So to say economy is the backbone of a nation.

The protests are against **CAA** (Citizenship Amendment Act) which was enacted into law on 12 December 2019 and again NRC (National Register of Citizens) a non issue has brought in public front by the Government making it a burning topic in front of the public keeping the economic front behind. Why? The simple answer is how to get majority Hindu votes discarding the Muslim votes to the greatest extent. Here in Assam the Protesters do not want Indian citizenship to be granted to any refugee or immigrant, regardless of their religion, as they assume that it would alter the region's demographic balance, as they are original (Khilangia) inhabitant of the region and they are in no way in favor of accepting the **CAA** resulting in a loss of their political rights, culture, and the land. In Assam naturally it raises two hidden questions in order to implement the issue of CAA & NRC (i)

"That are the original (Khilangia) inhabitant" and (ii) "The reasons for the formulation of Law". The government is successful to bring division, mistrust and sectarian thought among tribals-nontribals, Hindu-Muslim religious conflict and again Assamese-Bengali language conflict to divide the people in order to divide the votes so that the government could remain in power for all the time. To solve the problem of refugee there need not be necessary to bring the law of CAA and NRC what is done in other nations by the normal procedure. A person who is living here generation to generation is a citizen; a person who is a voter is a citizen. Why government did brought CAA and NRC to high light the issue so that the government could claim credit and ask for votes mainly of the Hindu votes.

A government who is thinking in terms of religion could never do anything good to the nation because it is against humanity. However great Gandhi created India based on religion, against the ethics of humanity, how the country could see the light of prosperity. Any country what is said to be developed was due to the efforts of all of its citizens. As such the policy of Gandhi was against the growth of the nation and against the nature of humanity. Similarly the present government is also working looking to the same ideals of religion and also further stimulated by the other side of humanity to stop the religious out cry of Pakistan in the border of India out of rivalry based on the theory of tit for tat, which was nothing but the creation of Indian great ever skilled leader Gandhi. The solution is not the outburst of "Delhi Rioting" or "Delhi Disturbance" but a call for revival of true humanity what was once the ideal of Jinnah who said keep religion away from politics but Gandhi never heard of it. Today in Pakistan everything is based on religion, because after the formation of Pakistan ethics of humanity is completely forgotten whereas so long Pakistan was in India, the same people were with the feelings of same Indian culture of love and brotherhood but today most of the individuals in Pakistan think Indians are enemy to Pakistan. Is it carrying the greatness of Gandhi? How the Indians could think of to honor him as the FATHER of the nation?

To find out the NRC for the original inhabitant under the current procedure one has to go a long way in the discussion of natural and political history of the region and the state. Before going to answer the problem (i) who are the original (Khilanjia) inhabitant of Assam, it is necessary to know who were residing in Assam before 1228 A.D. when the people from Thailand came and established the Ahom Kingdom. For that it is necessary to discuss few earlier Kingdoms. Let us begin with **Kamarupa Kingdom**.

Beginning with the naming of Assam, the name of Assam was found as 'Pragjyotisha' and 'Kamrupa' in the ancient Sanskrit literature. Its antiquity is established for the fact that it has been mentioned in the two great epics- The Mahabharata and the Ramayana and also in the Puranas. The analysis of meaning writes that Prag means 'former' or 'eastern' and Jyotisha means 'a star', astrology, shining. Therefore as such Pragjyotishpur was taken to mean the 'City of Eastern Astrology'.

The name is originated from mythology where Kamarupa tells us the story of Sati who died due to the rudeness shown to her husband by her father Daksha. Overcame by grief, Shiva carried her dead body and wandered the dead body throughout the world. In order to put a stop to the madness of Shiva, Vishnu cut the body into pieces by his discusses, which then fell into different places. One such piece fell down on Nilachal hills of Gauhati and henceforth the place became sacred and named as Kamakhya. But Shiva's atonement did not stop, so the God Vishnu sent Kamdev, for the development of love. Siva enraged and burnt Kamdev to ashes. Kamdev eventually regained his original form by God's grace and the country came to be known as Kamarupa (Where Kama regained his Rupa).

Assam is a state in **Northeastern Regions of India**, surrounded by hills of Himalayas and coming down to River Brahmaputra River and Barak valley. It is bordered by Bhutan and Arunachal Pradesh towards the north; Meghalaya, Tripura, Mizoram and Bangladesh to the south; Nagaland and Manipur in the East and West Bengal to the West.

The Origin of Assam starting with its name: The name 'Aham' or 'Asom' (because of Hills and Planes) was most likely given by the Ahoms who came to Assam in 1228 A.D. The Ahom, a Shan prince in course of time fully assimilated with the locals. Thus Ahom dynasty was established by Sukaphaa who ruled Assam for nearly six hundred years. But there were other groups of people in Assam even before 1228 A.D. The Bodo-Kachari, to which the Bodo people belong, is thought to have entered Assam from Southeast Asia who had settled in the region. The Bodo-Kachari was also some of the first people to produce silk material and was considered to be advanced in rice cultivation in Assam during that time period.[Ref[(Sen1999:44)]] (Bhatt2005:20), ^ (Dikshit 2013:376)].

The kingdom of Kamrup came to an end in the 12th century A.D. The Chutiya Kingdom controlled the entire region of present Assam districts of Lakhimpur, Dhemaji, Tinsukia and other parts of Jorhat, Dibrugarh, and Sonitpur. The hostilities with the Ahoms began when the Chutiya Kingdom expanding its territory towards the south. Due to hostility Ahom king, Sutuphaa, was once attacked by the Chutiya king during a friendly negotiation. The conflict triggered a number of battles between the two kingdoms, which saw great loss of men and money. The staggering dispute often flared up till 1523, when finally Ahoms took Sadiya killing the then king Nityapal. At last the Chutiya had dispersed to the frontier regions, but continued raids against the Ahoms time to times till 1673, and finally the Chutiyas fall under the domination of the Ahoms.

Kamarupa Kingdom of the 7th and 8th century included the entire Brahmaputra valley and at various times and also included present-day Bhutan and parts of Bangladesh, the southern boundary was near the border between the Dhaka and Mymensingh districts in Bangladesh. However the kingdom had broken up entirely by the 13th century into smaller kingdoms and from among them aroused the Kamata kingdom, Dimasa kingdom and the Chutiya kingdom as the main successors. Ahom dynasty of Sukaphaa who entered Assam in 1228 later took power and ruled all over Assam. In the 16th century the Ahom kingdom came into prominence and took over the political and territorial legacy of the Kamarupa kingdom.

Koch Dynasty (1515 - 1949): The princely state of Cooch Behar is also intimately connected with Kamrupa Kingdom since the established of the Ahom Kingdom in the 13th century.

In the 17th century the Ahom-Mughal conflicts, occurred in which the Ahoms kept the Mughals at bay in the Battle of Saraighat of 1671. After that the Ahom kingdom reaching at its highest picks but failed to preserve the Kingdom because of internal problems. Burmese invasion took place in the early of 19th century.

Due to heavy torture of the Burmese Army, Ahom King along with his workers and many people were compelled to take shelter in the adjacent state of Bengal. The young Maniram Dewan also fled to Bengal along with his father. Assam came under British India in 1828 due to the effort of Maniram Dewan by the defeat of Burmese Army and making the Yandabo agreement. The British with Indian soldiers attacked the Burmese army on two fronts, one through Chittagong from Arakan in the southeast region, and the other through Sylhet from Cachar and Jaintia in the north. Many of the people of Chittagong and Sylhet who join the British army to save Assam from Burmese army died in the War but in the end Burmese had to leave the place. That signifies the district Sylhet was also a part of Assam long before the attachment of Sylhet with Assam by the British. (Ref.1).

Under the efforts of the British the jungle regions of Assam has been transformed into Kaziranga National Park and Manas National Park, and made the area a centre of wildlife tourism. The economy of Assam began to increase through tourism. The beautiful Assam valley became more beautiful by the growth of Tea under the guide lines of the British bringing European Tea-planters and lakhs of Tea workers from distant places of India and sometimes even from China. Maniram Dewan played a major role in the production of tea. Assam became known for Assam tea and Assam silk. The state was the first site for oil drilling in Asia. In course of time the underground wealth were discovered- Coal and Oil. The source of huge economy was discovered.

Henceforth, the control of Assam came under the hands of the British, which marked the beginning of British rule in the state. The British set out to organize the administration, transport, and communication systems within Assam. Some of the major changes that came during the colonial rule include the construction of railways, establishment of tea plantation areas and discovery of coal and oil. However, in the post independence period or post-colonial rule, Assam saw the separation of territories, like the partition of Arunachal Pradesh in 1948, Nagaland in 1963, Meghalaya in 1972 and Mizoram in 1987. The population of Assam mainly comprises of the migrants from Burma and China, thus presenting a fusion of Mongol-Aryan culture.

Assam lost much of its territory to new states that emerged from within its borders. The British annexed Cachar in 1832 and Jaintia Hills in 1835. In 1874, Assam became a separate province with Shillong as its capital. Sylhet was merged with East Bengal on partition of India. With the partition and independence of India in 1947, the district of Sylhet (excluding the Karimganj subdivision) was ceded to Pakistan (the eastern portion of which later became Bangladesh).

However, like all other states of India, Assam was also involved in various freedom movements. With the enthusiastic participation of many courageous activists of Assam, however, the united Assam became a constituent state of India in 1950. But very soon it saw reduction of its area when Dewangiri in North Kamrupa was ceded to Bhutan in 1951. The capital of Assam was formerly in Shillong (now the capital of Meghalaya), and later shifted to Dispur, a suburb of Guwahati, in 1972. The States of Meghalaya, Nagaland, Arunachal Pradesh and Mizoram got their own separate states.

Let us see the old history why did Assam remain under Bengal during the Rule of British?

The Battle of Plassey: The Sea-port of Bengal being a gateway to India, a land full of riches and a ministerial although fortified by a strong naval presence, could not face the British because of few factors. It was the mistake of Mirza Muhammad Siraj ud-Daulah, who was the last independent Nawab of Bengal, gave the British a commercial license to buy Muslins and jute from Bengal. The British manipulated Siraj's ministers and bribed them to stand against the Nawab. It was a catastrophic betrayal. The British consolidate their hold in Bengal as rulers, after the Battle of Plassey (June 1757). Siraj was betrayed by his most trusted ally Mir Jafar and few other ministers. He lost the Battle of Plassey and finally Bengal went to the command of the western colonizers. Thus the British had established its command over Bengal.

The rule of Ahom Kingdom (Tai-Ahoms) for five hundred years collapsed due to the Burmese invention. But untiring efforts of Maniram Dewan succeeded to evade the Burmese Army with the help of the British, who by the time already being made their occupational influence in Bengal. During Burmese aggression Maniram Dewan encouraged the British general Davit Scot to proceed to Assam to fight against the Burmese. The colonial era of Assam began with the establishment of British control after the Treaty of Yandaboo in 1826.

Assam became an independent State after independence of India in 1947. Gopinath Bordoloi, became the first Chief Minister of Assam followed by Bishnu Ram Medhi, who took over as the next Chief Minister of Assam in 1950. During his tenure from 1950 to 1957, who gave importance only in the agricultural product Bimla Prasad Chaliha became the third chief minister from 1957 to 1970. His remarkable contribution was the construction of Saraighat Bridge over the River Brahmaputra in 1965, and an Oil refinery at Noonmati, Guwahati in 1962. But he too followed the process of disintegration by the introduction of "Language" which was Assamese Language in the fore front replacing all accepted "English" during his time instead of taking up the policy of the development of the whole region by the policy of creating industries utilizing the natural resources of the region, and the natural beauty of the region in the tourism sector.

The 1959-60 the language revolt took away Assam far behind and set the ingredient of dissatisfaction and disintegration throughout the whole region resulting the formation of many smaller states. The

Cachar District of Barak Valley could also have been like a region of Assam Valley in course of time by accepting the local language of Assam like that of the Tai-Ahom in order to form Ahom Dynasty or as that had happened in the USA where all immigrants accepted American English as their language of state in course of time without imposition. But due to imposition Cachar fought for Bengali language and got it only for Cachar bringing an under current sentiment of disintegration. However, still to-day the Cachar District of Barak Valley having with its Bengali Language because of the imposition of Assamese Language is remained with Assam taking active parts in the efforts of the development of the region.

A state or a region nowhere can develop without the good wishes and whole-hearted participation and sacrifice of the people of the region, however small for the development of the region. The sense of separation and isolation cannot bring a state in the front of development rather the sense of expression of integration only could bring a state in the frontal row of development. America became a country of Super-power by the integration of the intelligence of the young-youths of the world forgetting the human bitterness between Black and white; the Arab-World became one of the richest countries of the world for making business with all countries rich or poor with its huge resources of Oil making good relation with most of the people of the world. It is a concluding fact that a region or a country get richer and flourished with the fruits of development only through the good wishes of all irrespective of religion, language or customs, as because all are human beings and acceptable to each other in the course of time and patience in the long run.

Now Assamese became the official language of the State and Bengali also enjoyed by the Cachar District of Barak Valley with the same spirit of status. These are nothing but political gain to acquire political power but against the unity of the state. Next Mohendra Mohan Choudhury became the chief minister of Assam in 1970. He carried out the formation of Bongaigaon Petro-Chemicals, Paper Mill at Jogighopa and Jute factory at Silghat, few small factories here and there to reduce the unrest of the youngsters as he failed to bring big industrialists to set up big-industries in Assam in the atmosphere of unrest. The question of creating tourist centers also failed in spite of the existence of so many spectacular centers rarely found anywhere in India because of the existing unrest started with the language movement. In 1972 Sarat Chandra Sinha came to power after Congress securing absolute majority. To increase his popularity he shifted the capital from Shillong to Dispur in 1974 and thereby he had done the greatest blunder whereby the people of Assam lost their right over Shillong as well as in Meghalaya for all the time for ever. If he could make a second capital at Dispur keeping a part of Capital in original place at Shillong, where the people of Assam could enjoy the full right at least over Shillong, the beautiful Capital what was once made by the Assamese people of Assam and Bengali people of Sylhet together?

The Assam Movement took a new turn in 1979 that was again a popular movement against illegal immigrants in Assam. The movement was led by All Assam Students Union (AASU) and the All Assam Gana Sangram Parishad (AAGSP). In the atmosphere a mighty force ULFA (United Liberation Force of Assam) came into existence and finished the least probability of setting up any kind of big-industry in the state of Assam. The ULFA violence spoiled the existing business in all sectors. Thus an atmosphere of unemployment and unrest prevailed in the state. Educated youths get disheartened and some are lucky to get a job in distant Madrass or Bengalore.

The agitation after agitation was going on in Assam although agitation was largely non-violent, but the Nellie massacre was a case of extreme violence. The undeclared agitation continued and at last the agitation program was ended in August 1985 following the signature of an Accord, goes by the name as Assam Accord in between the leaders of AASU-AAGSP and the Government of India. By the long agitation almost 860 young lads lost their lives. The result was the formation of a political party, AsomGana Parishad. It came to power in the state of Assam in the Assembly elections of 1985 and later in 1996 but without eviction of a single infiltrator. In the end

Assam lost its progress in the sphere of development. Assam being remained attached with Bengal in the British period for a long period of time. It is astonishing to count that when Bengal was developed under the British period why Assam did not developed?

On this occasion, let us first know in detail the rich history of Bengal where Assam, a beauty of natural heaven was a part of Bengal. Under the Mughals, Bengal Subah or Mughal ruling Bengal had generated almost 50% of the empire's gross domestic product (GDP) having with of 12% of the world's GDP- such a rich and flourishing region including Assam could not see the destiny of prosperity. Why? The people of this region suffered the most before independence and after independence. It was the people of this region Hindus, Muslims, where its Bengali & Assamese people suffered the most to get Indian Independence for India as they fought against the British the most but get little after independence because the leaders of Uttar Bharat Petal, Nehru and Gandhi had taken their activity vigorously in the Eastern regions so that Jinnah turned his attention towards the Eastern region as such thrust of Pakistan turns towards Eastern Region. It was the reason the maximum killing, the "Calcutta Killing" had happened in Calcutta and the demand of Pakistan was with Assam-Bengal and not with the Delhi, Lucknow, Agra of any regions, and the greatest ruling regions of Muslim-Mughal. Bengal was divided and Assam survived luckily having being to be a part of East Pakistan. But after independence people of this region remained as the most neglected people of India again and the people of the region became a subject of mercy for shelter, progress and prosperity- a fact of truth remained under dark. Let us proceed to know the history of ancient, medieval, and present condition of the region including Bengal that only can explain the law related with CAA.

[5.6]

Role of British Bengal Including Assam: The Fort William in Calcutta (now Kolkata) was the first British stronghold in India where the British rebuilt it and made it into a fortified, cannon-fitted military base. After the fall of Mughal Empire, the focus of Indian culture and politics shifted from Delhi to Calcutta where the British rebuilt the Capital at Calcutta by the development of three villages into a modern City. The city gradually became the capital of the British India and it remained so until 1911.

Bengal has seen two catastrophic famines in 1776 and 1942 and two partitions in 1905 and 1947 under the British Raj along with the regions of Assam because the people of these regions fought for independence not for themselves but for the people of Uttar Bharat and that was realized afterwards. The province endured three unforeseen migrations in 1905, 1947 and 1971 under immature political leadership suffering the regions including the whole of North East to the catastrophic feature of human slaughter. The spree of development even after partition remained centering towards Gujarat and Delhi and nothing towards Bengal and Assam. Bengal and Assam was kept at the thrust to destruction with the internal fight of uncounted refugees without taking any effective step for rehabilitation of these people and cleverly Assam was kept engaged in the issue of language by bringing the three language formula in disguise by central administration and encouraging the different units of Assam to demand union territory leading to states without carrying any heavy industry or IT-industry for the development of the region.

Bengal province had produced many geniuses at the earlier time and in the recent time a progressive young stalwart Subhas Bose in the 20th century that had created unrest in the name of independence that had also destroyed the industrial progress of the region. Many freedom fighters of Bengal, under the Revolutionary units such as Anushilan Samiti and Jugantar sacrificed their lives for the so called independence movement. Many others such as Khudiram Bose, Surya Sen, Binoy, Badal and Dinesh sacrificed their lives but today nobody is ready to accept their sacrifice. Why did Bengalis fought against the British? Is it to pass a life of hawker and beggar? The remote region of Assam was not remained in behind. The sacrifice of **Maniram**

Dewan was the glowing example who was the only sacrificing hero among the Indian political leaders to sacrifice life for the nation, but instead of making him a national hero, Nehru unilaterally made Gandhi as the FATHER of the nation to compensate Gandhi in making him the PM of India in place of Sarder Petal, a selected candidate of the Congress.

Netaji Subhas Chandra Bose (Netaji), the face of Indian armed freedom struggle, formed the Azaid Hind Force and fought against the British till death. Many Bengali youths sacrificed their lives in the Cellular Jail of Andaman to fight against the British for Independence. Is it justified their sacrifice to live in Indian Union as an unwanted refugee. There is no point to keep the earlier united Assam and Bengal under the leadership of Delhi to pass a beggar's life in spite of the presence of so much of mineral wealth.

Post-Independence of Assam-Bengal: Indian politics now became Delhi centric and became indifferent to Assam-Bengal. Delhi remained indifferent although Assam-Bengal faced two back-to-back partitions and migrations in 1947 and 1971. The indifferent attitude of Delhi administration annoyed the youths of Assam-Bengal leading to witness the largest youth revolution in the form of the Nasality movement in 1970-71. The unrest continued in Assam as well as in Bengal.

Assam-Bengal region a state supreme in economic front in British period remained at the bottom list in the economic front after Independence of India. Where laid the Assam-Bengal's sacrifice for Independence of India? Assam, a remote region of Eastern India remain attached to the mainland of India crossing Bengal, as such the unrest in Bengal prevented the progress of Assam due to the narrow passage of land-route but again Assam is surrounded by East Pakistan on three sides that prevented the progress of Assam in the progress of trade through the obstacles in sea-route. Moreover, Delhi government never gave attention to develop international trade in the region through Myanmar (Burma). The lookout was towards West via Bombay and not towards East via Myanmar or Bengal. The whole region was exploited before partition and now exploited after partition.

The British took control of the region following the Battle of Plassey in 1757. The British utilized the wealth of Bengal to the Industrial Revolution in Britain. The prolonged administration of British in Bengal resulted unrest in Bengal and that became breeding grounds for Northern political leaders to utilize it for their benefit for the Indian independence movement in the early 20th century. The result was India's independence in 1947 on the religious lines into two separate entities without taking a single Hindu Bengali into confidence on the committee of the final resolution of agreement. West Bengal—a state of India—and East Bengal—a part of the newly created Dominion of Pakistan was formed where Assam was saved luckily to be a part of East Pakistan. There was lot of immigration in Bengal as well as in Assam. Thus unless the earlier destruction of Assam-Bengal was not taken into consideration the question of the Law of CAA could not be ascertained correctly.

Very soon a new Viceroy of India, Lord Curzon took up the British administration. Looking to the activity of Hindu youngster's secret killing activity of British, Curzon took up a firm decision to learn a lesion to the Hindu Bengalis. He thought to reduce the power structure of Bengali Hindus. In one stroke he thought to divide Bengal as East Bengal and West Bengal and by the second stroke he thought to shift the British Capital from Bengal to Delhi. Even in the Bengal Ministry he kept sufficient Muslim reservation beside other reservation so as to reduce the power structure of Hindus. Lord Curzon announced the division of Bengal on 19 July 1905 and implemented the same in the same year separating the largely Muslim eastern areas from the largely Hindu western areas. Assam became a part of Eastern Bengal as it was kept along with East Bengal. The Hindus of West Bengal was kept along with the province of Bihar and Orissa. The British applied the "divide and rule" policy for the sake of administration. In 1909, separate elections were arranged for Muslims as well as for Hindus.

The Bengali peoples particularly the Bengali Hindus started protest and procession against the decision of Curzon. Congress arranged meetings and petitions submitted to the authorities against the partition formula. At last in order to appease Bengali sentiment, Bengal was reunited by Lord Harding in 1911. Bengali spoken areas were once again unified, but Assam, Bihar and Orissa get separated and the capital was shifted to New Delhi. In 1947, again Bengal was partitioned, but here the partition was not done by the British but by the Indian leaders on the basis of religion, no where present in the world, for self interest without caring the welfare of the common people. Today after independence people of Bengal particularly the Hindu people of East Bengal who had been uprooted from their parental land being compelled to migrate to India leaving their ancestral home due to partition of Bengal have no place to take shelter. Where is the truth of Indian civilization where Indian claim India has an unparallel ancient civilization?

The analysis of the earlier history of India would reveal the failure of Indian political leaders for their narrow mentality. Gandhi brought the devastation by creating Hindu-Muslim rioting through the movement of NON-VIOLENCE. He brought the division of Bengal on the basis of religion, destroyed the industry and the overall economy of the region. Assam was a part of East Bengal as such the economy of Assam was also destroyed and devastated and transformed the region into a region of poverty and hunger.

Mohammad Ali Jinnah strongly claims Assam to be included in Pakistan but the other Congress leaders did not wanted to go against Jinnah for the greater benefit of bargaining in Uttar Bharat. However, Gandhi supported Assam to be included in India. Gandhi never went against Muslim to divide the country, and also never went against the killing of Hindus in Calcutta, the reason was clear; he was not against the formation of Pakistan in his inner mind, definitely because of certain hidden facts. Again Gandhi never went against in the inclusion of 98% Buddhist region of Chittagong Hill Track to Pakistan, because he did not wanted to annoyed Jinnah for greater interest of few regions of Uttar Bharat. It was a fact of the matter that appeared in the partition of India in the formation of Pakistan where

Jinnah behaved like a dictator and Gandhi along with other congress leaders behaved like an obedient disciplines. The matter lies in the violent nature of Muslim League with militant volunteers under the guidance of Jinnah while the submissive nature of Congress workers under goes under the guidance of Gandhi. The aim of Jinnah was to create Pakistan, a Muslim country and become the Chief of the new country as he could not achieve it in India because of the Hindu ethics of Gandhi.

On the other hand the aim of the Gandhi was to make Nehru the Chief of the country of India at any cost to flourish his name and fame under the new discovery of the ethics of "Non-Violence". The new ethics of "Non-Violence" was dearer to him than the country or the people of the country. Bengal and Punjab are the two progressive, advanced and strong state of British India, as such the look out of Gandhi was how to destroy the two states and how to eliminate or downgrade the leaders of the two states. Keeping it in mind he initiated his strongest effort in the two states in the form of "non-violence". He was instrumental to initiate violence under the cover of "Non-Violence" in Punjab through the sacrifice of Bhagat Singh but indirectly, he became a favorite person of British in disguise by withdrawing the movement and approving the hanging of Bhagat Singh. Similarly in Bengal he initiated the "Non-Violence" movement and continued the movement in spite of non-cooperation of the Muslims till the Muslims get ready to carryout violence and announced a particular date the 16th August 1946 to achieve Pakistan by "Calcutta Killing". Keeping himself in dark he engaged Petal to create Pakistan. He was so clever that in order to keep him away from violence, he went underground in Sabarmati Ashram and remained in silence for a while then he appeared in public along with the Bengal PM Suhrawardy to ask the public to maintain peace in Calcutta to earn the name, as a man of peace, and an international icon of peace.

Role of Gandhi and Bordoloi in the efforts of Assam: In February 1946, Pethic Lawrence, the then secretary of state for India, circulated a note where he included Assam in Pakistan for the cause of viability of Pakistan due to economic, defense and financial considerations. An impression was that the Cabinet Mission of Congress was not serious about exerting pressure on Assam going against the consonance with the Muslim League's demand. On May 16, 1946, the Cabinet Mission recommended that Assam and Bengal be tagged together to frame the provisional constitutions for the provinces despite the objection raised by Assam Premier Gopinath Bardoloi before the Mission.

However, Saadullah, leader of the Muslim League in the Assam assembly, suggested the attachment of Assam with Bengal. This helped the belief of Lawrence that Assam had such a close connection with Bengal that its separation from Bengal was impossible. The Congress leadership seemed to remain indifferent to Assam's case. The Congress apprehended that taking up the issue of Assam at that stage might result in confusion and a stalemate of the larger priority of India's freedom along with few important regions of Uttar Bharat. But it was Gandhi who supports the Congress Working Committee to take a more responsible attitude to the Assam problem.

On the other hand Gandhi even suggested to a Congress delegation from Assam that they should leave the party if the CWC did not support their stand. Ultimately, it was Bardoloi's credit supported by Gandhi to keep Assam away from grouping and thereby Assam became a part of India. Thus in spite of Gandhi's failure everywhere, at least in one occasion in the case of Assam, Gandhi was successful. Thus the record of history says Nehru in 1962 during Chinese aggression gave good-bye to Assam but Gandhi in 1947 well come Assam to India. As such Gandhi will remain ever great in Assam. But it had a under current reason, the reason was the arrival of Netaji, Assam a non Bengali region would support Gandhi but the Bengali region of Sylhet district would not support Gandhi that might be the reason to get it separated from Assam by referendum. How far Gandhi was humanitarian is yet to be known. Who was responsible for the division of the Country Gandhi or Jinnah or who was communal Gandhi or Jinnah, all were very clear in the record of history.

6. THE REASONS OF DESPAIR AND DESTRUCTION OF ASSAM

[6.1]

Since the independence of India and division of Bengal on the basis of religion and restructuring of Assam, communal tensions and violence remained in Assam and that flared up time to time under the patronage of few political leaders for their vested interest. In 1961, the government of Assam passed a legislation making the use of the Assamese language compulsory as the center is trying to impose Hindi all over India. However, that created unrest and unhappy atmosphere in different regions of Assam. Separatist groups began to form along ethnic lines, and demanding autonomy and sovereignty.

The government of India, which has the unilateral powers to change the borders of a state, divided one unit of Assam into several states beginning since 1963.The Naga Hills district became the 16th state of India under the name of Nagaland in 1965. In 1970, in response to the demands of the Khasi, Jaintia and Garo people of the Meghalaya Plateau, the districts containing the Khasi Hills, Jaintia Hills, and Garo Hills were formed into an autonomous state within Assam and later on that led to the formation of a separate state under the name of Meghalaya. In 1972, Arunachal Pradesh (the North East Frontier Agency) and Mizoram (from the Mizo Hills in the south) were again separated from Assam as union territories; both became states in the year 1986 according to the desire of the central government.

In the 1980s the Brahmaputra valley saw a six-year long Assam Agitation triggered by the discovery of a sudden rise in registered voters on electoral rolls. It tried to force the government to identify and deport foreigners illegally migrating from neighboring Bangladesh and to provide constitutional, legislative, administrative and cultural safeguards for the indigenous Assamese majority, which they felt, was under threat due to the increase of migration from Bangladesh. The agitation ended after an accord (Assam Accord 1985) between its leaders and the Union Government, which remained unimplemented, causing simmering discontent.

The post 1970 experienced the growth of armed separatist groups such as the United Liberation Front of Asom (ULFA) and the National Democratic Front of Bodoland (NDFB). In November 1990, the Government of India deployed the Indian army, after which low-intensity military conflicts and political homicides have been continuing for more than a decade. Lachit Divas' is celebrated to promote the ideals of Lachit Borphukan – the legendary general of Assam's history. Sarbananda Sonowal, the present chief minister of Assam took part in the Lachit Divas celebration at the statue of Lachit Borphukan at Brahmaputra river front on 24 November 2017. He said the first country wide celebration of 'Lachit Divas' would take place in New Delhi followed by state capitals such as Hyderabad, Bangalore and Kolkata in a phased manner.

In the earlier history we find Muslim League calls for direct action on 16th August 1946 demanding Pakistan. Massacre happened in the streets of Calcutta killing 5 to 10 thousand Hindus. The news of killing spread the violence in other places. Lord Louis Mountbatten formally gave a proposal what was "the proposal" to divide India to stop rioting.

In public front Gandhi appeared to be annoyed but he silently engaged Petal to complete the task. Patel gave his approval for the Mountbatten's plan "the plan of 3 June 1947" hoping to become the PM of India as his name was selected by the Congress and accordingly he lobbied Nehru and other Congress leaders to accept the proposal. Calling a general meeting Petal had taken the consent of the Congress. This was the history of surrender of the leaders of

90% Hindus to Jinnah, a leader of Muslim League of less than 10% of Muslims.

There was politics in Assam just before Independence. Muslims Leader Muhammad Saadulah became the Prime Minister of Assam in April 1937 because of Muslim Majority. Saadulah encouraged Muslim immigrants from East Bengal to consolidate his power of Chair. In 1938 Netaji Subhash Chandra Bose became President of the Congress; he could not tolerate the conspiracy in bringing Saadulah in the ministry as Prime Minister. He came to Assam and replaced Saadulah with Gopinath Bordoloi by the support of the members of Surma Valley.

At the beginning A K Azad, the veteran Congress leader of Bengal was sent to Assam to sort out the Assam problem, but Netaji was not satisfied due to the prevailing communal tension being existed in Assam for which he himself came to Assam as Congress President to solve the Assam problem. He instigated Bordoloi as PM of Assam as the members of Surma valley were convinced to support Bordoloi under the patronage of the Congress President. But very soon Bordoloi had been asked by the Gandhi to resign in view of the congress movement against the British after the declaration of the War what was objected by Netaji as because of the unique vulnerability of Assam on the borders of India before his leaving the country. However, judging the condition of Assam later on Gandhi expressed his opinion that Subhas was justified.

Assam's Prime Minister Gopinath Bordoloi expressed his views at the time of partition that Assam was not homogenous because of the presence of the Sylhet District. Bordoloi was an outstanding farsighted leader because of his leadership ability he had been chosen by the Congress President Subhas Bose himself coming from long distance of Congress Office to Assam in 1938 to install him as the Prime Minister of Assam. At that time Netaji's influence acted like a spirit for the elected people of Surma Valley to support Bordoloi to become the PM of Assam. Afterwards Subhas Bose left the country to liberate India through Azaid Hind Force. War II ended.

India achieved Independence, with a divided Bengal. Gandhi was interested to see Nehru as PM for his personal image no matter with the division of the country, and without division he could not kick out Jinnah. So long Jinnah was in India he could not succeed to fulfill his secret mission. Gandhi was not interested with Bengal and Bengal leaders particularly with Netaji. He was humiliated several times by the remarkable personality of Netaji, a young leader of Bengal. He could not succeed to make Sitaram Patto-via as Congress Present who miserably get defeated against Netaji, again he was humiliated as he failed to raise his voice of "Non-Violence" against Netaji's powerful voice of "Give me blood I would give you freedom".

What was necessary to develop a region, the exploration of the region, the proper utilization of the minerals of the region, utilization of the techniques, labor, and intelligence of the people of the region irrespective of religion, caste or community? It is the effort of all together when a region becomes spectacular and beautiful in all respect. It is quite natural when the people who are residing in a region for a long time accept the culture and language of the region. The glowing example is the country of USA. But in India, the short sided Indian leader Nehru in particular immediately after independence imposed Hindi neglecting the English used by the British in the multilingual country of India for long two hundred years. The result was out broke of revolt in the South. Still the short sided selfish leaders imposed Hindi in the back door through the formula of three language system. The then Assam Chief Minister followed the short sided policy of center and imposed Assamese in the united Assam blindly, thereby destroyed the amity, friendship, brotherhood and what not of the whole region of the United Assam. This kind of imposition of language had not only destroyed the amity of faithfulness of living together but even had created an atmosphere of enmity. Thus in course time every region except Cachar (Barak Valley) went away from Assam. Barak Region having with its Bengali language remained with Assam hoping in course of time to regain the earlier friendship as the two regions differ neither much in language nor in culture. One day by the lapse of time all would be the true citizen of Assam, who would work for the welfare of the state in spirit and heart. However, the land of Sylhet district except a town of Karimganj because of river line demarcation went to East Pakistan (now Bangladesh) but most of the people shifted to different places of Assam and in Cachar.

Partition of Bengal in 1947 is a tragedy for Bengal and Bengalis. Lord Curzon partitioned Bengal in 1905 that left a deep impact on the people of Bengal. The breakdown of Hindu-Muslim unity was caused by the "Non-Violence" Movement of Gandhi. The uncertainty in the Muslim minds led the All India Muslim League to demand the partition of India in line with the Lahore Resolution, which called for Assam-Bengal to be included in a Muslim-majority homeland. The sense of Hindu Muslim identity compelled the Majority-Hindus to demand a Hindu-majority districts a part of the Indian dominion. But again the farsighted matured few individuals in the Bengal Legislative Assembly voted to keep Bengal undivided. The Prime Minister of Bengal supported the proposition of a United Bengal as a sovereign state. However, the Indian National Congress (INC) supported by Petal and Nehru and the Hindu Mahasabha under the command of INC forced the British Viceroy Mountbatten to partition Bengal along religious lines. As a result, Bengal was divided into the state of West Bengal of India and the province of East Bengal and later named as East Pakistan. Assam was placed in India under the patronage of Assam Prime Minister Gopinath Bordoloi but the Sylhet region of Assam was allowed to join East Bengal after a referendum on 6 July 1947.Had the district Sylhet remained in Assam, the trade of Assam could have been improved through the passage of Sylhet and the present Mizoram to build a port like CHITTAGONG PORT near the area of Bay-of –Bengal. Assam would have explored by the export of tea through the sea port of Assam.

7. ACTIVITY OF SIRAJUDDAULA AND THE ENTRY OF EAST INDIA COMPANY IN ASSAM UNDER BENGAL

[7.1]

The new nawab Sirajuddaula was only 23 when he ascended the throne of Bengal. Soon he could realize that he was surrounded by enemies, local as well as by foreign powerful persons. Even in his own house he was surrounded by enemies. His greatest enemy was **ghaseti begum** (Meherun-Nisa), the eldest sister of his mother, Shawkatjang, his cousin, who was another great rival. Then it was **mirjafarali khan** who was the commander-in-chief of Alivardi's army, but again he was a part and parcel of the family as he was also the husband of a half-sister of Alivardi Khan. Beside these, the other dangerous persons were the Jagath Sheth family which controlled the Bengal money market and lastly the English East India Company, which was quite openly ignoring the Nawab. Without taking any permission from the Nawab, East India Company were fortifying the Fort William of Calcutta and taking all other military preparations. The Fort William was made a safe haven for the criminals and violators of the law of the land who were protected by the people of East India Company.

To bring the English under law, the young Nawab Sirajuddaula thought to attack Calcutta, when the English left the city for a distant place. East India Company brought Colonel **Robert clive** who entered into a conspiracy with the disaffected officials of the Nawab, Mir Jafar, Jagat Sheth, Rajballabh and many others. A secret agreement was formed between the Fort William Council and Mir Jafar agreeing to place Mir Jafar on the throne, and the latter agreeing to grant territorial, financial and trade facilities to the English. After the treaty of agreement Clive arrived at Palashi and took position on 23 June 1757. Sirajuddaula also came to face to the company's army. But to his dismay he could discover that the larger part of his own army defied his command and stood silent. Finding the situation not favorable Siraj tried to flee away from the field, but he was captured and brought back to the capital and killed. Clive, in accordance with the secret agreement, placed Mir Jafar on the throne. The Mughal sovereignty was virtually over with the war of Palashi and finally the English took the total control of power.

Revenue administration: Mughal revenue administration in Bengal was elaborately chalked out by Alivardi Khan (1756-1765) before his death he nominated his grandson Sirajuddaula (son of his daughter amina begum) to the masnad of the subah as he was not having son of his own. Sirajuddaula, a young man of independent spirit and indomitable character, was not prepared to follow the appeasement policy of his predecessors. He found the conduct of the English was wrong or unfair and unbearable. Immediately after his accession to the masnad he issued to the company a proclamation directing that the unauthorized fortification works in and around Calcutta must be demolished, that they must pursue their legal trade strictly according to the law of the land and finally, they must obey the laws now under the protective umbrellas of the Fort William. The company refused to accept the nawab's conditions and Siraj also refused to accept the trade right of the company. Under such conditions he dispatched troops, took control over all the English trading factories; and finally expelled them from Calcutta in June 1756.

But he could not sustain the initial victory. From Madras soon Robert Clive arrived in Calcutta and started the campaign to recapture the city in January 1756. The nawab being unable to face a trained naval force he was under compulsion to formulate a formal peace treaty (**alinagar treaty,** 9 February 1757) with the company to the effect that the company would enjoy all the privileges accorded to the company by the imperial Farman of 1717. In addition of that the nawab would also give due compensation for the losses sustained by the company and others consequent upon his Calcutta campaign.

Robert Clive, who was a soldier as well as a diplomat, took the Alinagar Treaty as a truce rather than a durable peace accord. His next attempt was to make necessary preparations for overthrowing Sirajuddaula who appeared to him to be hostile to East India Company. As a first step he tried to identify and win over nawab's enemies to his side. He set up secret communication connection with the amirs actually or potentially opposed to the nawab. A conspiracy was hatched up against the young **Sirajuddaula** and a secret treaty was concluded in May 1757 with the conspirators particularly with Jagat Sheth and Mir Jafar. The battle of Palashi started but Clive and the conspirators proceeded according to the secret pact and the downfall of Palashi came on 23 June 1757 disposing Siraj and inducting Mir Jafar into the masnad.

The event of Palashi and post-Palashi developments gradually had established the political dominance of the company. But yet, at that time the company was neither oriented to civil administration nor adequate enough to rule an extensive kingdom like Bengal. But the course of subsequent developments led the company along with few enemies of Siraj to move consciously to the goal of sovereignty. Mir Jafar, although became the puppet nawab had failed to compensate the company according to the secret treaty with Clive. Very soon in 1760, he was replaced by his son-in-law, **mirqasim**. The new nawab quickly settled the indemnity affair by relinquishing the three large and resourceful districts- Burdwan, Midnapur and Chittagong to the Company.

But Mir Qasim had his own plan in his mind how to get rid of Clive's constant harassment and then his plan of asserting himself as the real sovereign authority of the country. To control the aggressive Clive he made a plan, accordingly he shifted the capital from Murshidabad to Mungher, a distant and not easily accessible hill-fort in Bihar and far away from the reach of the English marine strike. He raised a new army for defense and established a new bureaucracy. Finally he tried to assert his sovereign status and called upon the company and other private traders to refrain themselves from resorting to unlawful trading activities and asked them to abide by the laws of the land. The English under Clive did not paid scant regard to the order.

The enraged nawab attacked Patna (July 1763) under compulsion and captured all company establishments. Many resisting Europeans and supporters of company people were killed. This kind of action had triggered off a full-scale war between the company and the nawab. Mir Qasim persuade the emperor and the nawab of Oudh to join him in his war against the English. The combined forces met the British in a battle of no return at Buxar (23 October 1764). The English army defeated the allied troops although Mir Qasim won a number of sporadic battles. The battle of Buxar led the company to control the accession of Diwani in 1765, and finally close to sovereignty. Clive's acquisition of the diwani of Bengal, Bihar and Orissa solved the problem to become the absolute authority of the sovereignty. Thus Bongo –Bihar-Orissa was ruled under Bengal Presidency.

8. ASSAM EMERGED AS AN INDEPENDENT STATE

[8.1]

The Government of India Act 1935 provided provincial autonomy with an enlarged elected provincial legislature consisting of 108 elected members. In 1937 elections were held in Shillong for the newly created Assam Legislative Assembly. The Indian National Congress had the largest number of seats, with 38 members, but declined to form a government under the guidance of Gandhi. Therefore, the Muslim League's Sir Syed Muhammad Saadulla formed the ministry. Saadulla's government resigned in September 1938, when Gopinath Bordoloi formed the ministry including Fakhruddin Ali Ahmed, the future President of India. Again all of the Congress ministries in British Indian provinces resigned, for the declaration of Second World War by the British, when Sir Syed Muhammad Saadulla was again invited to form a ministry.

Saadulla remained the Premier (Chief Minister) of Assam up to 1946. During the Japanese invasion of India in 1944, some areas of Assam Province, in the regions of the Naga Hills district and in some parts of the Manipur princely state, were captured by the Japanese forces. When fresh elections to the provincial legislatures were held in 1946, the Congress won a majority in Assam, and Bordoloi again became the Chief Minister of Assam. On 15 August 1947 Assam became part of the Indian Union, when Bordoloi continued as the Chief Minister even after India's independence in 1947.

The first Governor of independent Assam was Sir Muhammad Saleh Akbar Hydari and Chief Minister was Gopinath Bordoloi who witnessed the foundations laid for Gauhati University (1948), Gauhati High Court (1948) and Guwahati station of All India Radio (AIR). When Gopinath Bordoloi passed away in 1950, Bishnu Ram Medhi took over as the next Chief Minister of Assam. During his tenure from 1950 to 1957, the First Five-Year Plan was started, Panchayat system of governance was introduced and the agricultural sector got more importance. Bimla Prasad Chaliha was the third chief minister from 1957 to 1970. In 1958 the 66th session of Congress was held at Jalukbari, Guwahati. The Saraighat Bridge was constructed over the Brahmaputra River in the year of 1965; an Oil refinery was established at Noonmati, Guwahati in the year of 1962 during his time period. In 1959-60 the famous language revolt took place in Assam, and as a result Assamese became the official language of the State and Bengali also enjoyed the same status in the Cachar District of Barak Valley.

Mohendra Mohan Choudhury assumed the mantle of chief minister in 1970. The foundation of Bongaigaon Petro-Chemicals, Paper Mill at Jogighopa and Jute factory at Silghat in Nagaon were laid in his tenure. In 1972 Sarat Chandra Sinha came to power after Congress secured absolute majority. In 1974 the capital was finally shifted to Dispur in Guwahati.

The Assam Movement (1979-1985) was a popular movement against illegal immigrants in Assam. The movement, led by All Assam Students Union (AASU) and the All Assam Gana Sangram Parishad (AAGSP), developed a program of protests and demonstration to compel the Indian government to identify and expel illegal, (mostly Bangladeshisi), immigrants and protect and provide constitutional, legislative and administrative safeguards to the indigenous Assamese people. The agitation programs were largely non-violent, but the Nellie massacre was a case of extreme violence. The agitation program ended in August 1985 following the Assam Accord, which was signed by leaders of AASU-AAGSP and the Government of India.

The Assam Accord (1985) was a Memorandum of Settlement (MoS) signed between representatives of the Government of India and the leaders of the Assam Movement in New Delhi on 15 August 1985. A six-year agitation demanding identification and deportation of illegal immigrants was launched by the All Assam Students' Union (AASU) in 1979. It culminated with the signing of the Assam Accord.

The accord brought an end to the Assam Agitation and paved the way for the leaders of the agitation to form a political party and form a government in the state of Assam soon after. After Assam Agitation for a long period what was the output, nothing but the formation of a political party. Assam was neither connected with the main land properly, nor was its surrounding atmosphere improved adequately so as to increase its trade facilities abroad either in land route or in sea-route. The economy of the state could not show its growth and prosperity. It is an establish fact that economic prosperity is the sign of progress and prosperity to enjoy a better life what is seen in the western world.

The present state of Assam: The people could see the creation of detention camps, a massive operation of stripping citizenship of 2 million people. People are busy to check their names on the final list of the National Register of Citizens. What would people do if the country you born in, or the country you've lived in for decades, suddenly announced you had to prove your citizenship or else face detention and deportation? This is a situation for nearly 2 million people — most of them Muslims, some of them Hindus of Bengali origin, because their names do not appear on India's National Register of Citizens (NRC).

It is the part of the government's effort to identify and weed out the illegal immigrants in the northeastern state of Assam from the citizenship list. The political leaders of Assam for the sake of political power convinced the people by giving logical arguments that many Bengali Hindu-Muslims whose families originally came from neighboring Bangladesh (previously East Pakistan) are not rightful citizens, even though they've lived in Assam for decades. If anyone live in Assam and his or her name do not appear on the NRC, the burden of proof lies on the person to prove that he or she is a citizen of Assam. The obvious move would be to find out birth certificate or land deed, but many of rural residents don't know paperwork, because most of the population is illiterate. Everyone get the chance to appeal to a Foreigners' Tribunal, **the High Court of Assam or even the Supreme Court**, to prove their claim to citizenship. But if all that fails, one can be sent to one of the 10 mass detention camps the government plans to build, complete with boundary walls and watch towers.

In the economic front the government failed to show remarkable progress, to divert attention of the public the government indicated that it plans to **extend the NRC process** to the whole country. With so many people facing the threat of detention and for uncertain future prefer the path of suicide. Ultimately, it is going to be deportation from the world's largest democracy. In the name of patriotic service to the society, in order to make name and fame after capturing power, the Indian leader including Gandhi once divided the country **and that too on the basis of religion, nowhere present in the world. Thinking of the greed of power for the few political persons like that of the time of Independence of India, the United Nations, Human Rights Watch**, and the **US Commission on International Religious Freedom** all become very much concerns to see that this could soon be turned into a humanitarian crisis of horrifying proportions.

If the detainees in the camps end up being expelled from India that could constitute a wave of forced migration in the end, even greater than that triggered by Myanmar in 2017, when **hundreds of thousands of Rohingya Muslims** were displaced. If this looming crisis hasn't happened, humanitarian people or patriotic leaders should give their attention for the sake of humanity, before it escalates into a humanitarian catastrophe affecting millions.

A brief history of Migration in Assam: To understand the roots of India's plan for a massive detention system, it is necessary to go back to the 19th century, when the British occupied Assam by defeating the Burmese army and later for the sake of revenue set up big tea plantations in Assam. At that time it was a revolution to set up Tea-Garden in Assam by the big industrialists of Europe, when Labor was in high demand and many people from Bengal, Nepal, and elsewhere were brought into Assam to do the labor works. When British decided to plant tea in Assam through Chinese expert, they could not think at the beginning that Assam will grow into an enormous tea production state. After the discovery of the wild tea plant they devoted their energy in growing tea plant as they later could discover that Assam's tropical monsoon climate was the perfect weather environment for tea production. Their attempts in the set up of large number of Tea-gardens by the European industrialist became successful when found that Assam tea is worldwide famous as full-bodied tea with robust flavor and even highly liked in London market. It not only gave them an incentive to earn state revenue by the export of tea as well as a pleasure as it brings a kind of pleasure to his countrymen although the British administration was little concern with the development of Assam. In course of time the British could realize that it is the largest tea producing area in India, making up to more than 50% of all tea production in the country, where the Tea-planters cultivated Tea by bringing hundreds and thousands of Tea-Workers from other regions of India and engaging them in several restricted gardens extending the field area to about 304 thousand hectares. Assam tea also carried an important ingredient making it black for which in many places it is marketed as black tea blends, sometimes only as black tea.

The local Assamese were happy with local drinks and they were not interested with labor works. Then, in 1947, the subcontinent was partitioned, Jinnah became the Chief of Pakistan and Nehru was made the Indian Prime Minister by Gandhi. The power loving leaders never hesitated to create India and Pakistan amid bloodshed, and in the midst of rioting and transfer of many families rushing to the safety regions. That was the reason for a wave of migration of many Bengali people to Assam.

In 1971, the territory of East Pakistan has been turned into Bangladesh and that too due to the participation of the Indian Army. The cry of bloody independence war, turned millions of Muslims fled Bangladesh for India, and many of them remained in Assam, the public were not in fault but the situation was an event where government was compelled to respond for the future safety of the nation. Their lies farsighted view, Gandhi tried to divide India to get rid of Jinnah, but by giving East Pakistan he had created an absolute Muslim center for the creation of huge Muslim population without restriction to work as fire bomb as good as Atom bomb to disturb the nearby state, Bordoloi tried to get rid of Bengalese by separating Sylhet from Assam but instead of creating a happy future for Thai-Ohm, he created problem under compulsion to accommodate the unrestricted Hindu Bengalese by giving away the land of Assam (the district Sylhet) to Pakistan by pushing it to referendum at the joyful moment of getting Assam in India instead of getting it under East Pakistan what had been brought to Assam at an earlier time by the farsighted British snatching it by force from Bengal for the betterment of the whole North Eastern region creating the Capital at Shillong. Modi government getting failure in economic sector brought NRC in front and he is going to create another human bomb of illegal migrant accommodating them in detention camp, who knows one day the human bomb of detention camp would not bring a human holocaust bringing the militant force of international community to India and also to Assam?

It is a known fact that Bangladesh is not going to accept the newly stateless people. As the foreign minister of Bangladesh **put it**, "We are already in much difficulty with the Rohingya refugees, so we can't take anymore." Who knows where all these human beings will go if they're deported? According to Home Minister of BJP, it plans to **extend the NRC process across all over India**. If that happens, not India alone but the whole World would be looking at the biggest refugee crisis on the planet. Already, by the past few years the world had seen a movement of refugees around the world on a scale not seen since **World War II**. Muslim communities have been affected the most, the massive **6.6 million Syrians** had to flee their country due to civil war, **2.5 million refugees** had to flee from **Afghanistan**, and **700,000 Rohingya** had to flee from Myanmar in 2017.

In the atmosphere of high tensions of a massacre of Bengali Muslims slaughtering more than 1,800 in 1983, a peace accord was signed in 1985. It concluded with a commitment to create a method to identify people who came in after 1971 and their descendants including themselves would all be considered citizens of Bangladesh, not India. Plans were devised for a citizenship list, but it failed due to the complicated paperwork of millions of people. But **again due to** the rise of **Hindu nationalism** over the past several years and an associated rise in anti-Muslim sentiment collaborated with an order of Supreme Court in 2013 an up-to-date NRC was published hurriedly. In 2018, the state government finally published a draft of the NRC, whereby names of **Four million people** were left out of NRC list including some high-profile **Hindu and Muslim of Bengali origin**. Two prominent leaders from Assam's leading minority party, Maulana Badruddin Ajmal and Radheshyam Biswas, were left off the list.

After lots of public outcry and appeals, some people managed to get their names onto the NRC but many more to the extent of 1.9 million names remained out of list. It remained impossible to know how many of them have been left off the list erroneously. But many believe many rightful citizens were left out because of the non availability of birth dates in rural area. What's more, some and several are reportedly committing suicide as per the report of New York Times because of the anxiety they feel over the citizenship list, what was reported even in outside world. Noor Begum, who lived in a small hamlet in a flood-soaked district, spiraled into depression after finding out that she and her mother had been excluded from the citizenship lists. Her father and seven siblings had made it. It didn't make any sense when in a family if they all lived together and were born in the same place, would some be considered Indian while others illegal foreigners. On a bright morning in June, Noor, a family member hanged herself from a rafter. She was only 14.

"As human rights experts, now saying this process has been arbitrary and discriminatory," Meenakshi Ganguly, South Asia director at Human Rights Watch, concerns that the Foreigners' Tribunals may well go easier on Hindus than on Muslims who appeal for their citizenship determination. Some lawmakers are pushing a **Citizenship Amendment Bill**, which would carve out exceptions for immigrant Hindus, Sikhs, Buddhists, Janis, Parses, and Christians — but not Muslims — left off the NRC.

Destruction of Assam by the Assam politicians: Assam is one of the most naturally beautiful states but the state is still today the most backward states of the Indian Union. The reason is crystal clear because society is severely affected by insurgency, economic backwardness, and unabated foreign influx. The destruction of the state is also severely affected in the progress of economic development due to gross negligence of the center and also due to the inefficiency of the state government. It is true that social structure and politics of Assam is the by-product of the society and the nature of political patriots. The people could not see the foresighted ability of the political Patriots of Assam to bring any devise or enterprise in the progress of economy of the state. The progress of development is extremely slow that generated a peculiar discontent which resulted in the growth of the Assam movement followed by innumerable ethnic and sub-nationality movements destabilizing the entire social and economic fabric of the state. The movements virtually brought a change of mindset of the people of different community and the people turn towards regionalism and resurgent activity.

Access to power during the post-colonial period has been largely misused by the intra-party and intra-castes rivalries. More significantly the poverty and insolvency had turned the youngsters in the adversity of insurgency. Thus the problem of insolvency cum poverty added fire to the fuel turning the administration restless forgetting any kind of development project. Finally, the unabated illegal infiltration of the foreigners into Assam from neighboring Bangladesh already had created great havoc and poses a great existential problem for the native people. The Bangladeshi immigrants almost become the determinant factor in the politics of Assam that had generated a fear psychosis in the Asamiya minds that they would soon be the minority and numerically insignificant group in their own homeland. Here lies the political immaturity of the political stalwarts of India and Assam in particular as because Assam was the affected state.

Gandhi was highly honored in Assam as he was the only Congress leader who supported Assam to remain in India in 1947 during the time of partition of Bengal. Actually it was not for love of Assam but for fear out of Netaji if Netaji any time comes back as he was not declared dead in the war, Assam (except Sylhet) would support Gandhi and not Netaji. Gandhi was although a big religious leader but not a political leader having with of strong mind and spirit having of a leadership capacity and not at all a leader of farsighted intellect. Had he possess the farsighted intellect he should know in future the creation of East Pakistan would have been a small Islamic country where the growth of population would have been enormous because of the system of multiple marriage granted by the law of Islam. No body or no political party could form government in East Pakistan going against the rule of marriage permitted by Quran although any political patriot cannot accept it for cause of the prosperity of the country. Had it been in India it would not happen? If Gandhi really a well wisher of Assam he should not permit another Pakistan (East Pakistan) in the Easter part to destroy Assam, what is practically happening now in Assam.

India's Muslim minority is facing serious risks: Prime Minister Narendra Modi champions a hardliner brand of Hindu nationalism known as Hindutva, and his best companion Home Minister Amit Saha which aims to define Indian culture in terms of Hindu culture and Hindu values, which promotes an exclusionary attitude toward Muslims. That was nothing but the design of vote capturing what was present in 1947 among the Congress leaders to capture power based on Hindu- Muslim conflict being created by Great leader Gandhi by his "non-violence" movement taking only the Hindus based on Hindu Ethics. Gandhi's narrow minded farsighted thought created East Pakistan whereby the 3 core population has risen to almost 20 cores what had created the problem in the whole Easter regions of India disproportionally. Under Modi, vigilant-Hindus have increasingly perpetrated hate crimes against Muslims what was done once by Gandhi to kick out Jinnah as he was afraid of him because of his logical argument in abroad at London talk and again afraid of his militant activity at home. Congress remain in power of India by the appeasement of Muslims and by the appeasement of Muslim League being afraid of its militancy, and agreed in silence to make India a democratic country instead of the declaration of a Hindu country or a Hindustan against Pakistan's declaration of an Islamic country.

Now BJP coming to power after a long time trying its best to remain in power instead of failure in administration particularly in economic front just opposite what he had promised before election in the event of large public gathering. Forgetting the Indian culture of humanity and service to humanity now the leaders have gone to the lower strata of mentality for the sake of capturing power to scare the Muslim people and their communities to move away, or punish them for an effort for **selling beef** (cows are considered sacred in Hinduism). Again in the last month, **Modi erased the statehood of Jammu and Kashmir**, just to make the Indians happy what India should do in 1947 as per British declaration if India thought to be courageous and a fit administrator and fit enough to rule on its own the whole country. Kashmir was India's only Muslim-majority state, where the Muslims had shown their courage to punish anyone what they think not good for the state and the people, they compelled the Kashmiri Pundits to leave the state, where the Indian people had seen in front in silence that few lakhs of Kashmiri Pundits had to fled away from Kashmir although Kashmir belong to India. It did not reflect the courage and correct administrative policy of Democratic India or a Hindu India in term of Pakistan an Islamic country.

Gandhi was recognized as the Father of the nation and he is symbolized as a man of peace and he was considered as protector of humanity. But how a victim of partition can console himself to accept him as a man of peace when he was compelled to leave his ancestral home by the loss of half of his family members in the event of rioting at the time of Hindu-Muslim rioting and killing of human beings in the street when Gandhi neither could convince Jinnah by virtue of his humanity nor could stand like Hind-Krishna keeping Arjun by his side to protect the riot victims. If Gandhi was a man of humanity, how he could distinguish the Indians as Hindus or Muslims and accepted the partition of the country on the basis of Hindus and Muslims. Rather he had set up the seeds of Hindu-Muslim rivalry in India.

It was the reason why the present government is thinking in terms of Hindu-Muslim. It is estimated that the Muslims had formed approximately 14 percent of the national population but in Assam state it is more than twice. It was the reason why Modi in the 2019 Indian election campaign promises that if he (BJP) gets elected he would get the NRC in shape and deal with the Muslim migrants in Assam once for all. Other members of his ruling Bharatiya Janata Party (BJP) have used inhuman language against the Muslims. "These infiltrators are eating away at our country like termites," BJP president and home minister Amit Shah publicly **said** at an election rally that, "The NRC is our means of removing them". Shah has openly said our goal is to **deport** those deemed illegal immigrants.

It is said that India is a country of humanity but again the Indian leaders are behaving with the people inhumanly. If the leaders were human being, how they could keep away a section of the Indian people in a separate country because of the difference of religion? Now a separate country, an Islamic country exists nearby by the division of India. Many people in Assam of India are recognized as illegal immigrants. Does it not expose the inefficiency of the government to protect the border with full security? If we look to the history of these illegal immigrants they were nothing but the Hindus of India. There was a time when no Muslims were present in East Bengal. After the birth of Muslim religion, during Sufism the Sufis (religious preacher) came to Bengal and many people accepted the Muslim religion because of equality among all sections of people which was not present among the Hindu Brahmins and Hindu Dalits, unlike the forceful conversion to Muslims in the different other regions of India during the period of the Sultan Dynasty. On humanitarian ground why not these are accommodated in India claiming proportionate share of land from the adjacent country? After all they are also human beings and India having being a country of humanity should accommodate them, and make them a responsible citizen and a responsible human being above religion by giving education and modern technology. Every human being is a wealth of a nation if he is utilized properly as it is done in the USA or in Japan.

America was discovered by Columbus of Span, the highest number of Spanish people was settled in San Francisco but Spanish language did not become the language of America. English was not imposed in India by the British but it became the language of India by dint of which India get United. Hindi was imposed by the government of India just after independence but it was opposed by the South as such it is disliked by the people of Southern India. Similarly in Assam Assamese was imposed that disintegrated the United Assam; even in Barak it was opposed. If Sutapha coming from Tai-Ohm could create a new language ohm (Assamese)along with Chutetia, Morans and others in course of time, why not Assamese language would prevail all over Assam in the longer span of time, a fact of history but why imposed? Imposition had brought a human sense of repulsion in different regions of Assam somewhere openly and in some other places silently. A greater Assam with greater outlook could have been emerged only by the human wealth if the wealth is explored properly. America became a country of prosperity by the people of all kinds of all language, but India became a country of poverty even after 70 years of independence because of hatred of people of all kinds, hatred out of religion, out of language, customs and community. Out national policy is a policy of segregation while in other country the national policy is a policy of integration, where there is integration, there is progress and prosperity.

Contribution of Muslim immigrants in the progress of Assam:
The peasants of Mymensingh district were once brought to Assam under the Ministry of Saadullah in the district of Nowgang following the policy of "Grow More Food". The Census of 1931 table shows that population growth rates for all the Eastern Bengal districts went down sharply in each successive decades starting with 1901 while the population growth rates for Assam Valley districts rose sharply starting with 1911. The population of Mymensingh, Rangpur, Bogra and Pabna keep on decreasing while the percentage of population of Goalpara increases to 2 per cent in 1901 while in 1931 it increased to 15.8%. Similarly it increases in other districts as well. But after the 1937 elections, the United Muslim Party under the leadership of Saadullah formed a government in Assam. During the period of 1939-41, Saadullah government allotted one lac bighas of land in the Assam Valley for the settlement of East Bengal immigrants. Saadullah appeared to have maintained that the immigrants were mostly landless and the only solution was to provide them with available lands. But there was bumper agricultural growth out of their hard labor for which the food crisis in the Nowgong was eliminated.

In post-independence days Assam had provided shelter to a large number of people from outside the state. With the available resources at the time of independence the state was not in a position to welcome further immigration. But the partition of the country based on religion compelled a large number of Hindus to migrate to West Bengal, Tripura, Assam and various other neighboring states. Under compulsion of religious partition a large number of Bengali refugees were rehabilitated in Assam and given Indian citizenship. The district Sylhet of Assam was sacrificed to Pakistan but most of the Hindu people of Sylhet migrated to Assam, as because Sylhet was once a part of Assam. The sacrifice of Sylhet by referendum was right or wrong is realized now. The strategy is that the land of Assam was removed but not the people.

Immigration of Muslims in Assam: The land development scheme of Saadullah's government was subjected to severe public criticism.

This forced Saadullah to resign on 12 December 1941. But Saadullah became Premier once again in 25 August 1942. Since March 1942 till then, an area of seventy-five thousand bighas was settled with immigrants. But in the interest of the "Grow More Food" Campaign many pending evictions were stayed. The Government of India had desired the extension of cultivation in Assam from 52.8 lakhs of acres to 57 lakhs during the year of 1943, in order to get more food. The Assam Government adopted the policy to grow rice crops replacing jute crops and accordingly cultivators are encouraged. Government decided to accelerate land settlement in Kamrup, Nowgong and Darrang, to extend areas of immigrant colonies and to settle more lands with immigrants owing to the imperative need of growing more food.

Saadullah Government was encouraging immigration and opening out large areas to Muslims to increase their number. But the role played by his Hindu Cabinet colleagues has never been questioned or assessed the continuous immigration policy for "Grow More Food". The whole matter, however, was left to the Minister of information for a modified policy for submission to the Cabinet. As regards the "Grow More Food" Campaign, it was observed that the purpose being purely temporary for the duration of the war and it should not be confused with the long term land settlement policy of the Government. Rather it was admitted that the easiest means of growing more food was abolition of all restrictions on immigrant settlement. Thus considering growing more food by "A short term policy" more immigrants were allowed to come to Assam. The result was a vast land of Assam was occupied by the immigrant people. Saadullah's Muslim League coalition government threw new policies for settling immigrants; they were permitted to settle in forest reserves. However the Assam Jatiya Mahasabha, Sibsagar or Ahom Sabha, the Assam Provincial Hindu Sabha, the Assam Kachari Association and Assam Mouzadar association criticized the action of Saadullah.

After the arrival of Jinnah at Gauhati on 7 April, 1946, the situation changed as he made a remark that "if the government does not immediately revise its policy and abandon this persecution of the Muslims, a situation will be created which will not be conducive to the well being of the people of Assam". At the same time the Assam Provincial Muslim League Council, in a resolution adopted on 30th April, 1946 also moved the Central Council of action for launching direct-action against the Congress Government. They also made an appeal to the Muslim population to contribute generously towards an ad-hoc eviction relief fund. In 1946, Liaquat Ali Khan in his press conference criticized the government stand and stated that "to call these villages professional grazing reserves is a misnomer". It was nothing but a mere excuse for eviction of these poor Muslim peasants. He further pointed out in his statement that it was brutal and barbarous to evict the poor immigrants from their villages as they had spent time and labor to build up their dwellings. He also remarked that Cruelty and inhumanity of the Congress exceeded all bounds in the tyranny over the Muslim immigrants in Assam.

This was however, not appreciated by the Congress of Gopinath Bordoloi who went round the Goalpara and some areas of Barpeta where immigrants had settled. He was in favor of eviction of the Muslims. Accordingly fresh instructions on 14 May 1946, was issued for eviction of all these Muslim people. This was highly resented by the members of the Assam Muslim League and by organizing meetings, processions and hartals they registered their anger. Abdal Hamid Khan "gave a call to the evicted persons to return to the grazing reserves. He also resorted to a fast unto death in May 1946 in the evicted areas of Barpeta. His fast had the desired effect by 6 June 1946. This way to carry out the task of eviction became difficult, more so when the Muslim League members whole heartedly supported the cause of the immigrants. To counteract this opposition the Congress Government in Assam introduced stringent measures by promulgating the Assam Maintenance of Public Order Ordinance on 18 November 1946. The introduction of this ordinance was an indication of the firmness of the government to tackle the immigration problem. The Muslim League leaders reacted immediately against the stand taken by the Congress Government. They decided to launch a civil disobedience programme in protest against the eviction policy pursued by the Congress Ministry in Assam. Muslim League successfully carried out the civil disobedience movement. The effect of the movement was felt in those areas inhabited by the immigrants. On seeing the growing of communal feelings Gopinath Bordoloi decided to go slow with his policy and thereby he kept the province free from communal riots.

IMMIGRATION ISSUE after Partition: In Assam, the politics of immigration persistently overshadowed many other issues. In evaluating the trend and extent of immigration one cannot ignore the geographical realities and historical facts and compulsions which had undoubtedly governed the flow of population in Assam. The effect of the partition of the country was strongly felt in the eastern sector. One of the most important sections of the pre-partition population, whose contributions and sacrifices for the freedom of the country were second to none, found themselves third grade citizens of a hostile country. Partition brought endless misery for them and they eventually migrated to Assam. People outside Assam believed that there was plenty of waste land available in Assam. From humanitarian considerations, the Government of Assam rehabilitated few lacs Bengali Hindu refugees. The actual number of migrants however, was much more. More than thirty three years have passed since then, but the unending human flow from across the border is yet to cease. "THE RIOT OF 1950" the communal disturbances, before and after the partition (1947) had undoubtedly created tensions among the people. In Assam the riot of 1950 was a dreadful blow for the security of Muslims. Hundreds of Muslims were killed and their houses burnt. Both movable and immovable properties were damaged. The main ambition of the miscreants was to drive out the Bengali Muslims from Assam. Compelled by the constant fear for their lives and property and further bloodshed, many Muslims took refuge in East Pakistan. The number of Muslims migrated to East Pakistan was several lakhs. According to some it was eight lakhs. In the same way thousands of Hindus started to migrate to India and Assam as well under similar conditions.

The Immigrants (Expulsion from Assam) ACT, 1950: The influx of people from East Pakistan (present Bangladesh) has continued unabated and the Assamese people began to view it as posing a serious threat to the economic, cultural and political identity of the people of the state. Government of India seemed to aware of this problem and in the year 1950 passed the Immigrant (expulsion from Assam) Act empowering the Central Government to detect and deport infiltrators from East Bengal which was then East Pakistan. Accordingly a Bill was presented to Parliament. During the last few months, a serious situation has arisen in Assam due to immigration from East Bengal. Such large migration began to disturb the economy of the state, besides the law and order problem. At last an agreement was reached between India and Pakistan.

Nehru Liyaquat Agreement (1950): In order to reduce communal tension and to maintain peace between both the communities the Prime Minister of India, Shri Jawaharlal Nehru and the Prime Minister of Pakistan, Muhammad Liyaquat Ali Khan had signed an agreement on 8 April, 1950. This agreement was known as 'Nehru Liyaquat Agreement'. According to this agreement, the people who left their own country earlier with valuable property, due to the communal violence, may return into their own home on or before 31 December, 1950. If they return (from Pakistan to India and from India to Pakistan) within the appointed time, their citizenships along with the properties would be returned. The Indian Muslims who took shelter in East Pakistan started to come back to their own homes again. Thus Assam was populated by the immigrant Muslims. But the Hindus of East Pakistan particularly the Hindus of Sylhet who preferred to migrate to Assam as they were once in Assam never returned as they prefer to live with Hindus when they did not like to live in East Bengal being turned into an Islamic East Pakistan where the existence of Hindu culture became doubtful.

Lakhs of Indian Muslims took shelter in East Pakistan due to communal riot of 1950, most of them did not return to their own places of Assam before the Census of 1951. At the same time thousands of

Indian Muslims also decided to settle permanently in Pakistan, and thousands of the Muslims returned afterwards.

After partition the migration of Muslims to India or Assam was very rare. Bengali Hindus on the other hand continuously entered India from Pakistan to make their homes here. So the complete sealing of Indo-Pak border was impossible for India only for the protection of Pakistani Hindus. India always blamed Pakistan that they failed to protect the minority community. Pakistan on the other hand always condemned Indian Policy of deporting Muslims to Pakistan forcibly. In order to solve this problem Indo-Pak dialogue had been started. Letters were also exchanged between Field Marshal Ayub Khan and Jawaharlal Nehru. These exchanges were followed by a conference of the Home Ministers of the two countries at Delhi from 7 to 11 April 1964. The views of the Home Ministers were as follows: - "The Home Minister of Pakistan impressed upon the Home Minister of India the view that eviction of a large number of persons from Assam and Tripura and other Indian States had led to tensions and consequences thereof." "The Home Minister of India, on the other hand, explained his Government's position regarding the problems relating to the migration of minority communities from Pakistan into India the consequences arising there from. However, efforts were made to find out a good mutual solution to these questions. For the improvement of bilateral relations Home Ministers of both the countries forwarded some proposals.

Prevention of Infiltration from Pakistan (PIP): The Proposals of the Government of India were: Proposals for security, (a) Joint appeal by the two Home Ministers for communal harmony. (b.) Periodic meetings of representatives of the two countries for review and assessment of the implementation of Indo-Pak agreements and deviations in either or both countries and similar others. Similarly Government of Pakistan also said almost six lakhs Indian Muslims were forcibly deported from Assam to East Pakistan during the period 1961-66. Whatever, may be the exact number, it was true that lakhs of Muslims were forcibly deported from Assam to East Pakistan without any sympathetic consideration. After completing the checking the Government of Assam declared that, there were no more Pakistani foreigners residing in Assam.

On the other hand PAKISTANI BENGALI HINDUS ARE TREATED NOT as FOREIGNERS. It was because Bengali Hindus along with others fought for freedom of India. They were always in forefront for undivided Bengal as well as for undivided India. After the Bengal Partition they tried their best for the re-unification of Bengal. This endeavor was to some extent successful, when Lord Curzon was compelled to remove Partition in 1912. But it was again divided on the basis of religion as well as under the conceal Divide and Rule' policy of the British Government. Bengali Hindus of East Bengal, who would be minority, tried hard for the re-unification of Bengal, but Hindu-Muslim divergence still existed. The ultimate result was the Partition. After partition, Bengali Hindus of East Pakistan felt grief and sorrow as like the Muslims of India. Many Muslims started to go from India to Pakistan while many Hindus from Pakistan to India. But it was not possible to come all Hindus from Pakistan to India and all Muslims from India to Pakistan. At that time it was felt that the Hindus in Pakistan and the Muslims in India would be minority and they would be adversely affected by the policies of the respective Governments.

Therefore, Pandit Jawaharlal Nehru, the Prime Minister and Sardar Vallabbhai Patel, the Home Minister of India gave assurances that they would be friends and guides at any unhappy moment of East Pakistani Hindus. They committed to give rehabilitation as well as citizenship treating them as 'Refugees' or 'Displaced Persons', whenever, they (Hindus) would be compelled to come India due to atrocities. Thus there was a commitment of the Indian Government to provide settlement and citizenship to the Hindu Refugees or displaced Hindus. A new Department of 'Relief and Rehabilitation was opened both at the Centre and the states for their settlement in a planned manner. Even so, Bengali Hindus were deprived from the Government jobs, allotment of seats in educational institutions etc.

During Assam movement AASU and its allies demanded to deport both Hindu and Muslim migrants without consideration of caste, creed and religion etc, However Vishaw Hindu Parishad(V.H.P.), Bharatiya Janata Party(B.J.P.) and Central Government were not interested to deport Hindu Bengalis as they are treated as refugees. However, the emergence of Bangladesh altered the situation for the time being. Bangladesh became a good neighbor state as well as a friendly state. Mrs. Indira Gandhi, the then Prime Minister of India became very closed to Sheikh Mujibur Rahman, the then Prime Minister of Bangladesh. As a result a Treaty of Friendship, Co-operation and Peace was also signed on 19 March 1972 by Indira Gandhi and Seikh Mujibur Rahman whereby the war victims were send back to Bangladesh.

Contribution of Bengali Hindus in the progress of Assam: Bengali Hindus are Bengalis adherents of Hinduism, and are native to the Bengal region in the eastern part of the Indian subcontinent. Bengali Hindus speak Bengali, which belongs to the Indo-Aryan language family and adhere to the Shakta and Vaishnava traditions of their native religion, Hinduism. There are significant numbers of Bengali-speaking Hindus in different Indian states. During the Sena period (11th – 12th century) the Bengali culture developed into a distinct culture within the Hindu civilization. Bengali Hindus were at the forefront of the Bengal Renaissance in the 19th century. The Bengal region was noted for its participation in struggle for the independence from the British rule. At the time of independence of India in 1947, the province of Bengal was partitioned between India and East Pakistan, part of the Muslim-majority state of Pakistan. Millions of Bengali Hindus migrated from East Bengal (later Bangladesh) and settled in West Bengal and other states of India.

A district of Bengal called Sylhet was snatch away from Bengal in 1874 and kept under Assam for commercial and administrative facilities of Assam by the British. Most of the Hindu people of that district migrated to Assam as they had an affinity towards Assam because of long term existence with Assam. The migration continued in waves through the fifties and sixties, especially during 1964 East-Pakistan riots, and during the Bangladesh Liberation War, an estimated 2.4 million Bengali Hindus were massacred by the Pakistani army. The 1971 massacre again led to exodus of millions of Hindus to India and also in the border state of Assam, of course after liberation most of them returned to Bangladesh. During the decline of the Mughal Empire, Nawabs of Bengal ruled a large part of Bengal but the British East India Company captured Bengal overthrowing the Nawab Siraj ud-Daulah regime. The British rule destroyed the bases of Bengali Muslim society. Bengali Hindus got favors from the British rulers.

With rising nationalism among Bengali Hindus, the British rulers applied divide and rule policy, and started to make favors to Bengali Muslims. To keep the rising Bengali Hindu aspirations under control, the British partitioned the province in 1905 and along with some additional restructuring came up with two provinces – Eastern Bengal & Assam and Bengal itself, in each of which the Bengali Hindus were reduced to minorities. The Bengali Hindus, however, opposed to the Partition tooth and nail, and thereby created revolutionary nationalism, the British Raj finally annulled the Partition in 1911. The Raj, however, carried out some restructuring, and carved out Bengali Hindu majority districts like Manbhum, Singbhum, Santal Pargana and Purnia awarding them to Bihar and others like Cachar that were awarded to Assam, which effectively made the Bengali Hindus a minority in the united province of Bengal. The Britishers also transferred the capital from Calcutta to New Delhi.

The revolutionary movement gained momentum after the Partition of Benghal by the British in 1906. The British, unable to control the revolutionary activities, decided to hinder the Bengali Hindu people through administrative reforms. The Government of India Act 1919 introduced a change in the 144 member Bengal Legislative Assembly, 46 seats for the Muslims and 59 for the institutions, Europeans & others and left the rest 39 as General, where the Bengali Hindus were to scramble for mere representation. The situation worsened with the Communal Award of 1932, where in the 250 member Bengal

Legislative Assembly a disproportionate 119 seats were reserved for the Muslims, 17 for Europeans, Anglo-Indians & Indian Christians, 34 for the institutions, and the rest 80 were left as General. The Communal Award further divided the Hindus into Scheduled Caste Hindus and Caste Hindus. Out of the 80 General seats, 10 were reserved for the Scheduled Castes. Thus the British policy gave Bengal government indirectly to Muslims, the Muslims who were once enemy to British. The Hindus who were once friend to British became enemy to British. Who could say Bengali Hindus were intelligent but nothing but fool in politics even though Bengali Hindus were nothing but educated philosophers.

In 1946, the Muslim League supporters started a series of violent attacks against Hindus in Kolkata in the name of Direct Action Day, which escalated into the bloodiest communal riots between Hindus and Muslims of modern India. The key builder of communal riot through "Non-Violence" creating Hindus and Muslims for and against of "non-violence" remain in silence in a secured zone. After the initial attacks, rapes and killings by Muslims, Bengali Hindus joined hands with Sikhs and non-Bengali Hindus in attacking Muslims and ultimately it turned out to be a violent reprisal that resulted in heavy casualties of Muslims, finally forcing the government to stop the mayhem. Later in the year, the Muslim League government orchestrated the infamous Noakhali genocide.

After the failure of the United Bengal plan, it was concluded Partition of Bengal was the right decision under the atmosphere of communal tension. Thus the plan of Gandhi to bring division between Hindus and Muslims in order to divide under disguise to kick out Jinnah get succeeded what was initiated by the British based on divide and rule policy to administer India keeping the fighter Bengalis under control. Jinnah was clever than the Bengalis, the British who captured power from the Muslims favored initially the Hindu Bengalis but Jinnah win the heart of British by supporting the British in World War-II but the Bengalis were made fool by Gandhi to go against World War-II and in the end British came with the 3rd June

Plan for the division of India and Bengal as well. Gandhi's declaration in public front "the country would be divided over my dead body" gets down under the secret understanding of division of the country including the division of Bengal so that no Bengalis could look forward to Delhi Chair. Bengali Hindus get everything from the British but because of foolishness lost everything. Hindu Bengalis lost so many districts to Bihar and Assam because of their foolishness engaging themselves in the killing of the British; otherwise they could have been the owner of a big Bengal and the ruler of India. Gopal Krishna Gukley said "what Bengals think today India thinks tomorrow" that encourages the foolish Bengali sentiment to fight against the British and get finish what is today –Bengalis are beggar and hawkers and also Refugees.

Post-partition period: After the Partition, the majority of the urban upper class and middle class Bengali Hindu population of East Bengal immigrated to West Bengal. The ones who stayed back were the ones who had significant landed property and believed that they will be able to live peacefully in an Islamic state. However, after the genocide of 1950, Bengali Hindus fled East Bengal in thousands and settled in West Bengal. In 1964, tens of thousands of Bengali Hindus were massacred in East Pakistan and most of the Bengali Hindu owned businesses and properties of Dhaka were permanently destroyed. During the liberation war of Bangladesh, an estimated 2.4 million Bengali Hindus were massacred in Bangladesh. The Enemy Property Act of the Pakistan regime denied the property to Hindus. The refugee rehabilitation became an acute crisis in Orissa, Chhattisgarh, and Uttar Pradesh and in the Andamans. Apart from that thousands of Bengali Hindus had also immigrated to Assam.

Before India became independent, the city of Dhaka (present capital of Bangladesh) had a significant number of Bengali Hindus at 42.8%, but their numbers have since considerably dwindled, being outnumbered by Bengali Muslims. Bengali Hindus are at present the second largest community after Muslims in Dhaka (7%).

Indian States other than West Bengal: Bengali Hindus are the second largest community in Assam with a population of 3 million (9.12%). They are concentrated in the Barak Valley region and the population of Bengali Hindus in Barak valley is making up 50.1% of the total population of the region. As per 2011 census Bengali speaking population of Assam is about 29% of the total population of Assam. When people living together they became same in language and culture in the long run and became people of the state. This is seen in the USA. All people are no other than the Americans. In Assam the British applied the principle of divide and rule as such tribal people were kept separated from the plan people as such separate ideology of custom had developed when people of plan and hills could not mix together and get one and one human being. Our political thinkers also could not think like wise. Otherwise Dr Ambedkar, the father of the Indian constituent would not introduce reservation for Dalits and separate right for the regions of six schedules. Apparently at the time of independence movement the slogan was one India one nation and one law. It means we are one in all affairs. But at the time of practical application everything was forgotten. The ideal ethics became useless in front of the power of Chair. Forgetting the ideal ethics every Indian politician think for capturing votes how to satisfy every sections of the people forgetting greater benefit of the overall state or the country.

9. EVOLUTION OF DEMOCRATIC POLITICS IN ASSAM

[9.1]

The most influential meaning of democracy came to be synonymous with liberal representative politics. It is found that democracy as a form of politics involves principles of popular rule ensuring human rights and liberties and necessitating rule of law. The evolution of democratic politics in Assam has been a matter of serious discussion at different levels. Most of the historical works on the governance of nineteenth and early twentieth century Assam describe the functioning of the constitutional government put in place by the British. Political History of Assam described the main historical trends and developments from the period of 1826 to 1947 by emphasizing the significant role of the people of the state in the nationalist movement of India. He saw the agrarian riots as an outcome of the growing discontentment amongst the peasantry against the hasty and injudicious action of Britishers in raising the revenues on land without ascertaining the actual capabilities of the riots. He found that for a discussion on the resistance movements organized by the Ahom monarchy against the British rule, such as by Benudhar Sharma in 1950, Maniram Dewan since 1940 are a kind of democratic movement for human rights. These agrarian movements were the determined resistance of the riots indicating peoples' opposition to the authority. It was necessary to note here that these findings multiplied the conclusion about the realization of the masses about the futility of expecting better alternative to the British rule, drawn in the political history of Assam. Some works had been carried out to give an account of these agrarian unrests against high revenue demands and stagnant economy at various levels in Assam. Amalendu Guha while discussing electoral politics in Assam stated that the century old nationalism in Assam and its interaction with electoral politics referred that its evolution was simultaneous along with the democratic movements of all India. According to him, in the matter of peoples' political participation indicating involvement of common men in electoral politics, there was indeed a revolution. Guha however, narrated that peoples' political participation through the beginning of modern political consciousness led towards the growth and early developments of democratic politics.

The peasant upsurge of 1893-94 signifies the beginning of democratic politics in Assam. To quote Guha, in Assamese the word raij is used to protest against the administration that means people in general or in the context of a particular locality. It is found that the word is derived from the word Rajya which means a unit of administration in some parts of medieval Assam. Therefore, Raij-Mels are much more than what we understand elsewhere by a village Panchayat. They played a conspicuous role in the anti imperialist struggle in Assam. During the early British rule, the Raijmels were mostly organized for the redress of their grievances against the colonial oppression in the form of imposition of taxes on land, cultivation, fishing and cutting trees. In the Raijmels, people discussed and raised their protest against imposition of taxes on such matters and the decisions that were being taken to approach the government for the same. Thus a group of people in the form of association called Ryot-Sabhas demanded the employment of the Assamese people in the educational services however, without criticizing the employment of the non-Assamese are also a kind of democratic as well as humanitarian right which was present in Assam right from the beginning.

The new Ministry was formed on 18 September, 1938 under the leadership of Gopinath Bordoloi with the help and initiative of Netaji Subhas Chandra Bose. The new Ministry was hailed all over India.

Under the justified leadership of Gopinath Bordoloi many popular schemes were undertaken including the reduction in the land revenue and the salary of the ministers, improvement of the small-scale industries, introduction of reforms in jail and circular to the government servants particularly the police personals to consider as the servants of people not as their masters. The prohibition of opium in the province was regarded as the biggest achievement of the Bordoloi Ministry. However, it must be noted here that Assam after independence also witnessed many democratic movements mostly led by peasants and youth involving greater popular participation. From the middle of the twentieth century onwards large scale land reclamation at Nambor, Karbi Anglong had taken place with the demand of the land in these forests by the landless peasants. From the period 1948-52 there were intense peasant movements with the slogans like "land to the tiller" and "land for the landless peasants" under the influence of the Left peasant organizations which weakened the newly formed Congress led Provincial Government in Assam. It must be noted here that three non Congress political groups were present in the politics of Assam since 1940s which were-the Communist Party of India (CPI), Revolutionary Communist Party of India (RCPI) and Congress Socialist Party (CSP). The peasant fonts of these political groups successfully mobilized the peasant movements in Assam. Under their influence while the share croppers by giving only one fourth of their produce to the land owners waged an undeclared war against the absentee landowners, the landless peasants occupied lands inside the Reserved Forests or in the tea-gardens. Another peasant struggle in the form of anti-eviction movement became popular in 1973 where the All Assam Students' Union (AASU), the major student organization of the state also played a prominent role in mobilizing peasants.

The Role Gandhi in the destruction of India and Assam as well: Today we find Gandhi is the Father of the nation and the people of Assam remember Gandhi for saving Assam going to be a part of East Pakistan. But since the formation of Assam as a state of Indian Union the people of Assam are in agitation for protection of language, culture and development. But who was responsible for creating these problems. The language and culture was threatened because of non-stop immigration and development was neglected because of the short sided, selfish nature of Indian political leaders. The dream of Mani Ram Dewanin the endeavor of establishing the lost Ahom Kingdom was evaporated by the British by hanging him during the time of Sepoy Mutiny of 1857. In the British period of time Gandhi appeared in the political atmosphere of India since 1915, and started his political journey to increase his popularity as a supporter of British in the first world war, next a supporter of Muslim Khilafat Movement in 1920 originated in Turkey, next a supporter of Hindus through long journey of Salt Satyagraha (Dandy March) in 1929 and finally arrived in Calcutta in 1930 to carry on "Non-Violence" having with a half naked Dress exposing himself as if a Hindu SAINT to mislead the Hindus of Bengal just to finish the economy of the Bengal along with Assam and the leaders of Bengal to make the Delhi Chair safe for Nehru when he would be the Father of the nation by removing Jinnah through Hindu-Muslim religious fight.

His only objective was how-to become a political leader by misleading the people on the basis of religion as because Indian people Hindus or Muslims all are afraid of religion. The success of his religious fight came in 1947 by division of the country and making Nehru the PM of India and the supreme success came after his death by the declaration of the FATHER of the nation but will it give him peace even in heaven as he left here the poison of religious hatred due to which the two nation are at logger head and inside of India the two religious groups are suffering since 1947 in silence but exposing times to time that remembers the recent Delhi Violence. The Corona Virus has come from heaven to finish the mankind but left behind the message that human mankind cannot be divided as religious groups. Those who would survive should learn the lesson that they have to live as one individual of human being. No one has the power to divide the human being not even Gandhi.

By the time of his activity he had chosen a family, the Nehru family based on that family he would reach to his highest goal. By the

Blessings of Motilal Nehru he became the Congress President. His look out was how to be a great leader but he discovered he could not achieve it if he failed to corner Jinnah. He knows Jinnah was a popular advocate and successful advocate what he had already proved by releasing Bal GangDharTikal in a short span of time on the other hand he could not do anything in Bombay as advocate and returned empty handed at his early life which he could not forget. He knows he could easily win the soft Hindu minds by Hindu religion but it would be difficult to win the Muslim mind by the art of religion. But he got the opportunity in the period of 1920, to win over the Muslims when the Muslims of India call for a religious movement in India against the British what is called "Khilafat Movement" for the cause of the Muslims of Turkey. At that time the young Jinnah was also an active supporter of Congress. He failed to understand why Gandhi was supporting a religious movement and that too for the cause of the Muslims of Turkey. He disagreed with Gandhi and protested against Congress support. Jinnah warned Gandhi not to bring religion in Indian politics.

Not only that the Muslim militant activists of Khilafat Movement already started in attacking the nearby police quarters in Malabar of Bombay region warning the British administration to stop the killing of Muslim Caliph in Turkey. The British administrations getting the information through many Hindu workers immediately send the Gurka forces and began to arrest the Muslim militants. Many Muslim youngsters were arrested, beaten and even killed. The British Government put down the rebellion with an iron hand, British and Gurkha regiments were sent to the area and Martial Law imposed. One of the most noteworthy events during the suppression later came to be known as the "Wagon Tragedy", where 67 out of a total of 90 Mappila prisoners being destined for the Central Prison in Podanur get suffocated to death in a closed railway goods wagon. For a period of six months from August 1921, the rebellion extended over 2,000 square miles (5,200 km2) – some 40% of the South Malabar region of the Madras Presidency. An estimated 10,000 people lost their lives, although official figures put the numbers at 2337 rebels killed, 1652 injured and 45,404 imprisoned. Unofficial estimates put the number imprisoned at almost 50,000 of whom 20,000 were deported, mainly to the penal colony in the Andaman Islands, but around 10,000 went missing. The most prominent leaders of the rebellion such as Varian kunnath Kunjahammad Haji, Sithi-KoyaThangal and Ali Musliyar all went underground.

The Muslim activists on hearing the British torturer due to Hindu informer, many more Muslims attacked the Hindus and Christians, and torture the Hindus including the women, girls and children by burning their houses and throwing many of them into deep wells. On hearing that Gandhi was going to support the Khilafat Movement, Gopal Krishna Gukley informed Gandhi about the situation of Bombay where more than a lakh Hindu people are on the streets because of the Khilafat militants. In reply Gandhi said, now it is time to support the Muslims forgetting all other affairs. As such neglecting Gopal Krishna Gukhleyhe went on to support Khilafat Movement. In the Calcutta Congress meeting Gandhi vehemently supported the Khilafat Movement and announced the movement of Satyagraha. Jinnah could not tolerate the mischievous policy of Gandhi what he said it was nothing but a political anarchy in starting "Satyagraha" and he resigned from the Congress. Here Gandhi became successful to downgrade Jinnah but he did the greatest harm to India and Indian people by bringing religion in fore front in Indian politics.

Mahatma Gandhi played the central role in the juxtaposition of the Khilafat Movement with India's freedom struggle, primarily the Non Cooperation Movement. Mahatma Gandhi had already materialized his *Satyagraha*', the non-violent civil resistant nationalist movement reflecting a **Movement of Hindu Muslim Unity.** The Ali Brothers became extremely active towards the cause of the Khilafat Movement. Initially the Khilafat Movement saw the combined efforts of the Hindus and the Muslims under the supervision of the Indian National Congress against the British Raj under the guidance of Gandhi. Why? The reason was to get closer to the Muslims so that an opposite Hindu militant group gets formed. It was the reason why Hindu Mahasava

(RSS) came into being what Gandhi wanted in his hidden mind. It was a long time planning of Gandhi how to bring religious difference and how to corner Jinnah for his name and fame. His initial success lies in the formation of two militant religious groups, the Hindu Mahasava (RSS) and Muslim Khilaphat militant Party.

After the formation of two religious rival groups he turned his attention towards "Non-Violence". As such he started the long march of Salt Satyagraha and increased his popularity. By the time to make Nehru the PM of India he started to create the necessary field. He was man of Gujarat, the Capital of India was in Delhi but he had chosen Calcutta the best choice to start the movement of "Non-Violence" vigorously when the economy of Calcutta would go down. The Muslims did not join "Non-Violence" that became boon in disguise what he wanted. The two religious groups began to hate each other and finally that culminated with the "Calcutta Killing Day" resulting in the division of India and the division of Bengal and taking him to the throne of "FATHER" of the nation. Jinnah never wanted religious politics but Gandhi created religious politics. How could the Indians accept Gandhi is their well wisher although under politics the real history gets twisted when Indian had to accept Gandhi as the father of the nation?

Coming to Assam what kind of politics Gandhi had played here. Why did he, the only Congress became very much keen to keep Assam in India except the Sylhet of Assam, the reason is not for the future safety of Assam but for his future achievement of glory if Netaji any time comes back he might lose his path of destination to reach to the throne of the glory of the "FATHER" of the nation and a man of peace of international image even by the destruction of India and by the killing of the millions of its residents.

Ref. 1. ^ "Khilafat movement". *Encyclopedia Britannica*. Retrieved 9 October *2017*.

Aftermath of the Khilafat Movement in India: The unfortunate tragedy of "Non-Violence" occurred at Chauri Chauraon 5th February, 1922, where a mob of three thousand killed twenty-five policemen and one inspector that had changed the direction of the movement. Mahatma Gandhi on account of his selfless commitment to non-violence immediately ordered for the suspension of the movement. Simultaneously also the Khilafat Movement came to an end. After all Muslim militants never liked Gandhi's movement of "Non-Violence". Gandhi was the pioneer in the creation of militant Muslim force by joining Khilafat Movement and indirectly encouraging the militant activity forgetting his basic principle of "Non-Violence". His intention was to make himself popular not only among the Hindus by "Non-Violence" but also among the Muslims by supporting their cause by the support of Khilafat Movement to downgrade Jinnah where Jinnah was the most popular leader among the Muslims. The ultimate result was the creation of two opposing forces. A Force of "Non-Violence" based on Hindu ethics of "Tolerance "and Buddha ethics of "Ahingsa" a Hindu Force, while a Muslim Force based on "Violence" which is based on the teachings of Islam. The division of Indians based on religion how could be counted as a mission of humanitarian activity of Gandhi? The independence movement based on religion initiated by Gandhi through "Non-Violence" was the cause division of country. Even now in the atmosphere of Corona Virus, the common people could not think beyond religion as if the blood of Hindus and Muslims are also get populated by Corona Virus disproportionately due to religion.

10. THE SPECTACULAR BEAUTY & NATURAL BEAUTY OF ASSAM

[10.1]

Bengal was partitioned in 1905 as East Bengal and West Bengal, where Assam was kept as the Chief Commissioner's Province along with the District Sylhet. The Ruling of the new region, consisting of East Bengal and Assam including the whole of North-East was left with a Lt. Governor; and Dhaka was selected as its Capital. This province was formed with a 15-member legislative council in which Assam had two seats, the members for these seats were recommended by rotation by the British Administration.

Assam is a land of fairs and festivals. Tai-shans came to Assam in 1228 and under the leadership of Sukaphaa win the hearts of Chutiya, Koch, Kachari people and succeeded to form Ahom Kingdom. Since then most of the festivals celebrated in Assam under the spirit of accommodation and togetherness in the diverse faith and belief of her inhabitants. This perfect fusion of heritage of different tribes has made Assam the home of the most colorful festivals reflecting the true spirit, tradition and lifestyle of the people of Assam.

The major festivals celebrated in Assam are Bihu, Baishagu, Ali-Ai-Ligang, and many others. The people of Assam also celebrate Holi, Durga Puja, Diwali, Swaraswati Puja, Lakshmi Puja, Kali Puja, Idd, Muharram, along with the festivals of other states of India. Besides they perform Me-Dam-Me-Phi, the birth and death anniversaries of Vaishnava Saints Srimanta Sankardev and Madhabdev. The tribals of Assam have their own colorful festivals such as the Kherai Puja of the Bodos, the Baikhu and Pharkantis of the Rabhas, Ali-ai-ligang and Parag of the Mishing tribe.

Bihu is the most important festival of Assam related with harvesting of agricultural products. It is celebrated with joy and abundance by all Assamese people irrespective of caste, creed, religion, faith and belief, in a time period when farmers start sowing, and again in another time which is known as Kaati Bihu at the time of cutting and binding of grains and Magh Bihu marks the season of harvesting of grains.

Me-Dum-Me-Phi: It is one of the most important Ahom festivals in Assam which is observed by the whole Ahom community. This is performed annually on the 31st of January in order to develop social contacts and community feelings among the Ahoms. It is a belief among the devotees that if colorful processions are taken out on the day of occasion with traditional finery and dresses and the day of Me-Dum-Me-Fi is not celebrated in the customary way, the deities might be displeased and consequently there might be crisis in the State like political rivalry and infighting, increased activities of militancy, natural upheavals like floods and earthquakes resulting in loss of human lives and property. Therefore, the belief is that the performance of Me-Dum-Me-Fi is a must and a necessity for the interest of overall well-being of the people and the society. The beauty of Assam had attracted the British people and the British queens.

A-[BEAUTY OF KAZIRANGA]

The Kaziranga Park is existed by the side of the banks of the Brahmaputra River. In 1908, Kaziranga was designated and protected as "Reserve Forest" under the goodwill of Lord Curtozon due to Mrs. Curtozon who once visited the area and expressed her desire to protect the area.

[Picture of Kaziranga National Park]

In 1916, it was redesigned as "Kaziranga Game Sanctuary". Since then it was protected as reserve forest area and hunting was prohibited. Again since 1938 visitors were permitted to visit the Kaziranga Park.

B-[BEAUTY OF RANG GHAR]

Ahom Kingdom is the glory of Assam although its root lies in Thailand. Its royal palace is transformed in the spectacular view of Kareng-Ghar situated at Garhgaon, The Ahom Palace, is located in Garhgaon 15 kilometers away from original city center of Sivasagar, situated in the regions of Upper Assam, a region of beauty on the bank of mighty River Brahamputra. Of all Ahom ruins, the Kareng-Ghar is one of the grandest examples of Ahom architecture.

[Rang ghar of Ahom Kingdom]

Another earlier name of Assam is 'Pragjyotishpura', the meaning of which nothing but the astrology of the east as such Pragjyotishpur is proudly proclaimed as a 'City of Eastern Astrology'

C-[THE NAGA FORCE WITH NAGA MILITARY DRESS]

The state Nagaland was once a part of United Assam. It became the 16th state of the Indian Union on 1 December 1963. It is a hilly region but here it is the hard working people who utilized the art of Agriculture to bring advancement even in the region to upgrade its economic and thereby the state has brought a revolution in the growing agriculture sector of crops including rice, corn, millets, pulses, tobacco, oilseeds, sugarcane, potatoes, and fibers.

(ii) Naga Force with Naga Local Tribal Dress:

Other significant economic activity includes forestry, tourism and miscellaneous cottage industries.

The state is mostly mountainous having Mount Saramati as it's the highest peak with a height of 3,840 meters and its range forms a natural barrier between Nagaland and Burma. It's plain area lies along the bordering of Assam valley. It is well known for its discipline in military strength.

D-[BEAUTIFUL NIGHT VIEW OF KOHIMA]

People are here well-known for their bravery for head hunting out of matter related with dispute or enmity but again People are here also known for their good hospitality and their amazingly incredible sense of humor or sarcasm. A visitor cannot forget their hospitality in their behavior, in supplying food at a Hotel, or in giving other comfort and services.

[Beautiful Night view of Kohima of Nagaland]

People can enjoy local dishes made out of silkworms (very luxurious food), snail, bamboo pax, dried frogs, freshwater eels, spiders, along with hottest chilly, grown in Nagaland or in Bangladesh. The food cooked in the state is very hygienic with least amount of oil used. However, many people here prefer to eat boiled vegetables. Rice is easily available but surprising fact was that chapattis are not easily available. For non-veg lovers, amazing tasteful pork, beef and fish etc are easily available. The place is further become famous due to the presence of **"World War II cemetery and museum" where** - Kohima has a history of battles. It is the only place in India where Netaji reached here with his Azad Hind Force where one can see the remnants of World War II. The Naga people are Indian by birth but they became intimate friend of British as because they adopted the Christian religion. Because of their religious activity they get culturally a bit different from the culture of India and finally they get separated from Assam. Had the Nagaland not been separated from Assam, the North Eastern Region would have been a place of pride, with a mighty Military Force in Eastern India, what would have been no way less than any force of the world.

E-[BIHU DANCE OF ASSAM]

Bihu Dance of Assam is nothing but a minds blowing natural beauty of Assam. Bihu dance is the most popular folk dances or traditional art or culture of the north-eastern state of Assam, performed during the Bihu festival, the dance is an expression of the cultural metamorphosis of Assam. Men and women participate in the traditional art of cultural dance displaying the diversity of the indigenous tribes residing in the state since time immemorial. The youthful jolly appearance of the dancers and their rocking movement portray the essence of cultural impact still preserved in the naturally adorn beautiful Assam.

[BIHU DANCE OF ASSAM]

The various tribes residing in the state of Assam including Bado, Kachari, Mishimi, Karbi, Mising, Deoris, Nagas and Garos to name a few and also few tribal communities like the Mishings, the Morans and the Deoris celebrate the Bihu festival of Assam in their own style and traditional customs making the whole region a beauty of celebration along with the beauty of nature and turning the Easter region of eastern India a galaxy of beauty of humanity. The festival of Bihu can be broadly categorized into three groups – Bohag Bihu, Kaati Bihu and Magh Bihu. The festival occurred in general three times annually, the Bohag Bihu festival is celebrated during mid April, and Kaati Bihu is celebrated in the middle of October while the Magh Bihu is celebrated in the month of January. The beginning of the sowing season is the main theme of Bihu dance for the performance of good sowing expecting a good growth during this gorgeous spring time festival. The intriguing amalgamations of different tribes come to the forefront with this dance performance as the tribal people are also not behind in the natural growth with human affords.

F- [FALLS IN SHILLONG & IN ARUNACHAL]

Here it is the spectacular Elephant Falls in Shillong. Every resident of Assam will get pain as he or she is deprived of the ownership of the "Fall", as because belonging of "Fall" to any state encourages the right of ownership of every individual.

[Elephant Falls (Shillong)]

[Jung Falls (Arunachal)]

The **Elephant Falls** are a unique feature of Shillong, since the waterfall itself brings a thrilling beauty as the water rolls down step by step. The structure of the black rocks look likes an elephant so the name. The **evening view of Elephant falls** is a heart blowing feature for every individual in the midst of fading light. The crowd gets excited by the sheer gold glow of the water. The natural beauty and serenity of the falls make everyone spell bound with the pleasure of beauty and charm. Among the all waterfalls Elephant Falls is the most spectacular. There are other places to Visit in Meghalaya that include many other falls, besides Seven Sisters Falls. Meghalaya is blessed with so many unique places a visitor require at least a month time in exploring this beautiful state. There are many man-made lakes along with the natural lakes.

Jung Falls in Arunachal is one of the best waterfalls of the State. It is located at a height of approximately 100 meters. It offers a spectacular sight during monsoon. It was the place where Chinese explored their military journey to occupy Arunachal. Jung Falls is also known as Nuranang Falls, after the name of a local girl Nura, who helped an Indian soldier during the 1962 war. The locals thereby made a popular song out of her name. One can reach to the place by booking a cab.

[10.2]

[There is much other spectacular view but because of too much photo restriction, photos are not displayed everywhere.]

Since ancient times Kamrup of Assam is well known for **Kamakhya temple.** The Kamakhya temple is not just a famous pilgrimage site in Assam, but is also a unique temple in the country. It is located on the Nilachal Hill or Blue Hill, Kamakhya temple is not only a pilgrimage site in Assam but a unique temple where the deity of the temple is Kamakhya Devi, vagina of Goddess 'Shakti'. Giving birth to a living being is the superpower given to women by God and Kamakhya Temple & Deity is the celebration of this 'Shakti' within every woman. Amalgamation of traditional Nagara or North India and Mughal architecture, Kamakhya Temple discovered its unique style of architecture at Nilachal Hill.

Ambubachi Mela: Besides the cultural activity there is one most religious festival at Kamakhya temple of Guwahati which is held every year during monsoon (mid-June). It is a ritual of simple celebration with devotion to all powerful God, the power of creation based on

Tantra of Hinduism. It is performed in Kamakhya temple during Ambubashi by closing the doors of the temple for three days. It is a belief that the earth becomes impure for three days. During this time period of three days all kinds of farming work remain closed. The actual activity of Ambubachi mela begins on the fourth day onwards when the devotees are allowed to enter inside the temple for worship. Thousands of devotees from all over India and abroad paid a visit to the mela every year with devotion.

The natural beauty of Brahmaputra is better enjoyed at the foot hills of Guwahati which could be compared with the sea-side view of Singapore, a small city but the sea-water has enhanced its natural beauty like that of Guwahati but in addition it had increased its glamour by the increase of its economy. It became one of the economically strongest cities in the world by the administrative effort of its government in the progress of the economy. However, not the least a little of improvement is done at Guwahati in 1962 by establishing an Oil Refinery.

[Refinery at Noonmati in Guwahati]

Guwahati Refinery was set up at Noonmati in Guwahati on 1 January 1962. Guwahati Refinery is the first Public Sector refinery of India and belongs to Indian Oil Corporation Limited.

But no such progressive effort was seen in the Sinha Ministry. Singapore was once within in Malaysia but the union was unstable due to distrust and ideological differences between leaders of Singapore and of the federal government of Malaysia. The disagreement arises in the sphere of economics, finance and politics. In the Malaysian general election of 1964, the separation of Singapore was finalized. Now Singapore is economically one of the strongest cities in the world unlike Guwahati.

The contribution of **Maniram Dewan**, at the early stage of the development of Assam could not be neglected. His effort was to develop the Tea-plantation in Assam due to which the British brought a revolution in the setting of tea-garden throughout the whole region of Assam valley and thereby the beauty of tea-garden has enhanced the natural beauty of Assam. However, Maniram himself had established two tea- gardens on his own but the British did not allow him to do so. Even then he was the pioneer in the tea plantation in Assam and a versatile genius in the increase of beauty of the whole valley of Assam by the beauty of tea-plant.

Maniram started to build up Cinnamora Tea Estate at Jorhat, the British stood against it that made him hostile to the British. Maniram raised his voice against the British and revolted by opposing their policies. When the Indian sepoys started an uprising against the British, he could see an opportunity, and together with other activists like Piyali Baruah, he conspired against the British. Unfortunately, their conspiracy came to light and he along with other leaders was arrested. Maniram Dewan and Piyali Baruah were publicly hanged by the British for conspiring against them during the 1857 Sepoy Mutiny. Their death was widely mourned in Assam and resulted in an open uprising, which was suppressed brutally. At the turn of the century (1920), Assam joined the freedom movement led by Mahatma Gandhi. Assamese patriots like Tarun Ram Phukan, Nabin Chandra Bordoloi, Hem Baruah and others joined the National struggle for Independence. Even in the 1942 Quit India Movement, a number of martyrs laid down their lives, of which special mention may be made of Kanaklata, a teenage girl who died in police firing while trying to hoist the National Flag at the police station of Gohpur. Kushal Konwar, another young freedom fighter, was falsely implicated in a train derailment case by the Britishers and was punished to death.

Arunachal was a region of united Assam. Its natural beauty is unparallel but no government neither British Bengal nor Assam-Bengal of British India or Assam –India explored the beauty to convert the region into a destination of world tourists where **Bomdila** is the headquarters of the West Kameng district of the state of Arunachal Pradesh. It offers to the tourist visitors a panoramic view of the awesome Himalayan terrain with its snow-covered mountains. It is famous for its apple orchids with much plant having with beautifully colored flowers among many plants with three-part flowers. Travelers can take a walk through them to take the pleasure of nature. A visitor can take a monastery view of Bomdila, which is unparallel. In the year 1965, in the foot hills of Bomdila a community of monks were living there under religious vows. Again here a Sessa Orchid Sanctuary, covered with 200 species of orchids; Eagle-nest Wildlife Sanctuary, covered with beautiful birds like king-fishers, eagles, ducks, horn-bills, and pheasants, as well as animals like red pandas, black bears, and over 165 types of butterflies. It is also famous for its apple orchards. A visitor can take a bus or a shared cab or a private cab to reach to the place.

Let us see a place located in Tezpur, which is now designed with an amazing hill garden and sloping lawns with beautifully sculpted statues depicting stories of the Chitralekha all over the place. It is known as the **"Amazing Agnigarh"**, popularly known as the lover's site of Northeast. There is a history behind it. According to Hindu mythology, the site was a fortress surrounded by fire walls all over so that nobody could go in or out of the premises. According to Hindu mythology, it was built by Banasura, who was the son of Bali. He was very much powerful and terrible Asura even many heavenly Kings were afraid of him. But again he was a prime devotee of Lord Sibha. Banasura built the statue of **Agnigarh** to keep his daughter Usha in isolation. There is a legendary story behind it. His daughter Usha saw a handsome man in her dream and she fell in love with him. But he was no other than the Krishna's grandson Aniruddha. She did not see him before he appeared in dream. Usha's most dear companion was Chitralekha. She was a great painter. She drew a picture of the person based on the description given by Usha. It appeared exactly Aniruddha. She married him in secret under Gandharva rites. But Banasura, the father of Usha was not happy with the marriage. He immediately kept Aniruddha in prison. Hearing the matter Lord Krishna came to rescue his grandson Aniruddha. There started fierce fighting between them and finally Krishna succeeded to save Aniruddha and united them to live together. Hence forth it became a lover's site.

Bhutan is situated in the eastern end of the Himalayas. It's a beautiful landlocked country at the top of Assam. Its artistically designed beautiful monasteries attract every body's attraction. Paro Taktsang is commonly known as Tiger Nest Monastery in Bhutan that could be one the most awesome attraction. This is a place where the administrative headquarters, royal palace, and also a monastery remain together. A visit of the place in the evenings by anyone could discover its sheer brilliance and beauty.

[Here is a place of beauty of Bhutan where an administrative headquarters, a royal palace, and also a monastery existing together.]

In the end it was a fact to realize that the people of Assam along with its neighbor Bhutan is a little different than the people of India as the atmosphere is a little different than that of India, in summer time the whole of India is suffering with 40 degree temperature,

Assam is relishing the summer hardly with 30 degree and Bhutan is far cooler. The people of Assam is always calm and colder under cold atmosphere and as such they express their mind by saying that "Make a mind which never minds, make a heart which never hurts, make a touch which never pains and make a relation which never ends".

As the Assam's natural beauty is enhanced by the tea-plantation of tea garden, similarly plantation agro-plant such as rice also makes the nature beautiful by the growth of its green leaf before turning to fruit having being Assam is an agricultural State. Agriculture occupies an important place in the economy of the State. The principal food crop is rice. The cash crops are jute, tea, cotton, oilseeds, sugarcane, potato, etc. Noteworthy horticulture items are orange, banana, pineapple, coconut, guava, mango, jackfruit and citrus fruits. The State has an estimated 39.83 lakh hectares gross cropped area, of which net area sown is about 27.24 lakh hectare.

Assam's natural beauty is also increased by **"Forest Regions"** of Assam. The rich forest wealth of Assam constituted 26.22 per cent of the total forest area. The State has five National Parks and eleven wildlife sanctuaries. The Kaziranga National Park and the Manas Tiger Project (National Park) are internationally famous for one horned Rhino and Royal Bengal Tiger respectively.

Assam's industrial base is also based on natural wealth and Assam's all industry is enhancing the natural beauty of Assam. The nature based industry tea occupies an important place. There are six industrial growth Centers in the State and two such centers are being set up at Balipara and Matia. Presently four oil refineries have been working in the state including the one at Digboi. Construction of the Export Promotion Industrial Park (EPIP) at Amingaon near Guwahati is under construction. It is design as such that a Software Technology Park will be constructed at Borjhar near Guwahati.

A Central Institute for Plastic Engineering Technology (CIPET) has been designed at Amingaon near Guwahati to initiate the work very soon. Although Assam has always enjoyed the highest reputation for her arts and crafts associated with her cottage industries, the trade is not yet internationalized by the government by the trade of export. Besides these products, Cottage industries also include other products such as handloom, sericulture, cane and bamboo articles, carpentry, brass and bell-metal crafts. Assam produces varieties of silk, **Endi**, **Muga**, **Tassar**, etc. **Muga** silk is produced the best only in Assam in the world.

Assam was linked with mainland India through East Bengal through water ways, but after the advent of British the road and rail link was established. Tourism industry might be a lucrative business in Assam but the government gave little attention in the tourism industry. Few Important places of tourism in and around Guwahati can be named such as Kamakhya temple, Umananda (Peacock Island), Navagraha (temple of nine planets), Basistha Ashram, Gandhi Mandap, State Zoo, Sukreswar temple, and Saraighat Bridge.

Other places of tourist interest in the State those could be named as: Kaziranga National Park (famous for one horned rhino), Manas Tiger Project, Sibsagar (Shiv Temple-Rangghar-Karengghar), Tezpur (scenic beauty), Batadrava (birth place of great Vaishnava saint Sankaradeva) and Sualkuchi (famous for silk industry).

11. ECONOMIC GROWTH OF SINGAPORE & MALAYSIA VS ECONOMIC GROWTH OF ASSAM

[11.1]

Let us compare the economic growth of Assam with that of Singapore and Malaysia, the nearby two states, Singapore and Malaysia were once one state and they get separated for the cause of rapid development. Malaysia obtained independence much later than India. The country might be small in compare to India but there was no dearth of political patriots, who devoted their patriotic spirit for the development of the region unlike the selfish political stalwart of India to make the country economically strong and sound. However, small Singapore is now one of the economically strongest countries in the world. Singapore follows certain laws so as to create a prosperous society for its citizens. There has been little room for political dissent or for the cause of power or for the role of civil society. The trading of business is a democratic right for economic riches that has led to the creation of a model of development with a higher market economy. It has provided a blueprint for development that is now being followed by other countries such as Rwanda and Tanzania and perhaps even by China.

Singapore and Malaysia though separated yet both the countries are geographical neighbors, although their paths to development have not always been the same. Singapore has a highly-developed and successful free-market economy and has utilized most of its limited natural and human resources very successfully. It has enjoyed a remarkably open and corruption-free environment, having with stable prices, and having a per capita GDP higher than that of most of the developed countries. Its economy depends heavily on exports, particularly in consumer electronics, information technology products, pharmaceuticals, and on a growing financial services sector. Singapore had even utilized its hilly regions Santosa Hills in beautifully designed creative centers for entertainment to foreign tourists.

In regard to Malaysia, since achieving Independence from Britain in 1957, the Malaysian economy has been structurally reformed through the move from a heavy reliance on raw materials such as rubber and tin to an industrial based situation. The development of the heavy industries of Malaysian has been aided by government funded agencies such as the Heavy Industries Corporation of Malaysia Berhad (HICOM). Reform also had been brought in 1983, for economic betterment in line with the global spread of neo-liberal policies.

Assam is in no way less than Singapore or Malaysia and not less than the existence of several Hills and natural beauty spot. But no such effort of development was made in Assam either to make a center of big industry, or climatically favorable techno-center or the development of the Hills to beautifully designed creative centers for entertainment to foreign tourists to enhance the revenue of the state. Unlike Singapore Assam is not lacking in territory of natural resources but yet not developed whereas Singapore having being lacking in territory and natural resources, make remarkable economic progress. Fifty years ago, Singapore was an undeveloped country with a GDP per capita of less than $320. Today, it is one of the world's fastest growing economies. Its GDP per capita has risen to $60,000, making it the sixth highest in the world.

To reduce the crime related with theft and corruption, the administration of Singapore has introduced the death penalty for any form of crimes involving narcotics or corruption. Independent trade unions were replaced by a single umbrella group called the National Trade Union Congress (NTUC). Nobody has any right to threaten national unity, if so he would be jailed without recourse to the courts. These draconian but business-friendly laws attracted international investors who flocked to the city state. The result was heavy annual economic growth exceeding double digit. The port of Singapore is now one of the world's busiest transshipment port surpassing Hong Kong and Rotterdam. Now, Singapore has become the world's second busiest port after Shanghai. Singapore's economic model for the cause of economic growth even sometimes supersedes personal freedoms.

The successful growth of Malaysia in recent years can be explained in different ways. Firstly, it is one of the most open economies in the world, second it is open to foreign investment, and next Malaysia is governed following excellent macroeconomic management. It maintains a very low inflation system and it had never faced any balance-of-payments crisis. Besides, all these it has excellent physical infrastructure with good roads, harbors, and telecommunication networks, whereas Assam is lacking in good roads across all districts, no harbors or telecommunication networks. Assam was under British Rule for a time period but Assam was deprived of learning the administration under the British-style civil service, which has been maintained mainly in Calcutta. After independence Assam was under the command of Central government and failed to explore trade and industry because of western trade policy keeping eye to Bombay of Delhi administration. On the other hand Malaysia's economy depends heavily on exports, particularly in consumer electronics, information technology products, pharmaceuticals, and on growing financial services sector. In Malaysia the administration follows strict principles, such as labor force was strictly disciplined, political dissent was heavily punished, and the population control was maintained through a wide range of laws. Apart from that Malaysia enjoyed a remarkably open and corruption-free environment, stable prices, and a per capita GDP higher than that of most developed countries. Its economy is based on exports, particularly in consumer electronics, information technology products, pharmaceuticals, and on a growing financial services sector, whereas Assam is lacking in all these sectors as because Delhi government is less concerned with the Eastern regions of Assam, a place far away from Delhi.

Assam is not far away from Singapore and Malaysia and its geography and natural condition is also not very different from Assam. But unlike Assam both Singapore and Malaysia have displayed spectacular economic development over the past 30 years. Both are great trading nations taking advantage of their geographical locations at an international trading crossroads, and simultaneously developing their own capacities to manufacture, educate, innovate and finance commercial activity. This hasn't been attempted at all in Assam. Neither the government of Assam nor the central government of India has any look out in this respect how to enhance the economic growth of this region. The look out of the successive government was how to keep the administration under the control of Delhi government no matter of division or destruction leading to unrest for any cause of matter.

Singapore is the 7th least corrupt country and one of the most pro-business with low tax rates (14.2% of Gross Domestic Product, GDP) and has the third highest per-capita GDP in the world in terms of Purchasing Power Parity (PPP). However, it had overcome all exceptional challenges. Upon independence from Malaysia in 1965, Singapore had to satisfy with a small domestic market, high levels of unemployment and poverty to the extent of 70% of Singapore's households lived in badly overcrowded conditions. Besides, unemployment to the extent of 14 percent, GDP per capita was US$516, and half of the population was illiterate.

To overcome the existing conditions, the Economic Development Board was established to make Singapore attractive for foreign direct investment. By 2001 foreign companies made miracles. It accounted 75% of manufactured output and 85% of manufactured exports. However, in recent years, both inward and outward investment has exceeded all records in the financial and insurance service sector to approximately three times with that of manufacturing. At present Singapore's savings and investment rates are among the highest levels in the world, while household consumption and wage shares of GDP are among the lowest. Assam having being living in the neighborhood region did not get a taste of the slightest of that progress.

This successful economic growth of Singapore has been achieved partly through the efficient use of sovereign wealth funds (SWFs). These are investment funds kept reserved for the state that could invest globally and locally in real and financial assets such as stocks, bonds, etc. Singapore has developed from a "third world" city to one of the most competitive economies in the world today. It was because of its strategic investment policies and awareness of the city's environmental impacts. It had overcome all crises and in recent years it had accelerated its growth exceeding all records. By launching the Singapore Sustainable Blueprint, it had achieved the twin goals of economic growth and a good living environment. It is aware of its shortcomings, which include water scarcity, air pollution, island restriction and in the affairs of sustainability of air quality, transport, energy efficiency, and public health. It succeeded to overcome all shortcomings by its economic strength. Having being from the point of environmental aspect, Assam is the most identical region like that of Singapore but no such progressive environment is ever get visible. The question arises why not?

After the 1969 race riots, occurred between Bumiputera and ethnic Chinese, a New Economic Policy was devised to run for 20 years. The purpose was to redistribute the wealth, and enhance the growth. The target was to increase 30% GDP for Bumiputera by requiring all Initial Public Offerings (IPOs) on the stock exchange at a discount price. Again in 1975 the government created incentives to expand large-scale manufacturing and energy-intensive industries. The Heavy Industries Corporation of Malaysia (HICOM) was one such company formed to assist in the manufacture of pig-iron, aluminum die casting, pulp and paper, steel, cement, motorcycle, heavy engineering and simultaneously enhancing export incentives.

By 1997, the GDP of Bumiputera was increased from 20% to 23% and by 2011 poverty had been dramatically reduced to below 5%. The monthly income of ethnic Malays has increased at a greater rate than that of Indian and Chinese Malaysians since the NEP (New Economic Policy) get implemented. In addition to State-Owned Enterprises in water, power, rail, bus and air travel, telecoms, broadcasting, banking and oil and gas (PETRONAS is the 75th largest company in the world, contributing 45% of government revenue), the growth of economic progress is significantly influenced by the state-backed Sovereign Wealth Funds (SWF) and also by other financial institutions, such as the Khazanah National Berthed Ltd, the Employees Provident Fund, Malaysia Development Berthed and other development financial institutions.

Malaysia is a country of "pro-business" and, according to the World Bank in 2016, the country hold the rank 18th for "ease of doing business" and 6th in the case of attractiveness to foreign investment. The GDP growth to the extent of 5% p.a. has superseded many other countries. However, it was because of some of the ease of doing business at the expense of the environment for example the oil palm plantation expansion nibbling at the edge of National Park rain forest. Assam could not get the attention of the Delhi government to create any such progressive step to enhance the economy of the state although the state possesses many of the natural resources like that of Malaysia.

A key factor in the development of India is the level of corruption. This is one of the many factors held by many high intellectuals and economists to explain the so called 'Dutch Disease' where a developing country does not develop as rapidly as it might because wealth is diverted into the pockets of politicians and others. Corruption is regarded unofficially by the public as an endemic problem starting by many in India. It ranges from "community policemen" generating income by randomly stopping vehicles to fine them for a spurious violation, up to the core of defense and the Bank. The corruption in defense deal is a common feature of news in India apart from the huge siphon of money from Bank by many individuals as well as by many men in power through the loopholes of trade and business.

There are two predictions on how India would shape up in the hands of Indians when it became free, sprinkled all over the Internet Web sites. The first was a statement due to Winston Churchill, who made it in British Parliament during the debate on the Indian Independence Bill. "If Independence is granted to India, power will go to the hands of rascals, rogues, freebooters; all Indian leaders will be of low caliber and men of straw. They will have sweet tongues and silly hearts. They will fight amongst themselves for power and India will be lost in political squabbles. A day would come when even air and water would be taxed in India."

The second was from the Vellore jail diary of Rajaji, the tallest intellectual among India's political leaders in the last century who fought for India's freedom, dating back to 1921: He said-"We all ought to know that Swaraj will not at once or, I think, even for a long time to come, be better government or greater happiness for the people. Elections and their corruptions, injustice, and the power and tyranny of wealth, and inefficiency of administration, will make a hell of life as soon as freedom is given to us. Men will look regretfully back to the old regime of comparative justice, and efficient, peaceful, more or less honest administration".

The **economy of Singapore** is a highly developed free-market economy and ranked as the most open in the world. It is regarded as the 3rd least corrupt, most pro-business, having with low tax rates and a high gross domestic product (GDP)) and has the third highest per-capita GDP in the world in terms of purchasing power parity (PPP). State-owned enterprises play a substantial role in Singapore's economy. It is regarded as the regional hub for wealth management particularly in electronics, chemicals and services including Singapore's position as the regional hub for wealth management providing the main source of revenue for the economy.

Singapore has extended its strategic port which makes it more competitive than many of its neighbors in carrying out such entrepot activities. Singapore's trade to GDP ratio is among the highest in the world, averaging around 400% during 2008–11. The Port of Singapore is regarded as the second-busiest in the world by cargo tonnage. To preserve its international standing and further its economic prosperity in the twenty-first century, Singapore has taken extensive measures to promote innovation, encourage entrepreneurship keeping intake its workforce. The Singapore is engaged for setting, adjusting, and enforcing foreign worker immigration rules. At present approximately 243,000 foreign domestic workers are working in Singapore. So to say Assam is the neighbor of Singapore, the attention of Delhi government always towards Western ends of Bombay and feeble attention towards Eastern ends of Assam as because Assam is far away from Delhi.

There was a time when science was not developed and there was dearth of industrial products. The people of UK, French, Span or Portuguese were in search of food and in the process of searching food through trade they came once to the regions of South East Asia what was being the region naturally fertile at that period for trade and food. To make the communication easy through sea route, the Suez Canal was designed connecting the Mediterranean Sea to the Red Sea. This allowed easy travel from Europe to Asia enhancing a rise in trade volume in 1879. The nation saw a $32 million rise just after a year. The British came to India crossing Indian Ocean and established British rule in India. British also gradually occupied Malaysia including Singapore. With the progress of time science had developed, industries build up in Europe and the industrial product began to supply in India as well as in the countries of South-East Asia. Finally British left India in 1947, Malaysia in 1957. On August 31, 1957, Malaya's first Prime Minister Allahyarham Tunku Abdul Rahman proudly declared the independence of Malaya, what is now called Malaysia. Every country tried to increase its wealth and prosperity. Singapore and Malaysia make their country economically strong and sound by the concept of trade and technology. But the Indian political leaders never tried to set up the learning center for trade and technology in India rather most of the leaders involve themselves in the fight of occupying the power of Chair. Thus after 70 years of Independence, India could not see the industrial growth while the small country like Malaysia and Singapore became countries with industrial growth flourishing with modern technology while India is lacking behind in all industrial trade sectors.

In 1965 Singapore get separated from Malaysia, when Singapore faced a small domestic market, and high levels of unemployment and poverty. 70 percent of Singapore's households lived in badly overcrowded conditions, and a third of its people squatted in slums on the city fringes. Unemployment averaged 14 percent, GDP per capita was US$516, and half of the population was illiterate. But within a short span of time everything was changed and today now Singapore is the 6th economically strong country in the world.

It manages inflation to the lowest and provided workers with the proper machinery to sustain growth. In order to study the pattern of growth, the Singapore government has established the Economic Development Board to spearhead an investment drive, and make Singapore an attractive destination for foreign investment. The investment drive resulted 75% of manufactured output and 85% of manufactured exports. Meanwhile, Singapore's savings and investment rates rose among the highest levels in the world, while household consumption fell among the lowest. A small country like Singapore can manage its economic growth, the adjacent a bigger state Assam could not do anything, no investment drive has ever thought of neither by the Assam government nor by the central government.

As a result of investment drive, Singapore's capital stock increased 33 times and capital-labor ratio achieved a tenfold increase, as a result living standards steadily get increased. More families get moving from a lower-income status to middle-income security with increased household incomes. However, much unlike the economic policies of Greece and the rest of Europe, Singapore followed a policy of social safety net for each and every individual. This policy had converted Singapore into a welfare state. Singapore also developed a very self-reliant and skilled workforce well versed for a global economy, while India is only looking after internal economy involving state and center and not to think of external economy. Singapore transformed its industrial hub into an international hub of trade bypassing many other nations.

Economic electronic growth: Singapore's economic growth started since 1960 to 1999 to an average of 8.0%. Since the nations independence in 1965 Singapore GDP has stockpiled an average of 9.5% increase. The economic picked up in Singapore in 1999 was due to the effort of the Prime Minister of Singapore Mr. Go Chock Tong. A growth rate of 5.4%, increased to 9.9% by 2000. Instead of global financial crises in 2008, Singapore made a remarkable recovery and in the year 2010, the nation saw a 15.2% growth rate. It also has opened up activity in different sectors for economic prosperity. It had devoted its energy in the financial service sector, telecommunications, and in power generation in the atmosphere of global greater competition.

Growth in Banking Sector: Singapore is functioning as a global financial hub, having being a head quarter of banks of different countries. It is offering world-class corporate bank account facilities. In the 2017 Global Financial Centers Index, Singapore was recognized and ranked as the third most competitive financial centre in the world after London and New York City alongside bypassing the cities such as Hong Kong, Tokyo, San-Francisco, Chicago, Sydney, Boston, and Toronto. These include business involving multiple currencies, internet banking, telephone banking, checking accounts, savings accounts, debit and credit cards, fixed term deposits and wealth management services. Singapore has attracted assets which were formerly held in Swiss banks for several reasons. Assam what is almost identical with that of Singapore a nearby place lacking in all fronts due to a step-motherly treatment of the central government towards Assam.

Growth in Biotechnology: In the field of Pharmaceuticals Singapore is aggressively trying to increase its revenue. As such

Singapore is investing hundreds of millions of dollars into the sector of **biotechnology** to build up infrastructure. As such Singapore is recruiting top international scientists to carryout research and developing activity in **biotechnology** industry. Leading drug makers, such as **Glaxo Smith Kline** (GSK), **Pfizer** and **Merck & Co.**, have been invited to set up plants in Singapore. On 8 June 2006, GSK announced to invest $300 million to build a plant to produce **paediatric vaccines**, the first such activity in Asia. The investment in Pharmaceuticals now has increased more than 8% of the country's manufacturing production. Is there anybody in Assam or in India who is thinking to enhance **biotechnology** industry?

Energy and infrastructure: Singapore is the leading oil trading hub in Asia. The oil industry of Singapore is earning 5 per cent of Singapore's GDP, and because of that Singapore became one of the top three export refining centers in the world. In 2008, Singapore exported 68.1 million tons of oil to earn huge revenue. The oil industry is turned to the promotion of the chemical industry. Again in 2008, Singapore employed almost 70,000 workers to carry out 20% of the world market in ship repairing and the marine and offshore industrial works.

In summary, Singapore's total trade in 2014 amounted to S$982 billion. Singapore is a mini state compare to the United States. Despite its mini size, Singapore became the fifteenth-largest trading partner of the United States. In 2014, Singapore's imports reached to $464 billion, and exports reached to $519 billion. Singapore's major trading partners are countries such as Malaysia, China, Indonesia and South Korea besides EU27, United States, Hong Kong and Japan. Since 2009, the value of exports exceeded the value of imports for Singapore's trade with China. Singapore's principal exporting products are petroleum products, food/beverages, chemicals, textile/garments, electronic components, telecommunication apparatus, and transport equipment. Again Singapore's main importing products are aircraft, crude oil and petroleum products, electronic components, radio and television motor vehicles, chemicals, food/beverages, iron/steel, and textile yarns/fabrics. Assam is not only nearby to Singapore but also similar in many respects. If so where is so much production of goods as well as the market of exports?

Singapore is largely a corruption-free government. Its skilled workforce and its advanced and efficient infrastructure have attracted investments from more than 3,000 multinational corporations (MNCs) from the United States, Japan, and Europe. Foreign firms are engaged in Singapore in almost all sectors of the economy. MNCs are engaged in more than two-thirds in manufacturing output and direct export sales.

The government also encouraged firms to invest outside of Singapore. The country's total direct outside investments had reached to $39 billion by the end of 1998. The People's Republic of China was having the top accounting almost 14% of total overseas investments, followed by Malaysia (10%), Hong Kong (9%), Indonesia (8%) and US (4%). The recently growing economy of India, especially the high technology sector, is becoming an additional source of foreign investment for Singapore. Now the United States also appears to be keen to improve bilateral trade with Singapore and thereby recently signed the US-Singapore Free Trade Agreement. A country cannot develop without trade with other countries; Delhi is more concerned with party politics and less with international trade. The importance of Assam in the north eastern region is yet to be realized by the Delhi government. However, the trade activity of Malaysia or Singapore and their economic progress might have enlightened their outlook towards Assam, a gate way state for business in the Eastern regions of India.

12. CASTILIAN DEMOCRACY OVER RULED DELHI

[12.1]

Democracy through "CASTE" system: In the midst of Hindu-Muslim massacre India achieved her independence but Gandhi remained as a pioneer of peace through "Non-Violence" and exposed him as a man of peace and internationally an icon of peace. Nehru declared Gandhi as the FATHER of the nation remembering the contribution of Gandhi where at the point of independence Gandhi declared him as the PM of India discarding the selected candidate of the Congress.

India became the largest democracy in the world but very soon democracy has changed into a **"CASTE" system democracy where** everything is now decided in India by the caste doesn't matter what someone is doing what. Anyone who wants to go up to the ladder must play this caste card in India. PM Modi elected President of India by applying the CASTE card, no matter with other political leaders.

Everything in India is politically motivated as such all politicians are using this as vote bank tool. Politicians are dividing the people based on the caste system and keeping political future safe and sound. Every political party in India is now associated to some particular castes and they make people fighting so that they keep getting votes and can come into power. Political parties indirectly purchasing votes, as they offer everything for free and few trap works. Some states are there in India where the political parties openly declare many things free for the people if they come into power. People get everything for free, from sewing machine to two-wheeler, from jewelry to free food in the name of political leaders and on the condition of winning the election. Free things are also in education and other necessary things like free Wi- Fi although some promises are fulfilled, some are not, but politicians gets what they want.

Recent trend is **"Farmer loan waiver Scheme"**. Indian politicians can do anything or everything just for votes. Now it is common feature in news channel that running debate shows how the political party spoke persons and caste leaders marginalized votes by the policy of reservation. Before independence thinking of Politicians was remained center around religion now after independence it had changed its trend towards caste and cultism.

Educated audience does not give importance to caste system but in the working places where people work with many people, people of all religions and castes people never have any kind of discussion like one caste is great or some other is not great, but the politicians did their job to fulfill their desires. The problem lies with all uneducated people who watches these things gets inspired by one ideology and change their beliefs hearing some other and that is where the democracy dies.

The news of caste system changes the mentality of the people here and there. Politicians use this cast system as a great tool for their personal gain. Due to some of the legends, some casts were provided special facilities. Now people just need a cast certificate and they will get everything, subsidized ration, free education, free medical facilities, and reservations in jobs etc. So the conclusion is that caste system won't die, but rather democracy has to die. After independence peace and development is disturbed by the politics of Classism. This is India after independence.

Kashmiri Indian politician Markandey Katju has advocated the reunification of India with Pakistan under a secular government. It was a fact he stated that the cause of the partition was the "divide and rule" policy of Britain, which was implemented to spread communal hatred after Britain saw that Hindus and Muslims working together to agitate against their colonial rule in India. Katju once served as the chairman of the Indian Reunification Association (IRA), which seeks to campaign for this cause.

Similar views were also found from many others. Such as one Pakistani historian Nasim Yousaf, the grandson of Allama Mashriqi, has also championed Indian Reunification and presented the idea at the New York Conference on Asian Studies on 9 October 2009 at Cornell University; Yousaf stated that the partition of India itself was a result of the British interests and their divide and rule policy that sought to create another buffer state between the Soviet Union and India to prevent the spread of Communism, as well the fact that a "division of the people and territory would prevent a united India from emerging as a world power and keep the two nations dependent on crucial powers." Yousaf cited former Indian National Congress president Maulana Abul Kalam Azad, who wrote in the same stratum.

If a united India had become free in all respect then there would be little chance that Britain could retain her position in the economic and industrial life of India. By the partition of India, the Moslem majority provinces being formed a separate and independent state that had given Britain a foothold in India. A state dominated by the Moslem League as well as by the Congress had offered a permanent sphere of influence to the British. This had also indirectly influenced the attitude of Indians in India. The partition of India had materially altered the situation in favor of the British.

Historian Yousaf holds that "Muhammad Ali Jinnah, the President of the All-India Muslim League and later founder of Pakistan, had been misleading the Muslim community in order to go down in history as the savior of the Muslim cause and to become founder and first Governor General of Pakistan." Allama Mashriqi, a nationalist Muslim, had expressed his view where he pointed out Jinnah as "becoming a tool in British hands for his political career." Besides the pro-separatist Muslim League, Islamic leadership in British India rejected the notion of partitioning the country, exemplified by the fact that most Muslims in the heartland of the subcontinent of British

India remained where they were, rather than migrating to newly created state of Pakistan. India and Pakistan are currently allocating and spending a significant amount of their budget into military spending but instead of that money could be spent in economic and social development. Poverty, homelessness, illiteracy, terrorism and a lack of medical facilities, in Yousaf's view, would never be plaguing an undivided India as it would be more beneficial and advantaged undivided India "economically, politically, and socially." Yousaf has stated that as the Indians and Pakistanis speak a common language Hindustani, wear the same dress, eat the same food, enjoy the same music and movies, and communicate in the same style and on a similar wavelength, their unity would lead them to the highest peak of strength of heaven. He argues that uniting would be a challenge, though not impossible, citing the fall of the Berlin Wall and the consequent German Reunification as an example. The fear of Corona Virus has integrated the humanity, could it not integrated India-Pakistan and returns to British India to establish India a super-power.

But something was different in Pakistan. Afghanistan was once occupied by Russia in 1979. The USA, the country of democracy could not tolerate the forceful occupation of Afghanistan by the communist Russia. In order to evict Russia from Afghanistan, the USA engaged many Pakistanis after training in the guerrilla activity against the Russian forces. But Russia left Afghanistan in 1989. The USA stopped its guerrilla activity in Afghanistan. But many of the trained Pakistanis began to interfere in the administration of Pakistan. The Pakistan Army diverted these trained militants towards Kashmir to fight against the Indians. Thus peace and development was disturbed in Pakistan.

[12.2]

The Rise and fall of Delhi: The recent carnage in Delhi has demoralized the present government. US Congress woman Pramila Jayapal said "Democracies should not tolerate division and discrimination, world is watching". It was nothing but the effect of the division of India based on religion. Gandhi might be the father of the nation but his acceptance of partition was not accepted by the people heartily. The outburst of Delhi carnage was nothing but the outburst of hidden pain out of the partition of the country based on religion even after 70 years of independence. Delhi had a historic image but that had been deteriorated a little however small and brought a black spot to the historic city.

As per the ancient Indian epic Mahabharata, Delhi is called **Indraprastha**, the capital of the Pandavas. Delhi was the legendary ancient city is believed to have been established 5000 years ago, the oldest inhabited cities in the world. Afterwards the Delhi Sultanate is the name given for a series of five successive dynasties, starting with 1206 by Qutub-ud-Din Aibak; the relics of the Delhi Sultanate include the famous Fort. The Delhi Sultanate came to an end in 1526, when Babur formed the Mughal Empire. The fifth Mughal Emperor Shah Jahan built the walled city of Shahjahanabad within Delhi, and its landmarks, what is dazzling as the Red Fort and Jama Masjid even now in 21 centuries. At present New city, Delhi is built by the British, and declared Capital of British India on 12 December 1911. On 12 December 2011 New Delhi celebrated 100 years of serving as India's National Capital.

The ancient Yogmaya Temple claimed to be one of the five temples of Mahabharata days in Delhi. The iron pillar of Delhi is said to have been fashioned at the time of Chandragupta Vikramaditya (375–413) of the Empire. The Qutub Minar is the world's tallest brick minaret at 72.5 meters, built by Qutb-ud-din Aibak of the Slave dynasty in 1192 CE. From 1206, Delhi became the capital of the Delhi Sultanate under the Slave Dynasty. The first Sultan of Delhi, Qutb-ud-din Aybak, was a former slave who rose through the ranks to become a general, a governor and then Sultan of Delhi.

Qutb-ud-din started the construction of the Qutub Minar, a recognizable symbol of Delhi, to commemorate his victory but died before its completion. In the Qutb complex he also constructed the Quwwat-al-Islam (might of Islam) which was the earliest extant mosque in India. He was said to have destroyed twenty-seven

Jain temples initially housed in the Qutb complex and plundered exquisitely the carved pillars and utilized the debris for the construction of mosque. After the end of the succeeded Slave dynasty, in the late medieval period Delhi was built with a townships and Fort.

References:

1. *Chandra, Satish (2003). History of architecture and ancient building materials in India. Tech Books International. p. 107.* ISBN 8188305030..

2. ^ *Patel, A (2004). "Toward Alternative Receptions of Ghurid Architecture in North India (Late Twelfth-Early Thirteenth Century CE)". Archives of Asian*

3. doi:10.1484/aaa.2004.0004.

4. QutubMinarDelhi.com. "" Archived 25 July 2015 at the Wayback Machine. Retrieved on 5 August 2015".

5. Southern Central Asia, A.H. Dani, History of Civilizations of Central Asia, Vol.4, Part 2, Ed. Clifford Edmund Bosworth, M.S.Asimov, (Motilal Banarsidass, 2000), 564.

Once Delhi was Indraprastha, the capital of the Pandavas but later became the Capital of Sultans and Mughals. Muslim religion came in the Arab land only in 6 century, 1500 ahead but the religion expanded rapidly. The analysis will bring the question in front what was the reason? Whereas it is described by all religion that the main purpose of all religion is the same "the service to humanity".Qutb-ud-din Aybak, Sultan of Delhi destroyed twenty-seven Jain temples to built Qutb complex. Is it that Jain temples out of Hindu religion are not good enough to provide the service to humanity? It appears although the ultimate goal of all religion is nothing but the service to humanity but the path is different. The religious leaders of Hindus take the path of "Tolerance" to reach to the destination while the religious leaders of Muslims take the path of "Violence" to reach to the destination.

Thus in India the Muslims have taken the path of "Violence" to expand the Muslim religion and then to serve the people by rebuilding the towns or cities and expanding the trade to bring economic prosperity. In the history we find Timur Lang invaded India on 15 December 1398 and defeated the armies of Nasiruddin Mahmud of Tughlaq dynasty. Timur entered Delhi on 18 December 1398, and the city was sacked, destroyed, and left in ruins, and over 100,000 war prisoners were killed as well. But in recent time in the liberation war of Bangladesh we could see 93000 Pakistani war prisoners who were not killed by the Indian Force but released alive. Is it due to the path of "Tolerance" of the Hindu religion or due to the change of mindset of Indians for the cause of enlightened mind due to the advancement of education?

References:

1. *Beatrice F. Manz (2000).* "Tīmūr Lang". Encyclopaedia of Islam. 10 *(2ⁿᵈ ed.).* Brill. Retrieved 24 April *2014*

2. *Chaliand, Gerard; Arnaud Blin (2007).* The History of Terrorism: From Antiquity to Al Qaeda. *University of California Press. p. 87.* ISBN 978-0-520-24709-3. *isfahan Timur.*

3. Virani, Shafique N. The Ismailis in the Middle Ages: A History of Survival, A Search for Salvation (New York: Oxford University Press), 2007, p. 116.

4. *Singh, Raj Pal (1 January 1988).* Rise of the Jat power. ISBN 9788185151052. Retrieved 22 May *2012.*

5. *Kumāra, Mahendra; Śarmā, Parameśa; Siṃha, Rājapāla (1991). Jāṭabalavāna: Jāṭaitihāsa (in Hindi). Madhura-Prakāśana.*

6. Mallu, who later received the title of Iqbal Khan, was a noble in Siri and an ally of Muqarrab Khan, but later on betrayed him and Nusrat Khan, and allied with Nasir-ud-din Mahmud Shah. History Of Medieval India; V. D. Mahajan p.205

In 1526, following the First Battle of Panipat, Zahiruddin Babur, the former ruler of Fergana, defeated the last Afghan Lodi sultan and founded the Mughal dynasty which ruled from Delhi, Agra and Lahore. The early modern period in Indian history is marked with the rise of the Mughal Empire between the 16th and 18th centuries. After the fall of the Delhi Sultanate, the Mughals ruled from Agra, Sikri and Lahore. In the mid-17th century, the Mughal Emperor Shah Jahan (1628–1658) built the city that sometimes bears his name Shahjahanabad, the seventh city of Delhi that is more commonly known as the old city or old Delhi. This city contains a number of significant architectural features, including the Red Fort (Lal Qila) and the Jama Masjid. The old city served as the capital of the later Mughal Empire from 1638 onward, when Shah Jahan transferred the capital back from Agra. The Red Fort became the main residence of the Mughal emperors for nearly 200 years.

References:

1. "qila | Meaning of qila in English by Shabdkosh English Hindi Dictionary". *Shabdkosh Dictionary* |. Archived *from the original on 11 November 2013.* Retrieved 2 June *2018.*

2. "qila | Definition of qila *in English by Oxford Dictionaries". Oxford Dictionaries | English.* Archived *from the original on 3 April 2018.* Retrieved 3 April *2018.*

3. *William M. Spellman (1 April 2004).* Monarchies 1000–2000. *Reaktion Books.* ISBN 978-1-86189-087-0. Archived *from the original on 14 December 2011.* Retrieved 5 August *2012.*

4. *Mehrdad Kia; Elizabeth H. Oakes (1 November 2002).* Social Science Resources in the Electronic Age. *Greenwood Publishing Group.* ISBN 978-1-57356-474-8. Archived *from the original on 11 January 2014.* Retrieved 5 August *2012.*

The British East India Company established its power over India through Bengal. The Indian Rebellion of 1857 tried to end Company Rule in India. On 11 May, the mutineers reached and captured Delhi, and declared Bahadur Shah II the Emperor of India. However, the British returned and captured Delhi on 8 June 1857. On 21 September,

Delhi had fallen completely to the British. Delhi passed into the direct control of British Government in 1857 after the Indian Rebellion of 1857 and the remaining Mughal territories were annexed as a part of British India.

Calcutta was built by the British by the development of three villages and declared the capital of British India. But again the British Rulers were not happy with the Hindu Bengalis of Bengal during the British period of administration, the Hindu Bengalis particularly of the people of 24 –Pargona of Bengal being educated and absorbed in the administration in large number who was killing the British in disguise to capture power. The British Lord Curzon landed in India and very soon realizing the situation he decided to reduce the power of Bengal and Hindu Bengalis. In order to reduce the power of Bengalis he divided Bengal in 1905 and began to construct the Capital at Raisina Hills at Delhi. After political turmoil, Begal was reunited but the Capital was shifted to Delhi in 1911.

Thus New Delhi in Raisina Hill in the area of Lutyens' Delhi a monumental new quarter of the city designed by the British architect Edwin Lutyens to house the government buildings. Thus New Delhi was officially declared as the seat of the Government of India after independence in 1947. After the assassination of Mahatma Gandhi he was cremated at the Raj Ghat, of Delhi.

References:

1. Jump up to:**a b** *Centre, UNESCO World Heritage.* "QutbMinar and its Monuments, Delhi". *UNESCO World Heritage Centre.* Retrieved 11 December *2018.*

2. Jump up to:**a b** Hearn, The Seven Cities of Delhi 1906, pp. 134-173.

3. History of Modern India

It appears although the ultimate goal of all religion is nothing but the service to humanity but the path is different. The thinking of political leaders was different because most of the political leaders apart from few who were real patriot, think for personal image or personal power first and then the country and the people. Thus the political leader such as Gandhi thought for personal image and utilized the ethics of religion to reach to the goal instead of winning the opposite heart of opposite leader for the service of mankind what is called the service to humanity. Gandhi utilized the Hindus'religious path of "Tolerance" in the name of "Non-Violence" to reach to the destination while the Muslim leader Jinnah took the path of "Violence" to reach to the destination. The success came to Jinnah, Pakistan was formed.

It was a foregone conclusion as the record of past history shows that Muslim power was increased in India during Sultan or Mughal period due to the "virtue of violence" and due to power of strength. In the Second World War the Axis power (Germany, Italy, and Japan) fought against **Allied powers** (Great Britain, France, the **Soviet Union**, the United States and China). Finally the "Virtue of Violence" by the power of Atom Bomb wined the war which was also recorded in Mahabharata where Krishna asked Arjun to fight with arms but then why Gandhi followed the art of "Non-Violence" and the "Virtue of Tolerance". The reason was not to win the war but to continue the war so that his image as a popular leader to spread everywhere. Is he worked for the well fare of the humanity or for the down fall of humanity and for the well fare of the personal image as a man of peace through "Non-Violence"?

The Capital Delhi was built up by the Sultans and Mughals mainly with many achievements such as Qutub Miner, Red Ford etc but at the time of partition of India, Jinnah did not claim Delhi to be included in Pakistan. The reason was the greatness of Jinnah. Let us elaborate the fact. At the time of partition a big question lies with Bengal. Jinnah knows the formation of Pakistan became successful only because of Suharwardy, the then PM of Bengal. Jinnah wanted Pakistan in the North-West of India centering Punjab. But he failed to convince the Punjabi people where at that time Punjab was ruled under Umist-

Party (Hindu-Sikh & Muslim), any kind of religious violence was not encouraged in Punjab.

Jinnah was compelled to ask Suhrawardy to carry out religious violence in order to get Pakistan. The demand for Pakistan was encouraged on or before 16 August 1946. Accordingly arrangements were made to carry out rioting in the streets of Calcutta by bringing more than 5 lakhs Muslims from the Calcutta superb. A massacre of killing more than 10,000 thousands was completed on that particular day, calling it "Calcutta Killing" day. But after massacre the heart of Suhrawardy was changed completely thinking for the future of Bengal and Bengalis. He met with Sarat Bose, elder brother of Subhas Bose (Netaji) and ML (Muslim League) secretary Abul Hashim and thought of a Sovereign United Bengal. On 5 March, Kiran Shankar Roy, Home Minister of Bengal, met Fredrick Burrows, the then Governor of **Bengal**, when the latter asked Roy about the **Bengali Hindu** opinion on the question of a sovereign united **Bengal**.

"Let us pause for a moment to consider what Bengal can be if it remains united. It will be a great country, indeed the richest and the most prosperous in India capable of giving to its people a high standard of living, where a great people will be able to rise to the fullest height of their stature, a land that will truly be plentiful. It will be rich in agriculture, rich in industry and commerce and in course of time it will be one of the powerful and progressive states of the world. If Bengal remains united this will be no dream, a great country and great nation."

The United Bengal plan: **H. S. Suhrawardy, the last Prime Minister of Bengal, urged a separate independent status for the whole province.**

[Sarat Chandra Bose & H. S. Suhrawardy]

Sarat Chandra Bose, the elder brother of Subhas Bose supported the United Bengal plan as he was of the same blood of Netaji thought alike. After it became apparent that the division of India on the basis of the Two-nation theory would almost certainly result in the partition of the Bengal province along religious lines, Bengal provincial Muslim League leader Suhrawardy came up with a new plan to create an independent Bengal state that would join neither Pakistan nor India and remain unpartitioned. Suhrawardy realized that if Bengal was partitioned, it would be economically disastrous for East Bengal as all coal mines, all jute mills but two and other industrial plants would certainly go to the western part since these were in an overwhelmingly Hindu majority area. Most important of all, Calcutta, then the largest city in India, an industrial and commercial hub and the largest port, would also go to the western part. Suhrawardy floated his idea on 24 April 1947 at a press conference in Delhi.

Barddhaman's League leader Abul Hashim supported it. On the other hand, Nurul Amin and Mohammad Akram Khan opposed it. But Muhammad Ali Jinnah realized the validity of Suhrawardy's argument and future of Bengal. He gave his support to the plan. After Jinnah's approval, Suhrawardy started gathering support for his plan. Finally "Calcutta Killing" created strong rival force of Hindu Muslim. There were many Hindu leaders along with Hindu Mahasabha stood against the Muslims and wanted a Hindu Bengal. S P Mukherjee took the leadership for the creation of a separate Hindu Bengal. There lies the foresighted thinking of a leader for the service to a nation for the cause of service to humanity forgetting religion, caste or community. It was done by Abraham Lincoln in the USA, Mao Se Tung in China. Finally Bengal was divided based on religion. S P Mukherjee created West Bengal for Hindu Bengalis sacrificing a greater proportion of Bengali Hindus in Islamic East Bengal, undertaking a suicidal policy to finish the Bengali Hindus forever.

At resolution was passed at the Bengal Hindu Conference at Tarakeswar, authorizing Dr. Syama Prasad Mookerjee to constitute a council of action in order to establish a separate homeland for the Bengali Hindus. On 4 April, the very day the Bengal Hindu Conference was held in Tarakeswar, the working committee of the Bengal Congress passed a resolution demanding the partition of Bengal. The meeting was attended by Dr. Syama Prasad Mookerjee, Kshitish Chandra Niyogi, Dr. Bidhan Chandra Roy, and many others where the concept of emotion undermines the virtue of humanity leading the destiny of Hindu Bengalis to the sea of grief. After this, the Bengal Hindu Sabha and the Congress intensified their campaigns.

On 22 April, at a public rally in New Delhi, Dr. Syama Prasad Mookerjee declared that even if the Muslim League accepts the Cabinet Mission plan, a separate province needs to be constituted in the Hindu majority areas of Bengal and thereby be created a ditch of hell instead of heaven for the Hindu Bengalis, however big he was. Syama Prasad Mookerjee called a general strike in Bengal on 23 April demanding against the inclusion of the whole of Bengal into Pakistan. Out of emotion he was inside of bloody Pakistan and forgot to see the heaven of Sovereign United Bengal, and also out of emotion forget to see a country in front a United Kingdom that had emerged by integration as such and a bigger country the United State of America formed by the union of states. Out of emotion Syama Prasad Mookerjee forget to see the bright future of Bengalis where the Unity is the strength and Unity is the virtue of humanity and prosperity.

On May 8, 1947, Viceroy Louis Mountbatten cabled the British government with a partition plan that made an exception for Bengal:

it was the only province that would be allowed to remain independent when the units would be divided as Pakistan, United Bengal and India.

On May 20, 1947, a plan for a United Bengal was thrashed out between Suhrawardy and Bose (the details of the plan written afterwards).

But on May 27, Nehru formally announced that the Congress would not agree to the plan of the formation of "**A sovereign united Bengal**". It was because of the inner fear of insecurity of India being formed only with the regions of Uttar Bharat where the United Bengal might be a stronger country.

The Hindu nationalist party Hindu Mahasabha under the leadership of Shyama Prasad Mukherjee vehemently opposed it for a united Bengal. He also opined that even though the plan asked for a sovereign Bengal state, in practice it will be a virtual Pakistan and the Hindu minority will be at the mercy of the Muslim majority forever forgetting the nature of a nation with broader mindset. The Congress President Kripalani along with Nehru put forward their proposal against the formation of United Bengal. Gandhi by the movement of "Non-Violence" already created two religious groups in Bengal. Those who were supporting "Non-Violence" were Hindu Bengali and those who were not supporting "Non-Violence" were Bengali Muslims and thereby in the name of "Non-Violence" he had already created undercurrent hatred between the two groups.

A nation is not depended all the time on religion but depended on the patriotic performance of the leader. Netaji became congress President in 38 as well as in 39 because of his patriotic nature of performance and not because of language or religion. He formed Azad Hind Fouz consisting of a Sikh, a Hindu or a Muslim general. Thus the opinion of S P Mukherjee against the formation of a Sovereign United Bengal was a narrow minded suicidal policy to destroy Bengal otherwise today Bengal would have been a wealthy, rich and powerful nation like that of the UK, or USA, a country of Super-power. The formation of unity started from Thomas Jefferson (1801) to Abraham Lincoln (1861), where and how he united the black and white of two opposite human race different in language, custom and nature and get them united together and compel them to live as an equal citizen of a nation due to which today the country is a great nation.

However, the final decision was in favor of the division of Bengal. The East Bengal would be a part of Pakistan and West Bengal would be a part of India. The greatness of Jinnah lies to claim Calcutta as the Capital of East Pakistan sacrificing the demand of Delhi as the Capital of West Pakistan although Capital Delhi was a city of cities, built and destroyed by the Muslim Rulers several times and ruled by the Muslims at different periods. However the communal flare up prevents Calcutta to become the Capital of East Pakistan.

13. OPPOSITION TO THE PARTITION OF INDIA

[13.1]

The peace and development was equally disturbed in India as well as in Pakistan. Thus unity of the two is no way bad for the people of the two regions. Opposition to the partition of India was wide spread in British India in the 20th century and it continues to remain so in many countries in South Asian politics. Most individuals of the Hindu and Sikh faiths were opposed to the partition of India and many Muslims were also against the partition which was supported and were represented by the All India Azad Muslim Conference.

Pashtun politician Khan Abdul Ghaffar Khan of the Khudai Khidmatgar viewed the proposal to partition India as un-Islamic and contrary to the history of Muslims in the subcontinent, who had considered India as their homeland. Ghaffar Khan along with Mahatma Gandhi opined that "Hindus and Muslims were sons of the same soil of India; they were brothers who therefore must strive to keep India free and united".

Muslims in general argued that the economic development of Muslims would be hurt if India was partitioned, seeing the idea of partition as one that was designed to keep Muslims backward. They also expected "Muslim-majority provinces in united India to be more effective than the rulers of independent Pakistan in helping the Muslim minorities living in Hindu-majority areas and that the proposition for a partition of India was not justified from religious point of view". The Muslim leaders were farsighted, they thought that when all the Hindus were ousted from Pakistan, similarly all the Muslims are likely to be ousted from the Hindustan, if so what would happen to all the Muslims in Pakistan. After the formation of Pakistan actually that had happened in Pakistan almost all the Hindus were ousted from Pakistan by declaring Pakistan an Islamic Country and thereby they have proved that the Muslim leaders know how to establish the rule of administration at first which is the primary priority for a new country. But the Hindu leaders of India failed to do that, which proves beyond doubt that the Hindu leaders of India do not know how to establish the rule of administration at first in the case of the formation of a new country. The same thing was done by the British at the beginning after defeating the Muslim Rulers Siraj-uddlla, ousted all the Muslims from the administration and favored the Hindus. But subsequently the British had changed the policy of administration. A Ruler knows how to rule a country.

The leader Lama Mashriqi in the movement of Khaksar Movement opposed the partition of India because he felt that if Muslims and Hindus had largely lived peacefully together in India for centuries, they could also do so in a free and united India. Mashriqi saw the two-nation theory as a plot of the British to rule the region more easily, if India was divided into two countries that were pitted against one another. He reasoned that a division of India along religious lines would breed fundamentalism and extremism on both sides of the border. Mashriqi thought and explained to others that "Muslim majority areas were already under Muslim rule, so if any Muslims wanted to move to these areas, they were free to do so without having to divide the country". To him, separatist leaders "were power hungry and misleading Muslims in order to bolster their own power by serving the British agenda."

The Deccan Herald, in an article titled the tragedy of Partition, argued that the Muslim and the non-Muslim population lived together since centuries on the Indian soil, peacefully and harmoniously, without any major conflict. It was clear that if ever a separate Muslim country was formed, it could not possibly contain all or even most,

Indian Muslims. And there would inevitably be many non-Muslims and others in it. No amount of social and religious engineering could separate India's Muslims from non-Muslims since Hindus and Muslims living together for many years. It was practically not possible. The Indian Muslims did not have a common culture and moreover they speak not in same language. A Punjabi Muslim had very little in common with a Muslim in Bengal except, of course, religion. There was no single language that could be called a Muslim language. For centuries after century, the Indian Muslims shared the language and culture of the region along with non-Muslims. The second favorable argument was that the Indian Muslims were fundamentally different from non-Muslims that were even more absurd. Syncretism had been an important feature of Indian culture since early times. Culture and language were generally based on region, more than religion. And so a Bengali Muslim had much more in common with a Bengali Hindu than with a Punjabi Muslim and that became true by the liberation of Bangladesh. Considerable cultural diversity existed within Muslims and also between Muslims and non-Muslims. But even then it was not possible to draw a dividing line, between India's Muslims and non-Muslims.

After it occurred, critics of the partition of India pointing to the displacement of fifteen million people, the murder of more than one million people, and the rape of 75,000 women, view that Partition was a terrible mistake on the part of leaders of India. Both the countries are not in peace since more than seventy years even after independence. Leaders like Abul Kalam Azad, Abdul Matlib Mazumdar, Fakhruddin Ali Ahmed, Maulana Abul Kalam Azad and many others objected partition but leaders under Muslim league by virtue of militant forces succeeded in the partition of the country.

The cause of Partition: Responsibility for the partition of India continues to spark much heated debate. Among historians, some hold the British squarely responsible while others put the blame on the rift between Hindus and Muslims. Historians on the Left have argued that the partition was the result of both greed and convenience when capitalist supporters of the Congress struck a deal with their metropolitan counterparts. More lately, historians have argued that Congress leaders chose to have a strong Centre, rather than share power with the League. The popular perception is that lust for quick and easy power prompted leaders to settle for a hasty and imperfect division.

But however at the late hour it was also difficult to nullify the demand of Muslims for a separate homeland. Gandhi had done the greatest blunder by brining religion in Indian politics by the support of Khilafat Movement which was vehemently opposed by Jinnah. Getting failure in turning Gandhi away from religion in Indian politics being absorbed in the joy of the religious glory of the marriage of **"Non-Violence and Khilafat"** Jinnah left Congress and later get compelled to attach himself with the Muslim League to achieve a homeland for the Muslims of India against the formation of Gandhi's Ram-Rajya. But at the time of his death staying at death bed he had expressed his mental feeling by saying that the greatest blinder he had done in his life by the creation of Pakistan. It was because he thought of the future of the Muslims remained in India.

It was clear on seeing the millions of Punjabis who were shifting their places of resident from Pakistan to India after losing the family members in the thrust of communal rioting and the life saving household materials. Similarly afterwards millions of Bengali Hindus had shifted their residences from Islamic East Pakistan to India after losing few members and life saving household materials whereby 37% of Hindu population had been dropped down to 15 & and gradually to 7%. Muslims were the rulers that had been proved in every time in every activity of their administration. A Muslim ruler can think far ahead where a Hindu ruler cannot. Pakistan Prime Minister Liaquate Ali Khan earlier thought of the future of the Bengali Muslims in India after partition of Bengal on religious line. He was thinking if the Bengali Hindus could not live in East Pakistan (East Bengal), how the Bengali Muslims could live in West Bengal in India. But, however in opportune moment after forming the Nehru-Liquate Ali Pact in 1950, he could console himself as he had stabilized the future existence of Bengali Muslims in West Bengal, Assam and in the North Eastern regions. He was a farsighted administrator. He along with Jinnah was succeeded to create Pakistan for the Indian Muslims and in course of time made Pakistan absolutely for the Muslims by ousting the Hindus and later on by his own afford he stabilized the future safety of the Muslims left out in India after partition of India. But above all these he lost the glorious future of United India or United Bengal where in United India Hindu and Muslims could live together as the Blacks and Whites are living in the United States today, the United Bengal would be a store house of wealth by virtue of its Sea-Ports, Hills, Rivers and natural minerals which not only had attracted the Muslims, or the British and in the end India would have been a Super-Power having stronger in wealth as well as in strength in any regions of the world. But in reverse what is seen to-day government is giving more attention in defense expenditure in purchasing fighter planes to make the military efficient and stronger to fight against India and less in trade for economy leading the country towards poverty.

At the time of the entry of the millions and millions of Hindus from Islamic East Pakistan to India, he came to India by the call of Indian Prime Minister Pandit Nehru. He stayed in the Nehru palace and made an agreement to settle the issue permanently so as to stay the people on their own soil, which was known by Nehru-Liquate Ali Pact thereby Liquate Ali Khan by his political administrative maturity stabilized the existence of Bengali Muslims in Bengal or in Assam or in India permanently even after the division of Bengal including Assam on the basis of religion. A Bengali Hindu declined to live in Islamic East Pakistan but a Muslims agreed to live in secular India. The result was Bengali Hindus of Islamic East Pakistan shifted to India due to partition based on religion but the Muslims of Bengal and Assam of India had not shifted to East Pakistan because India is India and not a Hindu India after partition. Thus by the condition of the Pact a Muslim Ruler Khan converted a Pandit Nehru Ruler into a foolish Ruler. This is once again had proved beyond doubt that Muslims of India were the rulers while the Hindus were the subjects to be ruled by others.

Thus in the end the Hindu population in East Bengal dropped to 7% but Muslim population in West Bengal had never decreased rather the percentage of Muslim population had increased from 18% to 38%. It is better for a Bengali Hindu to live under the shadow of an intelligent Muslim Ruler rather than a foolish Hindu Ruler.

P. D. Tandon, Congress leader and Speaker of the UP Assembly, was an active proponent to apply force to achieve a united India. But Nehru was clear that use of the sword could not stem the communal forces– rather, it would ensure civil war that would have long term consequences. After Netaji, there was no other leader in India, not the question of Gandhi, who could bring victory for a United India as the example set by the American President Abraham Lincoln. He had given up his last breadth through the gun of a bullet, but his ideals of unity survived due to which the United States is now a Super-power, while M.K.Gandhi also had given up his last breadth through the gun of a bullet, but his ideals of disunity and division through religion survived due to which India remained a country of poverty destined to claim a developing country.

There were many Congress leaders in India without any leadership ability or any capacity of mental ability to see the farsighted destiny. A short sided political leader cannot think to build up a strong nation except to think the destiny of a community. In the period of 1947, a couple of months earlier, Congress President, Kripalani, had told the Viceroy Mount batten that "Rather than have a battle we shall let them have their Pakistan". Thus partition seemed inevitable, on 15 June 1947, Congress President, Kripalani, said that acceptance of partition flowed from the clause of no coercion in the resolution on the Cripps Plan. Nehru put this eloquently- "we have often to go through the valley of the shadow before we reach the sunlit mountain tops." Hence any measure that cemented Partition was to be avoided, be it dividing the army, transfer of population or parliamentary sanction for transfer of power to two dominions.

Ironically, for a believer in ahimsa Gandhi getting failure in all fronts finally he was willing to take the risk of civil war. He wrote:"Let

British leave India to anarchy, rather than as a cock pit between two organized armies" ('Harijan', 20 July, 47).

Congress and Gandhi then accepted partition on many grounds- that it reflected the will of the people that it was the only way out. Gandhi realized the British has come with the proposal of 3 June to hand over the administration with vivisection of India. The British Labor Government gave importance to logic of Jinnah. Gandhi knows the Indian people will make him responsible for the division of the country. To save his skin in the last moment he designed a formula. On 4ᵗʰ June, Gandhi made the arrangement to meet Viceroy Lord Mount Batten and kept the proposal to make Jinnah the PM of India so that the country people never blame him for the cause of Partition. Viceroy replied it is too late. Later on Gandhi, a Saint but the most clever politician held a meeting with Viceroy and other Congress leaders and said that the CWC had agreed to the vivisection of Pakistan and Hindustan not under any threat of violence but as there was no other option left of getting round the Muslim League.

Activity of Gandhi: Gandhi was a clever politicians, he carried out politics to earn his name and fame knowing well that he had little ability to rule a country. Getting failure in the profession of law he switched over to religion to increase his popularity. He created a new movement in the name of "Non-Violence" taking the advantage of the religious faith of the ordinary Hindu people. To increase his popularity he had changes his nature of thought time to time. He was a religious man of "Non-Violence" at the outset but at the beginning of his political carrier in India in 1915 after return from South Africa, he joined British in the First World War in the act of violence forgetting the principle of Non-Violence just to increase his popularity. He started the "Non-Violence" Movement, Jallianwala Bag massacre occurred on 13 April 1919 in Amritshore of Punjab; he stopped the movement at once to become a public figure and at the same time to become a favorable person of British.

Again he joined Khilafat movement in 1919; a movement was started by the Indian Muslims, a religious movement in support of the

Caliph of Islam of Ottoman Sultan of Turkey to get familiar and famous among the Muslims. Jinnah, a leader and a genius of law objected the support of Congress under Gandhi to Khilafat movement and at last he left congress. Afterwards, getting ousted from the Khilafat, and rejected by the Muslims, he again turned his attention towards the Muslims. To revive the Hindu sentiment, Gandhi thought of a long "Salt Satyagraha" starting from Gujarat Sabarmati Ashram to Dandi (24 March 1930 – 6 April 1930). In the procession of long distance of 384 km he could involve many people and many regions and thereby he could regain the lost set back of joint movement of "Non-Violence-Khilafat Movement". After regaining strength in popularity Gandhi again started the movement of "Non-Violence" along with the Hindus particularly in Calcutta. Looking to the violence activity of Muslim League demanding Pakistan, he left Calcutta and had taken shelter in Sabarmati Ashram and passing the days in his mental pleasure by sleeping with girls at night time in the Ashram. The Khilafat Militant turned to Muslim League, Calcutta massacre occurred on 16 August 1946 demanding Pakistan. Gandhi changes his political thought here after. To save his skin from the blessings of partition he thought of a new strategy to fool the people. He expressed his desire to bring Jinnah as the PM of India to keep the unity of India but that was not supported by other congress leaders because of the existence of communal atmosphere. After saving his skin from the curse of partition, finally he changes his thought along with other Congress leader from United India to a Divided India. But again he was conscious of his future image, Muslims made Pakistan an Islamic Pakistan, a home land for the Muslims of India but India was not a Hindustan, a home land for the Hindus because if so he could not increase his image as a leader of Hindu-Muslim, and a man of peace. He thought afresh and chock out a plan to stop rioting in the streets of Calcutta in spite of rioting in Dacca or in other cities of East Pakistan or East Bengal. He had taken the shelter under the virtue of Hindu-Religion, the tools of "Hindu ethics" the ethics of "Fasting' for any devotional works. Gandhi was finally succeeded to make himself an icon of peace by stopping the rioting in West Bengal by "Fasting" against the entry of Hindu Bengalis in millions due to rioting in East Bengal cum Islamic East Pakistan. He then went to Delhi to save the Muslims there but a Hindu patriot shoots him dead. Unlike Abraham Lincoln he failed to keep the country united.

Gandhi also had not forgotten to tell the people that Partition was nothing but temporary that it could be turned back, once the imperialists were out of the picture and once Muslim League realized its folly. Partition was seen by the leaders as better than civil war or balkanization. The AICC resolution on the 3rd June Plan made it clear that partition was accepted as a temporary arrangement that would bring violence to an end.

The failure of the Congress to draw in Muslim masses into the national movement was another factor at play. Gandhi's own reading of the communal situation having being his own creation through the marriage of "Non-Violence and Khilafat" had realized at late that both Hindus and Muslims had moved far away from non-violence. It was clear from his writing. The possibility of anti-communal struggle was limited as cadres and the ordinary people were already communalized. Gandhi was aware of his limitations, His writing was -: 'I have never created a situation in my life... People say that I had created a situation, but I had done nothing except giving a shape to what was already there. Today I see no sign of such a healthy feeling. And therefore, I shall have to wait until the time comes.' **(N.K.Bose, "My Experiences as a Gandhian-II, p. 53).**

Once Pakistan was announced, the Hindu Mahasabha raised the demand "to build up a real and powerful Hindu state". This was firmly opposed by Congress leaders. Gandhi fell to the bullet of a Hindu communal fanatic who was enraged at what the vivisection of India.

It was also a fact that Mount batten had a meeting with Jinnah where Jinnah said that the British had taken Indian administration from Muslims and so the British should hand over the administration to Muslims. Accordingly because of the protest from the majority Hindu people British had given a part of it to Muslims as Pakistan where the Muslim leaders were in a plan to create Darul-Islam. In the Pakistan area Muslims have established its superiority and in the remaining area under India, the Muslims have increased its population through religion by the principle of multiple marriage and by the creation of too many children and also by stabilizing the protection of Muslims in India by Nehru-Liquate Ali Pact expecting within ten years the Muslim population would be 50%. Thus in the end Muslims could rule India as well as Pakistan when the creation of India a Darul-Islamic country was not unnatural. It was because Muslims were the rulers and creator of the nations with courage and with the vision of foresight.

Gandhi stated that the decision had been arrived at after taking into account the pulse of the people of all communities, be they Muslims, Sikhs or Hindus. But he failed to exert his leadership ability to the destiny of unity except to divide the Indians as Hindus and Muslims by his political fight through religion throughout the journey of his political carrier. What he could give to the Indians, division, destruction and rivalry of Hindu-Muslims with which the Indian are passing their days since seventy years and now in front, the destiny of Assam to protect the language, the culture of Assam and the government in Delhi, what is burning under the hidden communal hatred with the religious blessings of Gandhi. But by virtue of the political genius of Gandhi, he could place himself even after death at the thrown of India as the FATHER of the nation and in the international level as a man of peace in spite of killing millions of people in the thrust of the division of the country.

The hope in India and Pakistan being reunited after some years reconciled leaders to the reality of division. The expectation was that once passions subsided, common interests would draw people together and partition could be revoked. Seventy years have passed and the two nations have come across with frontal fight on several occasions, now the emergence of Corona Virus should bring the two nations together after all they were the brothers of same boat. Before the boat gets sunk in the river brothers should extend their hands to pull each other.

14. GLOBAL UNITY DUE TO CORONA VIRUS

[14.1]

Let us see what is the effect of Corona Virus in other countries and is there anything to learn from them to reduce the tension of the two countries of India and Pakistan. The Partition of India was done with the concept that it could be turned back, once the imperialists were out of the picture and once Muslim League realized its agony of mistake. A longer period of seventy years had passed facing four frontal wars without the realization of the past mistake, now a new global threat had appeared in an invisible character; the two countries could think afresh forgetting the past to live together as friends and brothers as their destiny of origin was the same.

The World Health Organization has called on the global community to work together to fight the new corona virus that is causing an epidemic of viral pneumonia and deaths in China, Italy, Spane and USA including many other countries. WHO's director general, Dr Tedros Adhanom Ghebreyesus, said by the time that nobody should assume there was no risk that it would become a dangerous global epidemic. "Make no mistake; this is an emergency not only in China, but a global health emergency." It is an emergency to humanity. There have been several cases and several deaths reported to the WHO so far, Most of the deaths occurred inside of China, which is where all human-to-human transmission of the virus had so far occurred, said Tedros. "We know this virus causes severe disease and can kill, although for most people it causes mild disease," he added. A quarter of those who became ill had severe disease and most of those who died had underlying in poor health, such as heart disease.

Peter Piot, a professor of global health and the director of the London School of Hygiene and Tropical Medicine, said the outbreak was at a critical stage and international collaboration and more resources were vital in stopping it in its tracks. "There are still many missing pieces to fully understanding this new virus, which is spreading rapidly across China and around the world".

Anxieties in the UK and around the world are already running high. The Scottish government said more than five people were being tested for the novel corona virus. The Prime Minister Boris Johnson's spokesman was also worried with the spread of virus. Prof Jürgen Haas, head of infections at the University of Edinburgh, said he expected there would be many more suspected cases very soon in Scotland that emerged overnight. The Scottish government confirmed that the patients had been in Wuhan recently. "Following travel to Wuhan, China, two people confirmed as diagnosed with influenza is now being tested for Wuhan novel corona virus as a precautionary measure only. Three further people are also undergoing testing on a similar precautionary basis," said a government spokesman. He said they had "robust arrangements to manage emerging diseases and are monitoring this situation closely".

The US Centers for Disease Control warned citizens to avoid all but essential travel to Wuhan, in line with the advice from the UK government, while Egypt and Turkey joined the growing list of countries introducing screening at ports for travelers arriving from China. A programme has already been launched to speed up work towards a vaccine. Cepi, the Coalition for Epidemic Preparedness Innovations, said it hoped to have a vaccine in clinical trials within 16 weeks.

The head of the United Nations has called the corona virus pandemic the "fight of a generation" and a threat to world peace and security. The secretary general, Antonio Guterres, warned the UN Security Council that the pandemic had the potential to increase social unrest and violence, which would greatly undermine the world's ability to fight the disease.

It was said that it is the UN's gravest test since it was founded 75 years ago and had already hindered efforts to resolve international, regional and national problems. It was also said that "This is the fight of a generation and the *raison dêtre* [reason for being] of the United Nations itself,".

More than 95,000 people had died by the time after contracting Covid-19, according to Johns Hopkins University, which is tracking the figures. More than 1.6 million had been diagnosed as the economic impact continued to grow. One in 10 Americans had lost their job as a result of the virus and the IMF chief said the world was on track for the biggest downturn since the Great Depression. Guterres said the world was already seeing the "ruinous social and economic impacts. But the pandemic also poses a significant threat to the maintenance of international peace and security."He warned the pandemic could lead to opportunistic terror attacks, the erosion of trust in public institutions, economic instability, political tensions from postponing elections or referendums, and Covid-19 "triggering or exacerbating various human rights challenges". He said Security Council involvement would be "critical to mitigate the peace and security implications" and "a signal of unity and resolve from the council would count for a lot at this anxious time".

This week Donald Trump threatened to withhold funding from the WHO, but was accused of seeking to make it a scapegoat in order to distract from his own failings in preparing the US for its own outbreak, which had infected nearly 5 lacks and killed almost 15,000 by the time.

It is astonishing to hear that Boris Johnson, the British prime minister, was moved out of intensive care after being admitted three days earlier suffering from corona virus. Around the world people have been told to stay at home. Authorities in several other countries have warned of roadblocks to enforce social distancing. The New York governor said a record 799 people died from Covid-19 by the time, bringing the state's total loss to 7,067 people. Ti was estimated that the economic impact on the state was expected to be worse than 9/11. The South Korean city of Daegu, which endured the first large corona virus outbreak outside of China, reported now zero new cases for the first time since late February, as new infections across the country dropped to record lows because of efficient handling.

There have been calls for high-level inquiries into allegations of inhumane treatment in some aged care facilities. It has been reported in Spain where the army has reported finding dead and abandoned people in their beds. The death toll in UK care homes is likely to be far higher than reported, as per the report of the Guardian. The official death toll from the corona virus outbreak in Iran passed 4,000, the country's health ministry reported now and hereafter, 117 more people were confirmed to have died.

Many people blame the coronavirus epidemic due to globalization, but to prevent more such outbreaks, it is necessary to de-globalize the world, build walls, restrict travel, and reduce trade. However, short-term quarantine is essential to stop epidemics, but if it turned to a long-term isolation that would lead to economic collapse without offering any real protection against infectious diseases. The real antidote to epidemic is not segregation, but rather cooperation.

Remembering the past it is found that epidemics killed millions of people long before the current age of globalization. In the 14th century there were no airplanes and cruise ships, and yet the Black Death spread from East Asia to Western Europe in little more than a decade. It killed between 75 million and 200 million people – more than a quarter of the population of Eurasia. In England, four out of ten people died. The city of Florence lost 50,000 of its 100,000 inhabitants.

In March 1520, a single smallpox carrier – Francisco de Eguía – landed in Mexico. At the time, Central America had no trains, buses or even donkeys. Yet by December a smallpox epidemic devastated the whole of Central America, killing according to some estimates up to a third of its population. In 1918 a particularly virulent strain of flu managed to spread within a few months to the remotest corners of the world. It infected half a billion people – more than a quarter of the human species. It is estimated that the flu killed 5% of the population of India. Altogether the pandemic killed tens of millions of people – and perhaps as high as 100 million – in less than a year, more than the First World War killed in four years of brutal fighting.

In the century that passed since 1918, humankind became ever more vulnerable to epidemics, due to a combination of growing populations and better transport. The global transport network is today far faster than in 1918. A virus can make its way from Paris to Tokyo and Mexico City or in any other city or in any other place in less than 24 hours. We should therefore have expected to live in an infectious hell, with one deadly plague after another.

However, both the incidence and impact of epidemics have actually gone down dramatically. Despite horrendous outbreaks such as AIDS in the twenty-first century epidemics kill a far smaller proportion of human beings than in any previous time since the Stone Age. This is because the best defense for humans against pathogens is not isolation but it is information. Humanity has been winning the war against epidemics because in the arms race between pathogens and doctors, pathogens rely on blind mutations while doctors rely on the scientific analysis of information. Thus the system of isolation is not the ultimate solution, the solution lies in the scientific analysis in the discovery of preventive medicines to fight the Virus Corona.

The Black Death struck in the 14th century, people had no idea what causes it and what could be done about it. Until the modern era, humans usually blamed angry gods for diseases, malicious demons or bad air, and did not even suspect the existence of bacteria and viruses. People believed in angels and fairies, but they could not imagine that a single drop of water might contain an entire armada of deadly predators. Therefore when the Black Death or smallpox came to visit, the people began to organize mass prayers to various gods and saints. It didn't help. Then people gathered together for mass prayers, but the result was mass infections.

During the last century, scientists, doctors and nurses throughout the world get together and collected information and managed to understand both the mechanism behind epidemics and the means of countering them. The theory of evolution explained why and how new diseases erupt. Genetics enabled scientists to spy on the pathogens' while medieval people never discovered what caused the Black Death, it took scientists just two weeks to identify the novel corona virus, sequence its genome and develop a reliable test to identify infected people.

Once scientists understood what causes epidemics, it became much easier to fight them. Vaccinations, antibiotics, improved hygiene, and a much better medical infrastructure have allowed humanity to gain the upper hand over its invisible predators. In 1967, smallpox still infected 15 million people and killed 2 million of them. But in the following decade a global campaign of smallpox vaccination was so successful, that in 1979 the World Health Organization declared that humanity had won, and that smallpox had been completely eradicated. In 2019 not a single person was either infected or killed by smallpox.

What does this history teach us for the current Corona virus epidemic? Firstly, it implies that no one could protect himself or herself by permanently closing the borders. Remembering that epidemics spread rapidly even in the Middle Ages, long before the age of globalization, so even if reduction in global connections is completed still that would not be sufficient enough to stop epidemics.

Secondly, history indicates that real protection comes from the sharing of reliable scientific information, and from global unity. If one country is struck by an epidemic, it should be willing to honestly share information about the outbreak without fear of economic catastrophe – while other countries must trust that information without hesitation giving supreme value to humanity, and should be willing to extend a helping hand rather than ostracize the victim. Today, China can teach countries all over the world many important lessons about corona virus, but it is only possible if a high level of international trust and cooperation get supremacy above all.

Quarantine and lock-down are essential for stopping the spread of epidemics, but that requires trust of one another and each country when no governments ever hesitate to take drastic measures in taking any national under quarantine. In the discover of many corona-virus cases a country, could immediately lock down entire cities and regions provided the country is sure of getting help of other countries in the necessity of economic collapse.

The most important thing is to realize that the spread of the epidemic because of the evolution of viruses in *any* country endangers the *entire* human species. Viruses like the corona originate in animals, such as bats. After entering into human body, initially the viruses are ill-adapted to their human hosts but within humans, the viruses occasionally undergo mutations. Most mutations are harmless. But every now and then a mutation makes the virus more infectious or more resistant to the human immune system – and this virus can rapidly spread in the human population. Since a single person might host trillions of virus particles that undergo constant replication, every infected person thus gives the virus trillions of new opportunities to become more adapted to humans. Each human becomes a carrier to trillions.

The record of earlier history predicts perhaps a mutation in a single gene in the corona-virus affected a single person of Wuhan and that had infected some person in Tehran, Milan or Wuhan. If this is indeed happening, this is a direct threat not just to Iranians, Italians or Chinese, but to all human beings. People all over the world must share a life-and-death interest to fight against corona and for that it is urgent to protect every person in every country.

The mankind had seen the danger of human beings in the year 1970 due to smallpox but humanity managed to defeat the smallpox virus because all people in all countries were vaccinated against smallpox. If one country failed to vaccinate its population, it could have endangered the whole of humankind. It was because as long as the smallpox virus existed and evolved somewhere, it could always spread again endangering human beings *everywhere*.

In the fight against viruses, humanity needs to closely guard borders between the human world and the virus-sphere. Planet earth is teaming with countless viruses, and new viruses are constantly evolving due to genetic mutations. The borderline separating this virus-sphere from the human world passes inside the body of each and every human being. If a dangerous virus manages to penetrate this border anywhere on earth, it puts the whole human species in danger.

Over the last century, humanity has fortified this border by modern healthcare systems and border wall is protected by nurses, doctors and scientists who patrol it and repel intruders. However, long sections of this border have been left woefully exposed. There are hundreds of millions of people around the world who are lacking even in basic healthcare services. This endangers not only that country but all of human beings. It is necessary to think about health in national terms, how to provide better healthcare for Iranians and Chinese so as to protect Israelis and Americans from epidemics. This simple truth is true to everyone, but unfortunately it escapes even some of the most important people in the world.

President Trump leaves the podium after announcing a national emergency during a news conference about the corona virus at the White House in Washington, D.C., on March 13, of 2020 but requires more to do to save the mankind. The virtue of Faith and Trust become a necessity for the survival of humanity. Today humanity faces an acute crisis not only due to the corona-virus, but also due to the lack of trust between human beings. To defeat an epidemic, people need to trust scientific experts, citizens need to trust public authorities, and countries need to trust each other. Over the last few years, irresponsible politicians have deliberately undermined trust in science, in public authorities and in international cooperation. As a result, people are now facing the crisis bereft of global leaders that can inspire, organize and finance a coordinated global response.

The mankind had seen how the U.S. had taken leadership in the crisis of any epidemic. The U.S. served as leader in 2014 during

Ebola epidemic, the U.S. fulfilled a similar role during the financial crisis of 2008, remaining behind many countries to prevent global economic meltdown, but in recent time the U.S. has resigned from its role as global leader. The current U.S. administration has cut support for international organizations like the World Health Organization, and has made it very clear to the world that the U.S. no longer has any real friends. When the corona virus crisis erupted, the U.S. remained indifferent, and has so far refrained from taking a leading role. Now the trust in the current U.S. administration has been eroded to such an extent, that few countries would be willing to follow it. It was because the motto of US President is "Me First".

The void left by the U.S. has not been filled by anyone else. Xenophobia, isolationism and distrust now characterize most of the international system. Without trust and global solidarity human beings cannot stop the corona-virus epidemic, and it is likely to see more such epidemics in future. But every crisis is also an opportunity. Hopefully the current epidemic would enlighten the humankind to realize how the Mankind is confronted to face the acute danger posed by global disunity.

The epidemic could be a golden opportunity for the E.U. to regain the popular support it has lost in recent years. If the interested and fortunate wealthy members of the E.U. swiftly and generously send gift of money, equipment and medical personnel to help the people of hardest-hit colleagues of European countries, this would prove the worth for the people of Europe. If, on the other hand, each country is left to fend for itself, then the epidemic might sound the **death-knell** of the union.

In this moment of crisis, the crucial struggle is taking place within humanity itself. If this epidemic continues creating greater disunity and mistrust among humans, it would be the virus's greatest victory. When humans squabble – viruses double. In contrast, if the epidemic results in closer global cooperation, it would be a victory not only against the corona-virus, but also against all future pathogens.

To save the Mankind the human beings must stand united against the corona-virus pandemic. DonaMijatović, the Council of Europe Commissioner for Human Rights said "Millions of people around the world are living through extremely tough times because of the rapid global spread of the corona virus, COVID-19. All my thoughts are with the people infected, the families and people close to them and with those who have lost loved ones," He further said that "The situation in Europe are developing fast and governments are taking a great variety of measures to protect the population. I call on everyone - authorities and citizens - to do their part and uphold solidarity and unity while responding to the urgent challenges and concerns we all share."

European governments are fighting against the spread of the pandemic with a strong hand. This is necessary to respond to the unprecedented challenge that people are facing. At the same time, it is clear that the life and the enjoyment of human rights are affected by the pandemic and the measures must be adopted to encounter it. The right to health, the range of economic and social rights, and the right to civil and political freedoms, all are very relevant and correlated in the present context.

It is therefore crucial that the authorities take measures to prevent discrimination. It is also necessary to have a sound medical System to health care for all population groups. Positive measures are required to meet the specific needs of the groups at particularly high risk, such as older persons and those who may not fall under health coverage. It is also urgently required to take necessary measure to do more to mitigate the enormous pressure of health professionals in responding to the expectations placed on them.

It is essential that governments remain vigilant against racist, xenophobic or stigmatizing acts, and provide wide access to unbiased information on the public health situation, availability of services, and the measures undertaken.

Lastly, it is also necessary for all member states to ensure that the communication formats adopted reach to all people. Some governments have established communication channels via social media platforms, but transparency and accessibility are central for enabling the public's confidence and public participation in the governance of the current circumstances.COVID-19 poses a serious danger. But human unity, determination to protect human rights and solidarity, humanity would overcome it.

[14.2]

Experiment in search of Vaccine Discovery: The survival of humanity rests with the human affords of the exploration of unknown knowledge. In this respect the humanity gets a sigh of relief on seeing the Endeavour in different countries to find out appropriate medicines to kill the deadly Corona-Virus. Let us see the places where the experiment is going on to find the weapon to kill the virus.

WASHINGTON a global coalition founded by India and Norway, the US has begun a clinical trial of an investigational vaccine designed to protect against the corona virus disease which has claimed the lives of over 7,000 people globally. The trial also began at the Kaiser Permanente Washington Health Research Institute (KPWHRI) where a participant received the investigational-vaccine. An agreement between the Uruguayan and Australian governments was made to create a "sanitary corridor" to take the mostly Corona positive persons. In Rome the global corona virus death toll topped 100,000 on Friday as Easter celebrations around the world kicked off in near-empty churches with billions of people stuck indoors to halt the pandemic's deadly march.

It came to be known as the World Health Organization issued a dire warning that prematurely lifting lockdown restrictions could spark a dangerous resurgence of the disease affecting more than half the planet's population. Extraordinary measures is necessary everywhere to prevent the spreading of the Virus. It is natural as the governments struggling to cope with the COVID-19 pandemic, billions of people living in countries teetering on the brink of economic collapse.

The US has become the world's first country to have registered more than 2,000 COVID-19 deaths in a single day with 2,108 fatalities reported while the number of infections in America has crossed 700,000, by the time the highest number in the world, according to Johns Hopkins University data. China, where the deadly corona virus disease started in December last year killing more than 100,000, has so far recorded 81,000 cases. In the midst of a global pandemic that has sickened more than 60,000 people in Britain and killed more than 7,000, Britain discarded the most favorite night club activity. In Britain unprecedented phenomenon in the closing of pubs occurred. Never before in the history of the country have the pubs been closed outright.

Experiment in India in Search of Corona-Vaccine: Adar Poonawalla, the chief executive officer of Serum Institute of India (SII) said a vaccine for the corona virus pandemic is expected within one year although it will not be 100% effective. The medical experiment is at the forefront of developing the vaccine. It is further reported that vaccine will have 70% protection; the rest may still get the disease despite being vaccinated. Serum Institute of India Pvt Ltd (SIIPL) has announced that a vaccine candidate for the novel corona virus (COVID-19) is expected to progress to human trials phase within six months. It has been developed by SIIPL, in partnership with American Biotechnology firm Codagenix. It has progressed to the pre-clinical tests phase, i.e. the animal trial phase. Adar Poonawalla, CEO of Serum Institute of India, said, "I am glad to share that our combined efforts with the team at Codagenix have borne fruit, and we hope to save millions of lives with this vaccine".

The vaccine-virus strain will be the fastest 'Made in India' such vaccine to progress to the human trials phase within six months. The cost of the project is about Rs 300 crore, SII hopes to get external funding for the project via various global partners. Adar Poonawalla, CEO of SII, further said, "By August-end, we will have data on mice and primates to submit to regulatory authorities to enter into the human trials phase."

Covid-19 that is not a very severe disease in its own might but when it develops in a person with existing health conditions such as diabetes, cancer or ailments related to heart, lungs and kidney, the infection becomes potentially fatal. It can cause pneumonia, sepsis or even septic shock, where body's defense mechanism starts attacking protecting cells leading to death. Good thing is that corona virus cannot enter human body if effective step is taken in taking care of Mouth, nose and eyes those are being the principal routes through which the novel corona virus enters human body and then multiplies very fast.

The malaria medications chloroquine and hydroxychloroquine; a combination of two HIV drugs, are manufactured in India now thought to be an immune system messenger that are found to be effective in US and few other countries to cripple viruses. At a press conference on Friday, President Donald Trump called chloroquine and hydroxychloroquine a "game changer." Trump said " I feel good about it, "Indians become proud of it. His remarks have led to a rush in demand for the decades-old antimalarials products. Researchers in France have published a study in which they treated 20 COVID-19 patients with hydroxychloroquine. Hydroxychloroquine, in particular, might do more harm than good. The drug has a variety of side effects and can in rare cases even harm the heart. What's more, a rush to use the drug for COVID-19 might make it harder for the people to give some relief. Disregarding all factors that a vaccine is going to emerge in a time period of at least 12 or 18 months, but it's just one bright light in some way giving really a devastating news across the world.

News of Vaccine Testing in UK of University: News of Human trials of an eagerly-awaited vaccine, being developed by the prestigious Oxford University against the novel corona virus began in the UK now, with scientists expecting an 80 per cent chance of success, has startled the world of humanity. The UK government has pledged 20 million pounds to support the "ChAdOx1 nCoV-19" corona virus vaccine experiment and subsequent trial programme. The UK Health

Secretary Matt Hancock said that the government would "throw everything at" finding a vaccine as early as possible to fight against the deadly virus.

He further said "After all, the upside of being the first country in the world to develop a successful vaccine is so huge that I am throwing everything at it,". The trialed of vaccine is made on a harmless chimpanzee virus that has been genetically engineered. Now the testing is to be tested on volunteers aged between 18 and 55 who are in good health. Volunteers in the UK are being offered 625 pounds to take part in the landmark research, with a target of 500 to be enrolled by the middle of next month. The Oxford vaccine project is headed by Professor Sarah Gilbert along with other human genetics scientists who started work on designing a corona virus vaccine in January of the year. Professor said further - "Our brilliant team has been working tirelessly to get to this point using our skills and experience in vaccine development and testing, and will do the best job possible in moving quickly whilst at all times prioritizing the safety of the trial participants,".

The first patients will receive a COVID-19 vaccine developed at the University of Oxford very soon said the UK government, the project being developed on an emergency basis spending £20m (around $25m). U.K. Health Secretary Matt Hancock said another £22.5m is being made available to a second vaccine project at Imperial College London to carry out phase 2 trials and trying urgently to prepare a larger phase 3 study. A vaccine is the "best way" to defeat the virus and bring the UK out of lockdown.

He also reiterated an advance commitment to provide financial support to build manufacturing capacity for corona virus vaccines, so that stocks can be built up quickly if they prove effective in clinical testing. Hancock during the briefing said-"Both of these promising projects are making rapid progress and I've told the scientists leading them we will do everything in our power to support them,".

A Corona Center of 'Super Spreader': It is now reported Corona-Virus Victims in many states of India and the majority people get victimized by Corona in Nizamuddin building, a six-storey building in South Delhi where a good number of people of different regions and different countries, some were from Malaysia and Indonesia attended the religious prayer being organized by the Tablighi Jamaat - a global Islamic evangelical movement of Indian origin known as the Markaz. A good number of people get locked up in the building being deprived of travel vehicles and travel permit due to sudden lock down throughout India making it a source of center of Corona what many call a center of 'Super Spreader', leaving a trail of infection and death from Kashmir to the Andamans.

Plasma treatment for Corona Virus: What is Plasma in Blood? Plasma is the liquid portion of blood. About 55% of our blood is plasma, and the remaining 45% are red blood cells, white blood cells and platelets that are suspended in the plasma. It also contains 7% vital proteins such as albumin, gamma globulin and anti-hemophilic factor, and 1% mineral salts, sugars, fats, hormones and vitamins. It helps to maintain blood pressure and supply critical proteins for blood clotting and immunity; it carries electrolytes such as sodium and potassium to our muscles and helps to maintain a proper pH balance in the body, which supports cell function.

Plasma is commonly given to trauma, patients, as well as people with severe liver disease. Now in Delhi hospital Doctors have found plasma treatment is giving positive result for Corona positive patients. Delhi Chief Minister has given an appeal to the people who were being recovered from Corona Virus to donate Plasma voluntarily to the patients who were fighting for life against Corona. It is surprising to record that out of 200 recovered corona victim related with Markaz 150 people of them has expressed their willingness to donate Plasma. That shows that the Indian Muslims who were devoted to the religion of Islam being affected in the Delhi Markaz because of unforeseen lockout are in no way less patriotic than any other Indians. Is it justified to blame India's Muslim community for Tablighi Jamaat gathering uttering Corona Muslim gathering for outbreak related with Nizamuddin? It is still the pain of partition based on religion gets reflected in every sphere of life. The division of country occurred during the period of Gandhi, the leader is no more in India but why not Indians do their best to forget the pain of partition. It is possible only by the reunion of the two countries.

At present on 16 May 2020, U.S. President Donald Trump had a change of heart and he is saying he hopes there will be a **COVID–19** vaccine by the end of the year while officially announcing a new effort to combat COVID-19. "Its **objective** is to finish developing and then to manufacture and distribute a proven corona virus vaccine as fast as possible. Again, Mr. Trump said at a press conference "we'd love to see if we could do it prior to the end of the year," Priority in the discovery of Vaccine is given when Mr. Trump said former head of vaccines at pharmacy company Glaxo-Smith-Kline, and heads the U.S. Army's Material Command would lead the vaccine development and distribution effort.

Mr. Trump said that roughly 100 vaccines undergoing testing around the world out of which 14 were considered promising which are at work. U.S. Congress believes an effort of 12-18 month framework for vaccines was optimistic. However, the President's times cable for vaccine production was echoed by Mr. Slaoui.

"I have very recently seen early data from a clinical trial with a corona virus vaccine. And this data made me feel even more confident that we will be able to deliver a few hundred million doses of vaccine by the end of 2020," Mr. Slaoui said.

Mr. Trump also said that the U.S. was working with other countries on developing the vaccine and with "no ego." In response to a request for a message to Indian Americans, Mr. Trump said India and the U.S. were working together and that many Indian Americans were working on the vaccine. "And we're working very much with India too. And we have a tremendous Indian population in the United States. And many of the people that you're talking about are working on the vaccine too, Great scientists and researchers," he said.

U.S. to donate ventilators to India: Mr. Trump told reporters he was sending ventilators to India. "I am proud to announce that the

United States will donate ventilators to our friends in India. We stand with India and @narendramodi during this pandemic. We're also cooperating on vaccine development. Together we will beat the invisible enemy!"

It is reported so far, COVID-19 has infected more than 4.5 million people across the world and caused 3,03,651 fatalities. At the same time, scientists and medical researchers are working tirelessly to develop potential treatments and vaccine for corona virus disease. Meanwhile, health experts remain cautious and are strictly advising everyone to stay indoors and practice social distancing.

The US-based Modern a Therapeutics said that it had received approval from the FDA (US Food and Drug Administration) to conduct the phase 2 clinical trials of COVID-19 vaccine candidate. INOVIO Pharmaceuticals is developing a DNA-based vaccine candidate in its San Diego lab.

US drug maker Pfizer has teamed up with a German company BNTECH to develop a vaccine for COVID-19. Both the companies are working together on four RNA vaccine candidates. A potential corona virus vaccine is being developed by the University of Oxford and trying hard to develop the Vaccine under three month's time.

India will begin clinical trials of its Bacille Calmette-Guérin (BCG) vaccine on 6000 high-risk individuals. Bharat Biotech International Ltd (BBIL) has teamed up with the Indian Council for Medical Research (ICMR) to develop a COVID-19 vaccine.

[15.1]

If the threat of corona Virus failed to bring peace in Assam or in Delhi so to say in India the alternative method is to form one territory of British India giving independence to administrative units to Bangladesh as well as to Pakistan and by the elimination of the line of boarders as if British India is formed - one nation one country. This is possible to achieve either by

(i) Negotiation or by

(ii) The application of indirect force.

The country India was divided based on religion mainly sorted out by Petal, Nehru and Gandhi of Congress and Jinnah of Pakistan considering power, name and fame of few persons and neglecting the sufferings of the people. The leaders never thought it necessary to take the consent of the people by any kind of referendum. The temptation of power hungry leaders was how quickly to get the work done and how quickly to occupy the power of chair as the British was willing to hand over the administration to Indians even after winning the Second World War, although the hidden fear being lied in somewhere else, the fear of surrendered Netaji Force along with the British Indian Force being sympathized with the Netaji Force. And the temptation of power hungry SAINT, the cleverest politician Gandhi, ever born in India was hiding behind the international name and fame for the discovery of a new weapon of human being, a force of "Non-Violence" forgetting the virtue of humanity even in asking the most reliable few co-workers, or political friends such as Khan

Abdul Gaffer Khan who was the life partner of Gandhi in political fight against the British and not the question of the sufferings of the common ordinary people.

If direct negotiation gets failed, the use of direct force of violence would be the alternative means to bring unity and permanent peace in the Indian sub-continent. If Pakistan can send all the Hindus and Sikhs by force of violence to India, India also can send all the Muslims of India by force of violence to Pakistan when Pakistan would be compelled to come to the negotiating table to discuss the terms of equality with India. Similarly the present Bangladesh would be compelled to come to the negotiating table to find out the terms of equality with India on seeing all the Muslims of Bengal and Assam are going to proceed to Bangladesh as per the condition of partition of India, a division based on "Religion" when real peace would be prevailed in the Indian sub-continent.

The real peace in Assam would be prevailed only when Assam would be freed from all immigrants' and the peace in other regions of India would be prevailed when people could move to any region of his or her choice as was existed in the British India. If so, the leaders of India could boldly claim that Hindu Rulers of present India are in no way less than the earlier Muslim or the British Rulers. The example set by the earlier Muslims Rulers as well as by the British Ruler had shown how to establish absolute administration for a nation, Muslims did it by evicting the Hindus and the British did it by evicting the Muslims, now the time has come for Hindus of India to show how to set up administration of Unity and Equality and how to bring permanent peace in the region. The Muslims were the rulers, even with 10% supporting population; achieved a separate home land for the Muslims of India against the formation of Gandhi's Ram-Raja having with 90% supporting people.

But the formation of Pakistan did not brought peace in the minds of the leaders of Pakistan as their pleasure of happiness were not lied like the pleasure of Indian leaders with the power of chair only rather their mind was worried with the thought of the future safety of the Muslims remained in India. It was seen by Jinnah during his life time how at the time of partition in Punjab, the Muslims of Punjab and Delhi have been compelled to quit India in no time and how the Hindus and Sikhs have been expelled from Punjab and West Pakistan. The thinking of the future of the Indian Muslims made him sick and that was the reason why during the time of lying in the death bed he said the greatest blunder what he had done was nothing but the division of India and the formation of Pakistan.

The future thinking of Muslim was not less in the mind of Muslim Leader Liquate Ali Khan, the then P.M. of Pakistan although Pakistan was formed only with few Muslims but the greater part of Muslims had remained in India. He was restless after the formation of Pakistan and the eviction of Hindus particularly from East Pakistan. Truly, he was the real pioneer in the eviction of most of the Hindus from East Pakistan to India. Rather he was compelled to do so in all the seventeen districts of East Pakistan simultaneously in the month of January and February of 1950 taking the help of Punjabi and Baluchi Pakistani Army in civil dresses along with religious Mullahs of Bengal to teach a lesson to the Indian leaders for the affairs of Kashmir. The eviction was carried out in a plan strategy in all the seventeen districts of Bengal simultaneously. The process was to carry out the burning of houses in all the places in the darkness of night and taken out the materials in the day time. The lacking of safety and security had compelled all the Hindu inhabitants to leave their houses and proceed towards India crossing the border without rest.

West Bengal including Assam and the South Eastern regions of India were flooded with millions and millions of Hindu people and he was worried in thinking with the opposite reaction in which millions of Muslims were likely to be evicted from the Indian part of West Bengal, Assam and other adjacent regions. But by the sudden call of Nehru from Calcutta as the Indian P.M Nehru was summoned by the Bengal Chief Minister B.C.Roy to come to Calcutta immediately from Delhi to see the condition of Bengal, where on looking the horrible situation Nehru immediately call upon Liquate Ali Khan as he happened to be an old friend of Nehru at London during the study period of the graduation of law. Finding the opportunity he fixed a date and came to Delhi and settles the issue in the name of Nehru-Liquate Ali Pact of 1950 and thereby he could stabilize the security of the Muslims in India permanently. Thus once again a Muslim leader has proved beyond doubt that he was a Ruler, he knows how to create Pakistan absolutely for the Muslims of India and again how to stabiles the security of the Muslims in India that left off in India permanently.

Another glowing example is in front. It was finally decided among the leaders of the country that partition of India and the formation of Pakistan was the only solution for the peace of the nation. The British Governor Mount batten called the surveyor Radcliffe from London to India to sort out the line of demarcation of India Pakistan. The surveyor Radcliffe came to India first time as such he wanted one year time to visit the different places of India to give the correct picture of the line of borders of the division of Bengal and Punjab. But the Governor Mountbatten wanted to complete the task within a specific time period. Accordingly he said Radcliffe that he wanted the survey Report within 37 days and he said further that consider it as the order of the British Viceroy. It was because the Governor had fixed the days 14 August 1947, the day of the declaration of Pakistan which is only 37 days away.

Accordingly, without going to the actual place he did it seating in a room in the city of Calcutta taking the help of two Muslim advocates and two Hindu advocates. He had little idea about Chittagong Hill tracks and Chittagong district. A Chittagong Hill track is a region inhabited by 98% Buddhist considered as the place of Hindus while Chittagong district is a region of Muslim majority people. By mistake Radcliffe had enlisted Chittagong Hill tracks along with Chittagong district and included the whole region in Pakistan. The mistake could not be rectified before the 14 August 1947 for short of time although the matter had been brought into light to Governor Mountbatten and it remains as such under Pakistan.

Now after the formation of two nations, Chittagong Hill tracks, a Hindu region remains under Pakistan and Kashmir, a Muslim region remains under India for a longer period of time. By the time of long length of Pakistani administration the problem of Chittagong Hill tracks had been solved gradually and today there is no problem in Chittagong Hill Track, it is a peaceful area under East Pakistan and now under Bangladesh but Kashmir still today remained a hot spot, a center of violence and a topic of dispute. Who had shown the maturity of administration - a Muslim leader of Pakistan or a Hindu leader of India?

[15.2]

What is the Right Time: Now it is time for India and Indian people to forget Gandhi, the falsehood of "Non-Violence" and also to forget the damage done by Gandhi to India by bringing religion in Indian politics what was once rightly predicted by Jinnah, the religious politics of Gandhi was nothing but the signal of the danger of bloodshed in Indian politics and he then resigned from the Congress when Gandhi was mad to enhance his image by supporting the religious Movement of Khilafat, the origin of which was in Turkey. Now the people of India do not want to preserve any more the falsehood of Gandhi's "Non-Violence" and no more religion but want unity of the people and a unity for the cause of progress and prosperity. It is useless to deal with CAA or NRC to bring more unrest and chaos in India like that of Gandhi's "Non-Violence". Now it is the time for Hindu Leaders of India to exhibit, how to make the country, a country of super-power by the establishment of one country, one nation forgetting Gandhi's theory of "Non-Violence" in the process of the creation of Hindu-Muslim Unity through Gandhi's arranged marriage of "Non-Violence & Khilafat" finally resulting in the formation of militant Muslim League.

Let us analysis the contribution of religion. What are the contributions of the religions for the betterment of mankind? Hindu religion is the oldest religions of the universe. By the analysis of 21 century, it is observed that the Hindu religion is the most unorganized religion without any future strategy. At the beginning, it was only the Hindu religion existed in the Indian sub-continent. But it was observed a reign of fighting among the same Royal family bringing the end of Kingship with the creation of Hindu epics of Mahabharata. There was no development of mankind except the creation of bitterness among the mankind through Brahmans non-Brahmins or Dalit and subsequently the creation of few Hindu Rulers where the name of Asoka in the period of 300 AD in some way is worth mentioning. But he too left the Rule of administration and switches over to the ethics of "Ashingsha" of Buddha.

Looking the devastation of Hindu Kings as described in the Hindu epics of Mahabharata, Buddha, a philosopher, a spiritual teacher, and religious leader who lived in ancient India by the gift of God and had suggested the Rule of Administration through "Ashingsha".In the course of time what was seen the Rule of Administration through "Ashingsha" could not survive in front of the strength of the Rule of Administration of Islam. In the 20 century Gandhi also failed to exert the Rule of Administration through "Ashingsha" in the form of "Non-Violence in front of Islam, where 10% followers of Islam by dint of the strength of Islam (a Muslim religion) snatch away Pakistan from 90% of Indian followers of Hindu ethics of "Ahingsha" or "Non-Violence". Thus it is undoubtedly proved beyond doubt that the strength of Islam by virtue of its strength of violence is superior to the strength of Hindu religion by virtue of its strength of "Ahingsha" or "Non-Violence". As the gift of Islam what is nothing but "strength" is beneficial for the creation of trade and for the creation of a country is now required to be followed for the creation of a new India, a British India of one nation one country.

[15.3]

Teachings of Islam: It is a fact established by the Rule of Islam as well as by the Rule of British that a country is formed based on the strength of trade for economy and based on the strength of the Rule of Administration. Islam entered India through trade and established its strength of power and later created Pakistan by the strength of violence. Again the British make its foothold in India through the trade of East India Company and established its strength by the establishment of British administration in Bengal by the defeat of Nawab of Bengal Siraj-ud-ulla. Let us analysis how Islam emerging late in the 6 century but expanded rapidly first in the Arab country, Turkey and then in India and also in other European countries.

Many put forwarded the theory of reasons for the large concentration of Muslims in India because of the silent invasions of India by Arab and Persian Muslims. But other theories said that Arab traders were in contact with India since long before the life of Prophet Muhammad in the 600s. Arab Merchants used to visit India preferably the west coast of India to trade goods and sell different items like spices, gold, and African goods. The first mosque of India, the Cheraman Juma Masjid, was built in 629 during the period of Prophet Muhammad in Kerala. Thus the spread of Islam continued in the coastal Indian cities and towns, both through immigration and conversion. Expansion of Islam in Sind happened when the Muslim hero, Muhammad bin Qasim landed in India around the Indus River in the North-western part of the subcontinent, present-day Pakistan. He led an army of 6000 soldiers and encountered little resistance as he made his way into India when the Indians preaching "Ahingsha". Rather bin-Qasim was welcomed into the city by the Buddhist monks that controlled that area. Most cities along the Indus valley thus voluntarily came under Muslim control, without any fighting. In some cases, few oppressed Buddhist minorities reached out to the Muslim armies for protection against Hindu governors. Despite the little resistant of the Raja of Sindh, being stood against the Muslim expansion, Muhammad bin Qasim came out victorious. Thereby all of Sindh came under Muslim control at ease.

After the victory of the Muslims, there was peace in the area as the maintenance of peace was promised by bin-Qasim. There was no change in day-to-day life as Muhammad bin Qasim promised security and religious freedom to all Hindus and Buddhists under his control. The Hindu Brahmins were used in the job of tax collection and Buddhists monks were free to enjoy freedom to maintain their monasteries. Due to the existence of religious tolerance and justice, many people of the cities regularly greeted the victorious Qasim and his armies with the display of dance and music. Since then the Muslim armies continued to penetrate India, leaders such as Mahmud of Ghazni and Muhammad Tughluq expanded Muslim domains in India without altering the religious or social fabric of Indian society. The early history of India was entirely based on a caste system in which society was broken into several separate parts. It helps to spread Islam through easy conversion. Sometimes the entire castes get converted to Islam at a time. The equality in Islam had provided more attraction to Islam than the divided Hindu caste system. By converting to Islam, people had the opportunity to move forward in society, and no longer were they compelled to be submissive to the Brahman caste.

The Arab Muslims continued their entry into India more extensively since 711. They conquered the area known as Sind in the Indus River valley, which is nothing but the modern Pakistan. It is hard to imagine two religions and two civilizations Islam and Hinduism so different in their outlooks but still exists side by side though not always peacefully, since the Arabs arrived until the present day. Islam saw all people as equal before God, but India's rigid caste system presented a highly stratified social structure sanctioned by Hinduism of Hindu religion indirectly certifying that all people are not equal. Again Hinduism was incredibly tolerant of a multitude of gods, while Islam was strictly monotheistic.

Arab expansion was tried to stop time to time by various feudal Indian princes known as the Rajputs, but the warfare could not stop the Muslim advance across Northern India. Arab's tolerant rule won many converts to Islam in that region which means the Muslim of the day. This provided a solid base for further Muslim expansion into India. Although the Arabs only conquered the north-western part of

India, their tolerant rule won many converts to Islam in that region which remains the Muslim to this day. This provided a solid base for further Muslim expansion into India.

In summary, Islam is the second-largest religion in India, with roughly 15% of the country's population. It makes India a country with the largest Muslim population outside Muslim-majority countries. Based on trade and business, the religion started to arrive at the western coast of India in the 7th century CE in the Malabar Coast and 11 century in coastal Gujarat, and again in the 12 century in the North from the Arab Land. Over the centuries, there has been significant integration of Hindu - Muslim cultures across India and Muslims have played a notable role in economics, politics, and culture of India.

Buddhism, which was once very much popular in the subcontinent, slowly died down under Muslim rule. Though Muslim Force was powerful yet no evidence exists that shows forced conversions or violence against the Buddhists. Unlike Hindu traditions of casteism, Muslim scholars traveled throughout India, making it their goal to educate people about Islam. Many of them preached Sufi ideas that appealed to the people to change to Islam. In most cases, Muslim leaders replaced Hindu kings yet there was little evidence of violence and forced conversion. Indian leaders Gandhi, in particular, agreed to divide India based on religion were completely false and ill-motivated for self-exploration. Hindu and Muslim were a joint force of unity like that of Black and White of the USA. To-day America is a Super-power but India-Pakistan a divided nation surviving with begging bowel and fighting for right of existence. The greatest destroyer of the nation was no other than Gandhi; his ethics of "Non-Violence" that had created a Hindu Force of "non-Violence" and a Muslim Force of "Violence".

A Pattern of development: Since the period of 1000 years following the entry of the Arab Muslims into India, a basic pattern of development had emerged in India. Muslims had entered North-western India with a strong economic structure based on trade and also expanded to the south as well as to the east. Then another group of Muslims followed the same process to stabilize their existence as a trade partner. The Hindu Indian Kings never think for the people by the expansion of any kind of trade for economic growth but engaged the people in the prayer to God in Temple being constructed inside deep jungles here and there to get the blessings of Al-mighty. On the other hand the Muslims getting the teachings of Islam engaged themselves in the service of mankind by the growth of economy through the expansion of trade and by the expansion of Muslim territory by the god gifted virtue of strength. This pattern of utilization of strength repeated itself in three successive stages: the Arabs in the eighth century, Turkish started around 1000 C.E., and then the Mughal dynasty that entered India in 1526.

[15.4]

Growth of Islam in India: It is the second-largest religion in India with 14.2% of the country's population. It makes India the country with the largest Muslim population outside Muslim-majority countries. Islam in India existed in communities along the Arab coastal trade routes in Bengal, Gujarat, and Kerala as soon as the religion originated and had gained early acceptance in the Arabian Peninsula. The first incursion through sea occurred since 629 in Southern India. The Cheraman Juma Mosque was built up in Thrissur District in the Indian state of Kerala. The seafaring Arab Merchants built three mosques in Tamil Nadu. The Delhi Sultanate and the Mughal Empire have ruled most of the South Asia having being the Bengal Sultanate, the Deccan sultanates have played major economic and political roles in India. The introduction of further Islamic policies by Mysore King Tipu Sultan contributed to the South Indian culture. Over the centuries, there has been significant integration of Hindu and Muslim cultures across India and Muslims have played a notable role in economics, politics, and culture of India.

Muhammad bin Qasim (672 CE) at the age of 17 was the first Muslim general to invade the Indian subcontinent, managing to reach Sindh. In 1206 Islamic Delhi Sultanate control much of Northeren India.

Under the Delhi Sultanate, there was a synthesis of Indian civilization with that of Islamic civilization. So to say, the **Delhi Sultanate** was an Islamic empire based in Delhi that stretched over large parts of the Indian subcontinent for 320 years (1206–1526), extending a period of five dynasties ruled over Delhi. The sultanate reached to the peak of its expansion in the period of Tughlaq dynasty, occupying most of the Indian subcontinent. But a little decline happened due to Hindu reconquests of states such as the Vijayanagara Empire. In 1526, the Sultanate was conquered and succeeded by the Mughal Empire.

Economic policy and administration: The economic policy of the Delhi Sultanate was how to increase economy by the greater government involvement. They fixed penalties and increased penalties for private businesses that broke government regulations. Alauddin Khalji replaced the private markets with four centralized government-run markets, appointing "market controller". The main purpose was how to collect more revenue. The bulk of Delhi Sultanate's army consisted of nomadic **Turkic Mamluk** military slaves, who were skilled in nomadic **cavalry** warfare as such they were powerful in the application of the Rule of administration.

The Muslim Rulers have learned from their religion how to apply the gift of strength given by Allah in the expansion of economy for a better life and in the expansion of Muslim Rule of administration. As such they thought it wise to wipe out the non-Muslims for the future safety. Ghiyasud din Balban wiped out approximately 100,000 people, Alauddin Khaljikilled 30,000 people at Chittor and also in many in other places. The Tughlaq dynasty enjoyed the period of 1321-1330 AD as the Ruler of Delhi Sultanate. Muhammad bin Tughlaq ruled for 26 years. During his rule, Delhi Sultanate reached to its peak in terms of geographical reach, covering most of the Indian subcontinent. Muhammad bin Tughlaq ordered the transfer of his capital from Delhi to Devagiri in modern-day Maharashtra (renaming it to Daulatabad), by forcing the mass migration of Delhi's population. The capital move failed because Daulatabad was arid and did not have enough drinking water to support the new capital. The capital then returned to Delhi.

Revolts against Muhammad bin Tughlaq began in 1327. In 1338 his own nephew rebelled in Malwa, whom he attacked, caught, and flayed alive. By 1339, the eastern regions under local Muslim governors and southern parts under Hindu kings both had revolted against Delhi Sultanate Tughlaq but Muhammad bin Tughlaq did not have the resources or support to respond to the revolt. Muhammad bin Tughlaq died in 1351 He was succeeded by Firuz Shah Tughlaq (1351–1388), who ruled for 37 years. Firuz Shah Tughlaq also followed the same principle of jizya taxes. He raised taxes and jizya taxes form Hindus. The death of Firuz Shah Tughlaq created anarchy and disintegration of the Sultan kingdom. At lastly Timur arrived in India as Ruler of Delhi. He looted the lands with his army, plundered and burnt Delhi. His army carried out massacre and then returned to Samarkand. Nasir ud-Din Mahmud Shah Tughlaq, who had fled to Gujarat during Timur's invasion, returned and nominally ruled as the last ruler of Tughlaq dynasty. The period 1415 -1451 Delhi was ruled by Sayyid dynasty and then by Lody dynasty. Babur defeated and killed Ibrahim Lodi in the Battle of Panipat in 1526. The death of Ibrahim Lodi ended the Delhi Sultanate, and the Mughal Empire started its journey.

Desecration of temples, universities and libraries: Historian Richard Eaton has tabulated a campaign of destruction of idols and temples by Delhi Sultans. In his writing, he has listed 37 instances of **Hindu temples** being desecrated or destroyed in India during the Delhi Sultanate, during the period of 1234 to 1518. This was the policy of administration how to convert more Hindus to Muslims. He notes that this was not unusual in medieval India, as there were numerous recorded instances of temple desecration by **Hindu** and **Buddhist** kings against rival Indian kingdoms between 642 and 1520, involving conflict between devotees of different Hindu deities, as well as between Hindus, Buddhists and **Jains**. He also noted there were also many instances of Delhi sultans, who often had Hindu ministers, ordering the protection, maintenance and repairing of temples, according to both Muslim and Hindu sources. For example, Sultan **Muhammad bin Tughluq** also repaired a Siva temple in

Bidar after his **Deccan** conquest. There was often a pattern of Delhi sultans plundering or damaging temples during conquest, and then patronizing or repairing temples after conquest. This was the clever policy of administration. This pattern came to an end with the **Mughal Empire**, where **Akbar the Great's** chief minister **Abu'l-Fazl** criticized the excesses of earlier sultans such as **Mahmud of Ghazni**.

The campaign of temple desecration expanded later to different places of India. It is extended to Bihar, Madhya Pradesh, Gujarat and Maharashtra, and continued through the late 13th century. It also extended to Telangana, Andhra Pradesh, Karnataka and Tamil Nadu under Malik Kafur and Ulugh Khan in the 14th century and by the Bahmanis in 15th century. Even then the Muslim Rulers could not convert India in totality to Muslims. The successful Muslim conquerors retained their Islamic identity and created new legal and administrative systems although the non-Muslim population was left to their own laws and customs. Moreover they introduced new cultural systems. This led to the rise of a new mixed Indian culture different from ancient Indian culture.

During the period of the Delhi Sultanate, there was a synthesis of Indian civilization with that of Islamic civilization, and the integration of the Indian subcontinent with a growing world system. Thereby it had brought a significant impact on Indian culture and society, as well as over the wider world. During the rule of Sultanate, a reform took place which included the earliest forms of Indo-Islamic architecture, greater use of mechanical technology, increased growth rates in India's population and economy, and the emergence of the Hindi-Urdu language. Since 1526 onwards, the influence of the Sultanate was destroyed by the Mughal Empire.

The failure of Hindu Rulers: The failure of the Hindus and Hindu Kings was exposed for a long period of time. India belongs to Hindus right from the beginning as because it was only the Hindu religion was prevailing in India but the Rulers failed to protect its country and its religion. The reason was the Rulers were not sincere in their administration how to protect the land and how to do something for the betterment of the people. Most of the Kings in the different regions of scattered India remained busy with the well beings of the Royal family. However they constructed several Mandir and temples and diverted the attention of the people towards prayer as the Muslims in Arab land are sending the Muslims in Mosques for prayers after the discovery of Islam. But the Hindu Kings of India could not see how the Muslims of Arab expanding their economy by trade and expanding the Muslim Regions by using the gift of strength given by Allah being noted in the holy book of Quran how to use it for the protection and expansion of Islam. The Hindu Rajput Rulers were scattered and never thought of unity and the creation of an integrated force. Whereas Ala ud-Din Khalji in 1298, his ancestors being migrated to India from Arab Land modified his administrative set up how to acquire more revenue not for the luxury but for building a strong military force for the safety and protection of his region because he knows the Muslim population in the region is less in number in compare to Hindus. The same was followed by Muhammad bin Tughlaq starting with 1325 for a long period.

According to Hindu Religion under Lord Krishna killing of people for the cause of the legal right of the administration was not an inhuman work, (noted in Mahabharata asking Arjun to fight for right) similarly according to Islam, killing of people for the cause of the expansion of Muslim Religion in order to set up a better life style with a better economy with trade was also not an offence. In order to do that time to time the Muslim Rulers never hesitated to kill Hindu people and compel them by the destruction of idols and temples to get converted to Muslim by taking Islam. But the Hindu Rulers in spite of their supporters in large numbers could not get united to give a befitting reply.

[15.5]

The Mughal Dynasty (1526-1700 CE): The Mughal Emperor was founded by Babur, an Afghan leader claiming a descent of

Genghis Khan. By virtue of his mental strength and the strength of the combination of firearms, artillery, and nomadic cavalry, he was succeeded to win over the Sultan of Delhi having being equipped with a much larger army at the battle of Panipat in 1526 and later also he defeated a larger army of Rajputs. Before his death in 1530, Babur had established a Rule of Mughal in India.

The greatest of the Mughal rulers was Akbar the Great (1526-1605). Coming to the throne at the age of thirteen, he soon succeeded to crush any revolts and also expanded Mughal power into the Deccan Region. Like the Rulers of Sultan he also applied the gift of strength given by the Al-mighty Allah but in addition to that he also tried to apply the love of humanity and equality of mankind. To control the rebel forces of Rajputs, he made friendship with them, using them as his officers and government officials and even he agreed to marry Hindu princesses. To satisfy both the Hindus and the Muslims, he even tried to modify the religion, and transforming it into a new religion Din Ilahi. He was in favor of equal justice and prosperity for his subjects irrespective of Hindus and Muslims.

After the end of the ruling of Akbar, India had been ruled by three successors, Jahangir (1605-27), Shah Jahan (1628-58), and Aurangzeb (1658-1707), that was still in order to keep the trend of expanding Islam under Mughal monarchy. During this time, India experienced another flourishing development in the matter of the arts and fashion due to the fusion of Persian and Hindu styles. The art of architecture especially reflected Muslim influence as seen in the Taj Mahal, a mausoleum for Shah Jahan's wife what was considered still today as one of the world's most beautiful buildings.

Decline of the Mughals: It was during the reign of Aurangzeb that he followed a policy, just a reversal of the traditional Mughal policy of tolerance. He began to the persecution of Hindus that led the Mughal Empire to the extreme downfall. The Empire went into rapid decline after Aurangzeb's death in 1707, when a new people with a new culture, the British, had taken over the Empire.

The resulting Mughal Empire did not stamp out the local societies it came to rule, but rather balanced and pacified them through new administrative practices with diverse and inclusive ruling elites, leading to more systematic, centralized, and uniform rule. Eschewing Islamic identity, especially under Akbar, the Mughals united all through a Persianised culture of divine status.

In the 18th century, Mughal power had been severely curtailed by the Marathas who had routed Mughal armies and invaded several Mughal provinces from the Punjab to Bengal. By this time, the dominant economic powers in the Indian subcontinent were rested in Bengal Subah under the Nawabs of Bengal. And also to some extent the economic progress depended on the South Indian Kingdom of Mysore under Hyder Ali and Tipu Sultan. The economic progress was vastly devastated by the Maratha invasions over Bengal.

Finding the weakness of the Mughal Emperor, the British East India Company conquered Bengal in 1757 and then Mysore in the late 18th century. The last Mughal emperor, Bahadur Shah II, had authority over only the city of Shahjahanabad, before he was exiled to Burma by the British Raj after the Indian Rebellion of 1857. The contribution of Muslim revolutionaries is also documented in the history of India's struggle for independence. There were many Muslims such as Abul Kalam Azad, Hakim Ajmal Khan and Rafi Ahmed Kidwai and other Muslims who were engaged in revolt against the British Raj.

Khan Abdul Gaffar Khan (popularly known as "Frontier Gandhi") was a noted nationalist who spent 45 of his 95 years of life in jail; Barakatullah of Bhopal was one of the founders of the Ghadar Party, which created a network of anti-British organizations; Syed Rahmat Shah of the Ghadar Party worked as an underground revolutionary in France and was hanged for his part in the unsuccessful Ghadar Mutiny in 1915; Vakkom Abdul Khadir of Kerala participated in the "Quit India" struggle in 1942 and was hanged; Umar Subhani, an industrialist and millionaire from Bombay, provided Mahatma Gandhi his resources for Congress expenses and ultimately he died for the cause of independence. Among Muslim women, Hazrat

Mahal, Asghari Begum, and Bi Amma contributed in the struggle for independence from the British.

Maulana Azad was a prominent leader of the Indian independence movement and a strong advocate of Hindu-Muslim unity. He held discussions several times with Sardar Patel and Mahatma Gandhi in the period of 1940. Other famous Muslims who fought for independence against British rule were Abul Kalam Azad, Mahmud al-Hasan of DarulUloom Deoband, who was implicated in the famous Silk Letter Movement to overthrow the British through an armed struggle, Husain Ahmad Madani, Hakim Ajmal Khan, Professor Maulavi Barkatullah, Zakir Husain, Khan Abdul Gaffar Khan, Rafi Ahmed Kidwai, Fakhruddin Ali Ahmed, and many others.

Until 1920, Muhammad Ali Jinnah, later the founder of Pakistan, was a member of the Indian National Congress and was part of the independence struggle. Muhammad Iqbal, poet and philosopher, was a strong proponent of Hindu–Muslim unity and an undivided India, perhaps until 1930. Huseyn Shaheed Suhrawardy was also active member in the Indian National Congress in Bengal, during his early political career. Mohammad Ali Jouhar and Shaukat Ali struggled for the emancipation of the Muslims in the overall Indian context, and struggled for independence alongside Mahatma Gandhi and Abdul Bari of Firangi Mahal. Until the 1930s, the Muslims of India broadly conducted their politics alongside their countrymen, in the overall context of an undivided India.

The Partition of British India was based on religion; the heart breaking proposal was accepted and divided India into several regions. This led to the creation of the sovereign states of the Dominion of Pakistan (that later split into the Islamic Republic of Pakistan and the People's Republic of Bangladesh) and the Union of India (later Republic of India). The Indian Independence Act 1947 had decided 15 August 1947, as the appointed date for the partition. However, Pakistan celebrates its day of creation on 14 August.

The partition of India was set forth in the Indian Independence Act 1947 and resulted in the end of the British Raj. It resulted in a struggle between the newly constituted states of India and Pakistan and displaced up to 12.5 million people with loss of life varying from several hundred thousand to a million. The violent nature of the partition created an atmosphere of mutual hostility and suspicion between India and Pakistan that could not be imagined by the then great leaders of India, and the great Gandhi was an exception.

Khan Abdul Ghaffar Khan, also known as Frontier Gandhi, who was with Gandhi in 1930, Khan led the non-violent opposition against the British Raj and strongly opposed the partition of India but he was left out at the very vital meeting in accepting the agreement of partition. The partition included a part of division of the Bengal province East Bengal, which became a part of the Dominion of Pakistan. And West Bengal, the other part of Bengal became a part of India. Similarly the partition of the Punjab province became West Punjab, a part of Pakistan and East Punjab remain as a part of India. The saddest part also include the partition agreement involving the division of Indian government assets, including the Indian Civil Service, the Indian Army, the Royal Indian Navy, the Indian railways and the central treasury, and other administrative services. The most popular leader was M K Gandhi among the Hindus and also among the Muslims because of his skill of selfish exploration only for name and fame as an extra-ordinary person of international image but the country was divided in his presence and even taking his consent. Let us see Gandhi and his family and the contribution of real Gandhi family in the independence of India.

The Family of M.K. Gandhi: The Indian people know Mohandas Karamchand Gandhi who was once the most popular leader of India, thought for the people of India and also for the nation of India. He is now the Father of the nation. He had given his acceptance in favor of partition for the good of nation. But in the course of time people could know that he was thinking more for Nehru family than the family of the country people. Now the people often mistaken Nehru family is the Gandhi family. It was because of the change of Title of Indira Gandhi after her marriage from Indira Khan to Indira Gandhi as because M K Gandhi had donated his title to Feruj Khan, the husband of Indira Nehru. Hence forth Nehru family has been transformed into the name of Gandhi family. But M K Gandhi had his own family. It is not worthy if the Indian people do not know the real family of Gandhi. After all Gandhi is the Father of the nation of India.

The father of M K Gandhi was Karamchand Gandhi who married four times. His first three marriages ended with the deaths of his wives; among which two died immediately after giving birth to two daughters. He later married Putlibai Gandhi in 1859, and their marriage lasted till his death in 1885. This marriage produced four children - three sons and one daughter. Mahatma Gandhi was his youngest son. All his children got married during his lifetime.

The life of Mohandas began as such. In May 1883, the 13-year-old Mohandas was married to 14-year-old Kasturbai Makhanji Kapadia. In late 1885, Gandhi's father Karamchand died. When Gandhi was 16 years old, and his wife of age 17 had their first baby, who survived only a few days. The Gandhi couple had four more children, all sons: Harilal, born in 1888; Manilal, born in 1892; Ramdas, born in 1897; and Devdas, born in 1900.

In June 1935, Mahatma Gandhi wrote a letter to his eldest son Harilal, accusing him of "alcohol and debauchery". In the letters, Mahatma Gandhi stated that Harilal's problems were more difficult for him to deal with than the struggle for an Indian republic. **(ref-1).** In 2014 three letters were written by Mahatma Gandhi to Harilal in 1935 a translation of one of the letters was in Gujarati suggesting that Gandhi was accusing Harilal of raping either his own daughter, Manu, or his sister-in-law.**(ref3).**

Reference:

1. "Gandhi three autograph letters signed to his son". *Mullock's Auctions.* Retrieved 19 September *2016.*

2. *Sinha, Kounteya (22 May 2014).* "Gandhi's letters accusing son of raping grand daughter find no buyer". *Times of India.* Retrieved 3 April *2019.*

3. Jump up to:**a b** "Lost in translation, says Mahatma kin". *Telegraph of India. 15 May2014*. Retrieved 3 April *2019*.

Harilal Mohandas Gandhi was the eldest son of Mahatma Gandhi. In 1906 Harilal married Gulab Gandhi without informing father, with whom he had five children. In 1911, he severed all ties with his family in South Africas and returned to India. Gulab died in 1918 due to influenza. Harilal became detached from his children. Eventually, a disgruntled Harilal snapped all ties with his family. He went back to his old practices, embezzling, stealing, and soliciting prostitution in public places, and was arrested several times. In the late 1930s or early 1940s, Harilal embraced Islam and adopted the name Abdulla Gandhi. It is said that he did this because the Muslim leaders had promised to settle his debts. The leaders of the Pakistan Movement took him all across the country dressed in Muslim attire. But when his mother pleaded, he became a Hindu again with the help of Arya Samaj. When India became independent in 1947, Harilal was living like a beggar in the streets.

Gandhi was assassinated on January 30, 1948. He came to his father's final rites but few could recognize him. Gandhi's funeral was marked by millions of Indians. Gandhi's death was mourned nationwide. Over a million people joined the five-mile long funeral procession that took over five hours to reach Raj Ghat from Birla house, where he was assassinated. At his father's funeral, he was recognized by only a few people due to his derelict appearance. Devastated, alone, and a destitute, he himself passed away four months later.

The family history of Gandhi brings a big question in front of Indian people that M K Gandhi who was so honored in India and abroad failed to control his own son, how could he control the whole country. However, he controlled Nehru family as such Nehru family became known as the Gandhi family. He failed to control all the leaders with diverse views bringing the division of the country. The big question is when Gandhi failed to be a befitting father of a family, how the country people had accepted him as the Father of the nation.

There are other incidents the analysis of which never supports Gandhi was the right person to be accepted as the FATHER of the nation apart from the damage he had done to the country. Gandhi had fought the British, non-violently, for an independent and united India. In the end, he achieved independence but not unity. The British finally gave up the subcontinent in August 1947, they partitioned it, and Gandhi accepted it without any protest. Pakistan was explicitly created as a homeland for Muslims. But, owing to Gandhi's efforts, India itself was established as a nondenominational state, the new constitution forbade discrimination on religious grounds; the Muslims who remained were to be treated as equal citizens. Thus he agreed to grant right to Muslims and he denied giving the equal right to Hindus but instead he increased his image as a super-human being at the cost of Hindus.

But the people of other countries did not recognize his ill treatment. A statue of Mahatma Gandhi has been installed in the university campus in Ghana's capital, Accra in honor of his work as a young man he lived and worked in South Africa. In his early writings he referred the black South Africans as "kaffirs" - a highly offensive racist slur. Gandhi granted the Muslims a Pakistan but denied the Hindus the Hindustan, people of India accepted it as blessings but the law student of Ghana never accepted the racist slur of Gandhi and they demolished the statue of Mahatma Gandhi from the University Campus.

Gandhi's thought and ideas can best be understood in the background of Gandhi politics. Essentially Gandhi politics and his concepts gave a false dream to millions of Indians calling for non-violence against the industrial exploitation of British imperialism so as to create a Ramrajya. Gandhi's politics was to increase his popularity by the coalition of Khilafat Movement with Non-cooperation movement. Many people thought that the coalition of Gandhi with Ali brothers was the great mistake which had diverted the strength of Indian movement towards the happenings of Turkey. Others mostly thought as per Hindutva ideologists it was a sign of Gnadhi's leaning towards Muslims.

But on 5 February 1922 when non-cooperation was withdrawn by Gandhi at a time when the whole nation was full of energy and motivation and British government was paralyzed. Gandhi thought otherwise to give benefit to British Government so as to continue the movement for a long time only when his image would be increased. With the same spirit of thought he supported the hanging of Bhagat Singh by Gandhi-Irwin Pact. His personal image was more important than the love and affection of the country people. This can be seen in the protest of Gandhi in Karachi (during Karachi Session 1931 of INC) by the demonstrators crying slogans:"Gandhi Go Back!","Gandhi's truce has sent Bhagat Singh to the gallows", "Down with Gandhi" and "Long live Bhagat Singh". Those who loved Bhagat Singh and other revolutionaries started hating Gandhi.

Rivalry with Subhas Chandra Bose was also no exception. Subhas Chandra Bose became President of INC in 1938 and again in 1939 beating the candidate (Pattabhi Sitramaiyya) endorsed by Gandhi. But the members in the Congress Working Committee were Gandhi's supporting boy, so Gandhi made it impossible for Subhas to work as President and forced him to leave the Party.

The assumption that RSS hate Gandhi is entirely wrong. RSS considered Gandhi as a Hindu icon. It is also important to note that, Gandhi stood for all the Hindu ideals such as Ram rajya, Gita's importance, Hind swaraj, against cow slaughter etc, so how can a Hindu organization hate him. Clever Gandhi also played politics with Jinnah. It is believed that initially Ali Jinnah was Gandhi's boy and he was assured big position in the Congress and in the Government of Independent India. But later Jinnah found that he was betrayed by Gandhi and the same assurance has been given also to Nehru as well. In the course of time following Lucknow pact of 1916 between Congress and Muslim League Gandhi failed to recognize the growing powers of Jinnah which came on the surface in 1935 elections and afterwards in the support of new country Pakistan.

However, many argue that the British were forced to expedite the Partition by the events on the ground. Once in office, Mountbatten quickly became aware if Britain were to avoid involvement in a civil war, which seemed increasingly likely, there was no alternative to partition and a hasty exit from India. Law and order had broken down many times before Partition with much bloodshed on both sides. Mountbatten became worried assuming massive civil war. After the Second World War, Britain had limited resources, perhaps insufficient police force in keeping the order of administration. Another viewpoint was that while Mountbatten might have been too hasty with partition as he had no real options left and the best he could achieved under difficult circumstances. The historian Lawrence James concluded that Mountbatten was left with no option but to cut and run in order to save his prestige without involvement in a potentially bloody civil war from which it would be difficult to get out.

Abdul Kalam, one of India's most respected scientists and the father of the Integrated Guided Missile Development Programme (IGMDP) of India, was honored through his appointment as the 11th India. His extensive contribution to India's defense industry leads him to immense honor of fame being nicknamed as the Missile Man of India. His tenure as the President of India was affectionately known as People's President that goes against the concept of the partition of India based on religion.

The history of Muslim expansion was based on the policy of trade how to increase the economic power so as to bring a better life for human being. The same policy was adopted by the British. All religion is spreading the ideals that all human beings are equal the Hindu religion was not supporting the equality of human beings by creating Brahamins – Non-brahamins and Dalit -NonDalit. Indian political stalwarts were so powerful in their foresighted views that they had given the recognition of the Dalit and Non-Dalit even in the constitution. According to few such as Swami Vivekanda who said Hindu Religion is supreme as it involves all human beings of the Earth but the Indian Political thinker did not recognized it. Their outlook was all people are not same. Hindu people are different from the Muslims as such they require two different country. They divided the country based on "Religion". Again they had divided the Hindu community as Brahamins, Non-Brahamins, Dalit and Non-Dalits and so on. They had recognized the division in the constitution by giving separate right for the Dalit, Tribals and so on. The politicians should ask themselves why did the 90% Hindu could not Rule over 10% Muslims? Could they not learn anything from the politics of other countries?

Teachings of Indian Politicians: India was a country of Hindus right at the beginning but the Hindus failed to protect its country from the non-stop immigration of the Muslims from the Arab land since the emergence of Muslim Religion by Hazarat Muhammad in Arab Land in the period of 600 CE. The historic events of Delhi reveals that Delhi was a place a power center, most of the time, the city was used as Capital by the Sultans of Turkey and Mughals of Uzbekistan supported by Ottoman Empires.

In Mahabharat it was found the description of fighting between Pandabs and Kaurabs. It was described how the strongest fighter Arjun was reluctant to fight against Kaurabs who were no other than his brothers or forefathers. The Lord Krishna, the religious head of all Hindus asked Arjun to fight because the duty of a Ruler is to fight for the cause of right without looking who is brother or who is forefather. Thus the application of strength in right place in right time became the basic ingredient to establish the right of humanity as per Hindu Religion. But in the course of time many religious stalwarts twisted the Hindu Religion into a religion of "Tolerance" and "Ashinga". Buddha expanded Buddha Religion, a new Religion similar to that of the religion of Hiundus based on "Ashinga".

Many Indian Politicians appeared in the 20 century to capture power by evicting the British, by dint of force of strength, such as Bal Gangadhar Tilak, Netaji Subhas Bose but lost before the stronger opposite force. Looking to the stronger force, the greatest clever politician Gandhi had taken a new strategy to fight, a strategy of "Non-Violence" and correlated it with the Hindu religion of "Tolerance" and "Ashinga". He knows "Non-Violence" cannot stand against any mighty force but he can expose himself as a man of importance by continuing the movement for a longer period of time. He was a clever person, he knows how to face the problem, he appeared in London for studying law overcoming the orthodoxy religious barrier of his village but he was completely failed in practicing law at Bombay. After that he turned towards religion and thought wisely how to bring it in India for his exploration as a man of importance. Under such circumstances he had no other alternative but to convey himself as a SAINT with half naked Fakir Dress and continue with a new Hindu ethics of "Non-Violence". He had taken dual strategy to satisfy the common ordinary people as he was raising his silent voice of protest thorough "Non-Violence" against the British and again he was satisfying the mighty British by never raising any stronger voice of protest against the British fighting through arms. The mighty British was also happy with Gandhi as he was consoling the public through "Non-Violence" although some times for the sake of administration the British get compelled to arrest him but even then the British never kept him in any ordinary jail but kept him in palace to encourage him in Non-Violence.

Finally he was succeeded to raise his image in the international atmosphere at the cost of the sufferings of the Indian people and destruction of the Indian sub-continent. He knows how Russia achieved her freedom by Russian Revolution, how French established democracy through French Revolution and how the United States get rid of the mighty British Force. It was not his intension to do good to the people but to increase his image otherwise he had the plenty of opportunity to raise his voice of revolt as done in other countries. It was at the hanging of Bhagot Sing, at the cry of Unity of Khilafat Movement or in the latest after the end of War during the trial of the Force of the Azad Hind Force. But in every incidents he was with the British Administration and British Force and in the latest he agreed to partition hurriedly in secret betraying the country people without taking the consent of the Indian (without referendum) people and many sacrificing leader like Khan Abdul Gaffer Khan.

After the formation of Pakistan, rioting and killing of people and massacre of common people in different places, Gandhi no longer remained a sensible leader; he lost his mental balance which is reflected in the Extract of his Delhi Diary:

EXTRACTS FROM THE DELHI DIARY OF GANDHI

(i) **10th September 1947:**"Is it not our shame as a nation that there should be any refugee problem at all? Qaid-e-Azam Jinnah, Liaquat-saheb and other Pakistan leaders have proclaimed in common with Pandit Nehru and Sardar Patel that the minorities will be treated in the respective dominions with the same consideration as the majorities. Was this said by each to tickle the world with sweet words, or was it meant to show to the world that we mean what we say and that we will die in the attempt to redeem the world. If so, why are the Hindus and Sikhs and the proud Amils and Bhaibunds driven to leave Pakistan which is their home? What has happened in Quetta, Nawabshah and Karachi? The tales one hears and reads from western Pakistan are heart-breaking. It will not do for either party to plead helplessness and say it is all the work of goondas. Each dominion is bound to take full responsibility for the acts of those who live in either dominion. 'Theirs is not to reason why; theirs but to do and die.' No longer do we work willy-nilly under the crushing weight of imperialism. But this does not mean that there will now be no rule of law if we are to face the world squarely in the face. Are the Union ministers to declare their bankruptcy and shamelessly own to the world that the people of Delhi or the refugees will not cheerfully and voluntarily obey the rule of law? I would like the ministers to break in the attempt to wean the people from their madness rather than bend". Muslims must realize and admit the wrongs perpetrated under the Islamic rule.

(ii) **23rd September 1947:**"I am told that there are still left over 18,000 Hindus and Sikhs in Rawalpindi and 30,000 in the Wah Camp. I will repeat my advice that they should all be prepared to die rather than leave their homes. The art of dying bravely and with honour does not need any special training, save a living faith in God. Then there will be no abductions and no forcible conversions. I know that you are anxious I should go to the Punjab at the earliest moment. I want to do so. But if I failed in Delhi, it is impossible for me to succeed in Pakistan. For I want to go to all the parts and provinces of Pakistan under the protection of no escort saving God. I will go as a friend of the Muslims as of others. My life will be at their disposal. I hope that I may cheerfully die at the hands of anyone who chooses to take my life. Then I will have done as I have advised all to do".

Gandhi has not only destroyed the country but had destroyed the existence of Hindus and Sikhs and had not learnt anything from the liberation activity of other country. In 1776, Thomas Jefferson made the Transformation of the American Declaration of Independence. On July 4, 1776, the United States Congress jointly accepted and approved the Declaration of Independence. Its primary author, Thomas Jefferson, meticulously design and thought of the outcome to write the Declaration as a formal assignment of why Congress had voted on July 2 to declare independence from Great Britain. A year after the outbreak of the American Revolutionary War, the Congress came out with a statement announcing that the thirteen American colonies were no longer a part of the British Empire. The Declaration of Independence also initially published as a printed broadsheet that was widely distributed and read to the public and ultimately Independence came to the United States. The thrust of division of black and white was eliminated by Abraham Lincoln by giving his life. Winston Churchill kept the United Kingdom strong and sound at the point of collapse under the bombing thrust of Hitler. And again Mao Se Tung kept the growth of economy of China under the initial set back, while the Indian leader Gandhi utilized the religious weakness of the Hindus in the division of the country to make him icon and father of the nation thrusting the people in destruction of killing by communal violence and later in the atmosphere of famine in Bengal to finish his political rivals.

[15.6]

Argument in favor Unification: Indian reunification refers to the potential unification of India with what is now Bangladesh and Pakistan, the latter of which was partitioned from British India in 1947. Gandhi sensing Germany threatening the world peace and stability compelling Britain to declared war against Germany, then his Non-Violence is losing its importance. So in order to save his image through the protection of "Non-Violence" he wrote a letter on December 24, 1940 to the govt of German addressing Hitler as "Friend" and enlighten him giving a formidable argument in favor of non-violence as a force of power, and not weakness. He appeals to him to stop the war in the name of humanity and proposes for an international tribunal to determine "which part was in the right". He made a joint appeal to Hitler as well to Mussolini. According to him Victory attained by violence is tantamount to a defeat, for it is momentary. But the irony of the fact was that at the time of proposal of partition of India he could not prevent partition by satisfying Jinnah for the sake of humanity because that would prevent him to become a leader of international image and later father of the nation. His Victory attained by non-violence is tantamount to a win causing partition and bringing inhuman tragedy to millions thrusting rioting and displacement in millions. How could he justify the Victory attained by non-violence? By twisting the politics he became the Father of the nation.

Jinnah was at the beginning against of bringing religion into politics, but Gandhi was never against in brining religion into politics. According to Gandhi different religion would take different road, so long we reach the same goal. But what had happened "Non-Violence" of Gandhi reached to the goal of "the point of liberation" and similarly Muslim League by virtue of "Violence" under the guidance of Jinnah reached to the same goal of "the point of liberation". The liberation of India was attained but by the partition of India. Thus the theory of Great Gandhi was miss-fired and brought the irreparable suffering to Indians. On the other hand liberation by violence as it is seen in the U.S.A or French had brought unity, stability and prosperity. Thus the big question in front of the people of twenty century whether the activity of Gandhi was in favor of the unity of the country or in favor of the division of the country. We were one nation before British came to India. One thought inspired us. Our mode of life was the same. It was because we were one nation that we were able to establish one kingdom. Subsequently Gandhi coming from South Africa divided us with the theory of "Non-Violence. There are many youths who had taken training in arms believe in the method of violence. They believe if India resorts to arms in order to defend her honor than that of Gandhi's Non-Violence, India could do that. Indians should not be in a cowardly manner become or remain a helpless witness to her own dishonor in the partition of India. No one can honor it as the advice of a sensible leader. But above all this Gandhi is now occupying the highest position of India. Corona Virus has integrated all people of Indian sub-continent as the all people think alike, speak alike and get pleasure alike. Let us forget the past and get together to form one country one nation.

There were many wise politicians who were against the partition formula of India. In 1947, British India was partitioned into India and Pakistan the latter of which included northwest India and a part of eastern India. Those who opposed the vivisection of the country were the super human being and a follower of the doctrine of composite nationalism. Two national Party oppose the partition, one was the Indian National Congress, and the other was the All India Azad Muslim Conference, opposed the partition of India; the president of the All India Azad Muslim Conference and Chief Minister of Sind, Shadeed Allah Bakhsh Soomro. Bakhsh stated that "No power on earth can rob anyone of his faith and convictions, and no power on earth shall be permitted to rob Indian Muslims of their just rights as Indian nationals."

Khaksar Movement leader Allama Mashriqi opposed the partition of India because he felt that if Muslims and Hindus had largely lived peacefully together in India for centuries, they could also do so in a free and united India. Mashriqi had seen the two-nation theory was nothing but a plot of the British to remain in power from distance in the environment of rivalry of two regions. He reasoned that a division of India along religious lines would breed extremism on both sides of the border. Mashriqi further said that "Muslim majority areas were already under Muslim rule, so if any Muslims wanted to move to these areas, they were free to do so without having to divide the country." To him, separatist leaders were hungry for power and hungry for personal fame and pleasure. According to Maulana Husain Ahmad Madani, a Deobandi Muslim scholar and proponent of a united India argued that it was wrongly attempting to "scare Muslims into imagining that in a free India Muslims would lose their separate identity, and be absorbed into the Hindu fold". It was nothing but the destruction of the united force of India in the progress of development and security of the nation. The All-India Muslim League campaigned for a separate country; Pakistan was not good for the Muslims.

It was the belief of the Indian nationalists that after the departure of the British from the Indian subcontinent, Pakistan would be destabilized and reunite with India. Thus many of wise politicians thought it would be best for the British to leave sooner. On the other hand, Muhammad Ali Jinnah was not happy with Gandhi for bringing religion in Indian politics and out of rivalry of leadership he wanted Pakistan by division otherwise he was once the strong supporter of the United India before the bringing of Khilafat by Gandhi in Indian politics. The thinking of reunion made many **wise men** happy imagining the tragedy of the ordinary common people out of division of the country. Lord Listowel remarked that "It is greatly to be hoped that when the disadvantages of separation have become apparent in the light of experience, the two Dominions will freely decide to reunite in a single Indian Dominion, which might achieve that position among the nations of the world to which its territories and resources would entitle it."

Political thinker like Markandey Katju, former Justice of the Supreme Court of India, serves as the Chairman of the Indian

Reunification Association (IRA) also gave opinion in favour reunion for the betterment of the two nations. He advocated the reunification of India with Pakistan under a secular government. He stated that the cause of the partition was due to the divide and rule policy of Britain, to bring communal hatred. Pakistani historian Nasim Yousaf, the grandson of AllamaMashriqi, has also championed Indian Reunification and presented the idea at the New York Conference on Asian Studies on 9 October 2009 at Cornell University, where Yousaf stated that the partition of India was resulted for the interests of British so that united India never emerge as a country of world power. Yousaf also cited former Indian National Congress president Maulana Abul Kalam Azad, who wrote in the same vein of strength.

If a united India had become free then in time it would be a wealthy country when there would be little chance that Britain could retain her position in the economic and industrial life of India. Yousaf holds that "Muhammad Ali Jinnah, the President of the All-India Muslim League and later founder of Pakistan, had been misleading the Muslim community in order to go down in history as the savior of the Muslim cause and to become founder and first Governor General of Pakistan." AllamaMashriqi, a nationalist Muslim, thus saw Jinnah as "becoming a tool in British hands for his political career." Besides Islamic leadership the British India had rejected the notion of partitioning the country practically, exemplified by the fact that most of the Muslims in the heartland of the subcontinent had remained where they were, rather than migrating to newly created state of Pakistan.

India and Pakistan are currently allocating a significant amount of their budget into military spending—money that should be spent in economic and social development. Poverty, homelessness, illiteracy, terrorism and a lack of medical facilities, in Yousaf's eyes, would not be a problem for an undivided India as it would be more advantaged "economically, politically, and socially." Yousaf has stated that Indians and Pakistanis speak a common language Hindustani, "wear the same dress, eat the same food, enjoy the same music and movies, and communicate in the same process of custom and culture as such their living together must not be a problem. Two religions, two nations had no justification. He argues that uniting would be a logical conclusion forgetting the past bitterness, though not impossible, citing in front the example of the fall of the Berlin Wall and the consequent German Reunification.

Mehdi Hassan, when visiting Ajmer Sharif Dargah, always prayed for the "reunification of India and Pakistan in some peaceful form or the other." French journalist François Gautier wrote that: Kashmir may hold the key to India's reunification with Pakistan, either by force or by mutual consent. As long as Pakistan and India remain divided there will be other Kashmirs, other Ayodhyas, and so on.

For the unity India and Pakistan each and everyone should remember what was said Aurobindo. Sri Aurobindo's words in 1947, goes as "The old communal division into Hindu and Muslim seems to have hardened into the figure of a permanent division of the country. It is hoped that the Congress and the nation will not accept the settled fact as for ever settled, or as anything more than a temporary expedient. For if it lasts, India may be seriously weakened, even crippled: civil strife may remain always possible; possible even a new invasion and foreign conquest. **The Partition of the Country Must Go.**" Similarly let us remember what was said by others. Educationalist P. A. Inamdar commented at the Rangoonwala College of Dental Science in July 2017 that the reunification of Pakistan and Bangladesh with India would "keep India prosperous and peaceful". Similarly a Pakistani Communist activist Mr. Lal Khan, suggested that undoing the partition is a necessity because it would resolve the Kashmir conflict, as well as reduce the power of the "security-bureaucratic machine", thus guaranteeing a true democratic set up to build up the unity of democratic society.

Kingsley Martin observed that –"**Hindus**"… have not forgiven the Muslim League for destroying the unity of the subcontinent when the British agreed to independence." Many Hindus were devastated by the fact that "part of the motherland envisaged in the ancient Hindu scriptures" was partitioned from India. The Bharatiya Jana Sangh, a Hindu political organization never could forgotten that the creation of Akhand Bharat was not its objectives which was existed prior to its partition in 1947. Ram Madhav, a spokesman for the Rashtriya Swayamsevak Sangh, a Hindu nationalist organization, stated that "The RSS still believes that one day these parts, which have for historical reasons separated only 60 years ago, will again, through popular goodwill, come together and Akhand Bharat will be created."

Similar to RSS (Rashtriya Swayamsevak Sangh) a group of 200 Islamic clerics gathered in Pune in July 2017 and issued a statement calling for Indian Reunification. The partition of India had created India and Pakistan but the pain of partition is constantly hurting the common residents, Political leaders as well as religious leaders too. It is the general expectation "The Unity" the sooner the better. Until and unless the borders of India are peaceful there cannot be any success to achieve economical, societal and educational development. Tensions at borders are leading to enormous expenditures and destroying development work. The division made by British was unnatural it is better for honorable Prime Minister Narendra Modi to use all military options and unite Pakistan, Bangladesh and Afghanistan to make Akhand Bharat forgetting the recent Delhi violence concerning CAA and NRC. The dream saw by Indian leaders once before and after independence will come true and India will become most powerful country in the world.

The establishment of East India Company in Calcutta and the British administration in Calcutta had raised the status of Calcutta converting it the Capital of British India. Few politicians became power hungry who started to kill the British that compelled the British Rulers to shift the Capital to Delhi but yet the political activity did not get reduced. All political Party concentrated in Calcutta to exhibit their vigor of protest. The most popular leader Gandhi misleads the majority Hindus through the Hindu ethics of religion and never thought for the well fare of all people. In every country a popular leader is one who thought for all and does everything for the betterment of the country. But Gandhi was the exception. As such the country is divided and he gave his consent without any objection knowing well that the country is going to destruction through communal rioting and going to destruction losing the facility of trade and economy. He was a popular leader if he stood firmly against the division, the country would have not been divided and the country would have been a super-power. Now a change had occurred due to Corona Virus. The danger of Virus had united the humanity. Now the opportune moment had arrived the divided units of India to march together to build up the lost unity for getting the past history of rivalry. Calcutta was the place of center where Gandhi had started "Non-Violence" vigorously and again Calcutta was the center where ML of Jinnah had started "Calcutta Killing" demanding Pakistan. Let Calcutta be the center for the call of reunion. If it really comes true the mighty strength and energy utilized by the militant Muslims in the "Calcutta Killing" against the Gandhi's falsehood of "Non-Violence" would be the hidden energy of strength for the new nation of India, a future Super-Power of the Universe.

The Hidden Power of United Bengal: It was the hidden power like that of the United Kingdom or the United States of America. The United Kingdom once ruled the whole World and the United States of America is now the Super-power of the World. What is the future of the United Bengal?

The UK is short name of "The United Kingdom of Great Britain and Northern Ireland". It is made up of four countries; England, Scotland, Wales and Northern Ireland. Americans, have established the United States, similarly UK is formed with the union of four countries. In the year 925 – The Kingdom of England was established by the unification of Anglo-Saxon tribes across modern day England. In 1536 – Kingdom of England and Wales came together under the King Henry VIII. Accordingly a bill was enacted by King Henry VIII which effectively made England and Wales the same country and governed by the same laws.

In 1707 –The Kingdom of England (which includes Wales) joined with the Kingdom of Scotland to form The Kingdom of Great Britain. 1801 – United Kingdom of Great Britain joins the union of Ireland having with the name of United Kingdom of Great Britain and Northern Ireland. But in 1922 The Republic of Ireland (Eire or 'Southern Ireland') withdraws from the union, leaving just the northern counties of Ireland. This is the UK.

Similarly the United States of America was created on July 4, 1776, with the Declaration of Independence of thirteen British colonies. In the Resolution of July 2, 1776, the colonies resolved that they were free and independent states. Their independence was recognized by Great Britain in the Treaty of Paris of 1783, which concluded the American Revolutionary War. This effectively doubled the size of the colonies that was organized into territories and then states. The first great expansion of the country came with the Louisiana in 1803, the Spanish Florida, and the Texas and so on. In 1845 led directly to the Mexican–American War and made the state of California. However, as the development of the country moved west, the question of slavery, black and white discrimination came in front challenging the unity of the United States. This came to a head in 1860 and 1861, when the governments of the southern states proclaimed their secession from the country and formed the Confederate States of America. The American Civil War led to the defeat of the Confederacy in 1865 under the correct guidance of the President of the United States stabilizing the unity of the country and the eventual readmission of the states to the United States Congress.

The Black Death, also known as the Pestilence and the Plague, was the most fatal pandemic recorded in human history. The Black Death was a disaster affecting Europe in the 14th century and is estimated to have killed 60 per cent of Europe's entire population. The Black Death most likely originated in Central Asia or East Asia, from where it spread to Africa, Western Asia, and the rest of Europe up to Italian Peninsula. The pandemic of "Black Death" has brought a tendency of oneness among the people of different states of different regions, similarly the "Corona"pandemic has also brought a tendency of oneness among the people of Indian sub-continents particularly among the people of India, Pakistan and Bangladesh as the people of these regions once lived together for a long period of time enjoying almost the same culture, same language, same dress and the same food.

This has highlighted the possibility of a United Bengal. The United Kingdom or the United States of America was once created by the union of different states; as such the United Bengal is also likely to be formed by the union of two parts of Bengal. It was divided by the British in 1906 and again reunited in 1911. During Independence of India Bengal was divided again in 1947. Let us see how it happened.

Looming partition of Bengal: As 1946 drew to a close, India was in remnant. The British were desperate to leave but, somewhat tragicomically after two centuries of colonial Rule. A scheme to transfer of power under the 1946 **Cabinet Mission Plan** was designed to transfer power to India that had been rejected by the Congress. Some form of partition now seemed to be emerging as a Hobson's choice.

British Bengal roughly consisted of East Bengal (modern-day Bangladesh) and the Indian state of West Bengal. Like North India's Muslims, Hindus in Bengal were wary of the British exiting, leaving them a minority. Since 1937, ever since democratic government had been introduced in the provinces of British India, Muslim-majority Bengal had seen Hindus out of power because of communal hatred created by Gandhi's "Non-Violence". Matters were worsening by horrific communal rioting in August, 1946, in Kolkata. By the end of the year, there was a growing acceptance in the division of Bengal. The historian Joya Chatterji wrote, "Bengal must be divided and that Hindus must carve out for themselves a Hindu-majority province".

It was against these odds that HS Suhrawardy, the then premier of Bengal, addressed a press conference in Delhi on April 27, 1947, in order to make the **case** for an "independent, undivided and sovereign Bengal":

The plan did attract some intelligent support. The British saw in it a way to better protect their commercial stakes in Kolkata. On May 8, 1947, Viceroy Louis Mountbatten cabled the British government with a partition plan that made an exception for Bengal: it was the only province that would be allowed to remain independent should it so chose to. On May 23, in a cabinet meeting Prime Minister Attlee also hoped that Bengal would remain united.

However, by far the most-influential supporter of the plan was Sarat Chandra Bose, senior Congressman and elder brother of Subhas Chandra Bose (who was abroad, unreachable – probably dead). On May 20, 1947, a plan for a United Bengal was thrashed out between Suhrawardy and Bose. The proposed country would have joint electorates and universal adult franchise. Hindus and Muslims would have equal quotas in the military and the police which would be indigenized and "manned by Bengalis". A Hindu-Muslim coalition government would be set up with parity between the communities in the cabinet. The prime minister would be Muslim and the home minister a Hindu. The plan was made public on May 24, 1947, ten days before the final partition plan was announced.

MA Jinnah, the leader of the Muslim League, was not averse to the idea since, as he said in his talks with Mountbatten, "What is the use of Bengal without Calcutta". However, the Bengal Muslim League itself pulled in every direction. The Urdu-speaking Muslims in Bengal desired union of Bengal with Pakistan and not a Sovereign Bengal.

In the Congress, Mohandas Gandhi was an initial supporter of United Bengal but then backtracked given that the Congress Working Committee had "taken him to task for supporting Sarat Babu's move". Both Jawaharlal Nehru and Vallabhbhai Patel were implacably opposed to a United Bengal, because of a future threat. Nehru was very close to Lady Mountbatten; as such Nehru's opposition to the proposal was enough for Mountbatten to backtrack on pushing the plan any more with London.

But Bose did not back down. "It is not a fact that Bengali Hindus unanimously demand partition," Sarat Bose wrote to Vallabhbhai Patel on May 27, 1947. Bengal leaders of Bengal became administrator at the beginning of the British Rule as the British favored the Hindu Bengalis and not the Bengali Muslims as the British captured power by the defeat of Muslim Ruler Siraj-ud-ullah. The mindset of most of Bengali leaders like the other Uttar Bharat leaders became narrow. Such as Gandhi wanted his image through "Non-Violence" and by making Nehru the PM of the country, similarly a Hindu Bengali leader always think a Muslim will never do any good to Hindus. Of course it was due to the prevailing communal atmosphere present at Calcutta at that time. The leaders did not go deep into the matter to find out the reasons. They failed to assess the fall out of division. There were no Muslims in Bengal once; the Muslim religion came in Bengal after the emergence of Islam. At the outset, the expansion of Muslim religion was due to the sacrifice of Muslims and in course of time the Muslims had expanded their strength through trade and efficient administration. If the Bengali Hindu leaders could think likewise, they could also increase their strength through trade and intelligence creating an atmosphere of equality and humanity instead of inclining towards religion like that of Gandhi. A country is developed by the principle of unity and equality. The example is UK and the USA.

Eventually, the United Bengal plan came a cropper. On June 3, 1947, when Mountbatten announced his plan to transfer power to native hands, there were only two contenders: India and Pakistan. Bengal was partitioned, the western part joining the Indian Union and the eastern part joining Pakistan. The mass upheavals and the population transfers it caused are still buffeting the politics of Assam. However, Attlee's prediction wasn't completely off the mark: within just 24 years of the British transferring power, East Bengal broke from Pakistan to emerge as Bangladesh.

Attlee thinking Bengal was going to be an independent country in 1947-Why? Once it was almost certain that United Bengal is emerging as a Sovereign nation. It was the short sided

Bengali leaders and selfish power hungry Indian leaders prevented the formation of Sovereign United Bengal. It is little known, but in 1947, along with India and Pakistan, there almost emerged a third sovereign country: United Bengal. It was just before the partitioned of Bengal into West and East Bengal on August 17, 1947.

On December 28, Pakistan newspaper **Dawn** published a somewhat curious bit of news. "UK PM Attlee believed Bengal may opt to be a separate country," read the headline. As per recently declassified documents, Clement Attlee had briefed the US ambassador in the United Kingdom on June 2, 1947, about the plan to partition India. "A division of Punjab is likely," said Attlee, but he added there was a "distinct possibility Bengal might decide against partition and against joining either Hindustan or Pakistan".

People's lighting thought: All People are human beings but well fare of human beings is only learn by experience, it was the Empire of Buddha out of war of Pandab-Kaurab, it was Islam out of trade and violence, the same was followed by the British extraction under Rule of administration and violence, but apart from violence Unity is strength, Allied Forces survived over Axis Forces, German was victimized by bifurcation of East German-West German but in the long run people realized unity is strength and unity is prosperity, German get reunited. For India the theory of division between Hindu-Muslim, division of Dalit-NonDalit is completely wrong and against the betterment of a nation as well as humanity. The weakness of the Hindus of India is best utilized by the people of Turkey and Afghanistan in the name of Islam categorized as Muslims. Similarly the weakness of India is best utilized by the British to enrich the United Kingdom. But unlike the British, the Muslims never tried to enrich Turkey or Afghanistan but devoted their energy in India to fight to the last for existence and development. In the last turmoil of India it was seen by the Indians, under the guidance of Gandhi through the principle of "Non-Violence" that the country had reached to the extreme point of destruction, by communal fight bringing division and destruction of humanity through the color of Hindu-Muslim.

Now in the end it is proved beyond doubt that a teaching of all religion is the same that is nothing but the service to society and the service to human beings. The best way of serving the people is to bring Unity among all kinds of people and to expand trade to bring prosperity. Thus unity of India-Pakistan and unity of United Bengal is the best policy to bring prosperity and happiness to the people of this region.

The Pandemic of Black Death in the 14th century had estimated to have killed 60 per cent of Europe's entire population. But it had brought a unity among all the states of the Europe. Now Corona has brought fatal pandemic in the 20 century. The distant American President Trump had extended his hands of friendship with Indian Prime Minister Modi to fight against Corona jointly. Thus it is expected the near neighbor Pakistan would also extend the hand of friendship forgetting the earlier rivalry. If so the people of the region would feel peace and happiness even after the sufferings of corona and loss of lives beyond account.

A learning lesson from Corona-Virus: It was Mr. **Abdul Malabari has been undertaking unclaimed bodies for cremation. He never thought otherwise as he would have to bury people whose families wanted to say goodbye but couldn't because of Covid-19.** Mr. Malabari, 51-year person is ready to do the human work; he said "As soon as we get a call, we proceed with the kit."

What he's most proud of, he said that his team includes people of all faiths and castes. "We have Hindu volunteers who bury the bodies of Muslims, and Muslim volunteers who cremate the bodies of Hindus." Most often, he says, they end up with the bodies of the homeless or runways that are never identified. "We find bodies in rivers and canals, on railway tracks. We sometimes deal with decomposed bodies."

He says the effect of what they do is hard to express but, over the years, it has affected his sleep, appetite and even his ability to enjoy time with his family. But he has never considered stopping for the service to humanity.

Every time someone dies of corona virus in Surat - in India's western state of Gujarat - officials call Mr Malabari. So far the city has recorded 19 deaths, and 244 active cases. "In such difficult times, Abdul bhai [brother] has been of great help," says Ashish Naik, Surat's deputy commissioner of Surat.

Mr. Malabari says this is his job, and so he agreed to do it, despite the risk. His team now eats and sleeps at the office of their charities, to protect their families from infection.

Mr. Malabari said it was due to his change of heart through a service three decades ago. It was his compassion for a stranger three decades ago - when a different disease was snaking its way through the population - which led to his work today.

The stranger's name was Sakina, and she was suffering from HIV. Her husband and son had brought her to hospital, but then disappeared. Efforts to track them down after her death proved fruitless. And so, she had been lying in the morgue for a month. Local officials were desperate, and put an appeal out for a Muslim volunteer who would take on her burial. Mr Malabari, then just 21, was touched by the advert and decided to proceed to help. He contacted the only organization in Surat that was burying unclaimed bodies, but they told him the man who did the job was travelling so they would have to wait for him to return.

"I felt it was unfair," Mr. Malabari said. So he went to the hospital and told officials that he would bury Sakina. Her body, he recalls today, "was stinking". But he was not put off, approaching some women he knew to bathe the body as per Islamic custom. But they refused, he says, because Sakina had HIV, which was still little understood in 1990.

So Mr. Malabari decided to do it himself, pouring buckets of water over her body, before taking her for burial. He says that's when he realized Surat couldn't rely on just one man for this job. "It took me a whole day, and I also realized I could not do this alone." So he started his charity. He says his family, which runs a textile business, was initially against it.

"I remember telling them how Islam says it's every citizen's duty to help and carry out a person's final journey out of humanity and respect. I was just doing that as a fellow human being."

Today, there is as much fear surrounding the bodies of those who die with Covid-19 - although with far more reason as, although health experts say the virus cannot transmit after death, it can survive on clothes for a few hours. So once the body is sealed in a bag, no-one, not even family, can see it.

Mr. Malabari and his team take all the precautions - they wear masks, gloves and gowns. They have also been trained on how to prepare the bodies. First, they spray the body with chemicals and then they wrap it in plastic to avoid contamination, before transporting it in one of the two vans reserved for Covid-19 victims. The vehicles are sanitized after every trip, and the cemetery or crematorium is disinfected after each funeral.

Even so, fears over the virus have led to protests in some Indian cities by people who live close to the graveyards. Mr. Malabari says he has also encountered some trouble, but he has been able to reason with people so far.

The hardest part, he says, is dealing with families who can't say goodbye - many of them are also under quarantine.

"They cry a lot and talk about seeing the deceased. We explain to them that it's for their own safety and assure them that we will make the arrangements according to their religious customs."

He says sometimes a family member has been allowed to observe from a far: "We take them in a separate vehicle and ask them to stand at a distance and pray".

Now, he says, his three children - a daughter and two sons - are "happy" and "proud" of him. His charity has since grown to 35 volunteers and has some 1,500 donors, as well as the help and support of officials.

"In my heart I feel a sense of satisfaction from doing this that nothing else will ever give me."

It is a service to humanity irrespective of Hindu, Muslim or Christian. Gandhi should remember from heaven that all people of all religion could live together and the partition of India no longer is required. The Bengali Hindus of Bengal should know that it was necessary to live with people like Malabari for the service to humanity welcoming the formation of Sovereign United Bengal and asking for a unity of two Bengal.

———— The End ————

OTHER PUBLICATIONS BY THE AUTHOR

1. INDIA & THEGLOBE (N) published by Power Publishers.com. Kolkata.

2. MY JOURNEY & SOVEREIGN UNITED BENGAL Published by Partridge Publishing Ltd.

3. Control of Terror and Terrorists Published by Olympia Publisher, London.

4. AKHANDA BHARAT published by Power Publishers.com. Kolkata.

5. A Silent Patriot of Bangladesh Published by Partridge Publishing Ltd.

6. GANDHI VS JINNAH published by Eastern Book House.in Panbazar, Guwahati.

7. THE AGONY OF BENGAL AND ASSAM published by Power Publishers.com. Kolkata.

8. An autobiography of a STREETBOY Published by QUIGNOG.

9. The contribution of Maniram Dewan & M K Gandhi in the Independence of India. Published by Eastern Book House in Panbazar, Guwahati.

10. Hideous Barak Published by Power Publishers.Com. Kolkata.

11. INDIA my Country Published by Power Publishers.Com. Kolkata.

12. THE DARK SIDE OF GANDHI by notionpress.com Delhi.

13. **SELFISH LEADERS VS BENGAL & BENGALIS** by notionpress.com Delhi.

14. **NEW INDIA AFTER UNKNOWN VIRUS & KNOWN GANDHI** notionpress.com Delhi.